THE UNITED STATES AND THE EUROPEAN COMMUNITY IN THE 1990s

Also by Kevin Featherstone

POLITICAL CHANGE IN GREECE: Before and After the Colonels
(*editor with Dimitrios K. Katsoudas*)
SOCIALIST PARTIES AND EUROPEAN INTEGRATION: A
Comparative History
SPICERS' EUROPEAN POLICY REPORT: The Internal Market
THE SUCCESSFUL MANAGER'S GUIDE TO 1992: Working in
the New Europe

Also by Roy H. Ginsberg

FOREIGN POLICY ACTIONS OF THE EUROPEAN
COMMUNITY: The Politics of Scale

The United States and the European Community in the 1990s

Partners in Transition

Kevin Featherstone
Senior Lecturer in Politics
University of Bradford

and

Roy H. Ginsberg
Associate Professor of Government
Skidmore College, New York

St. Martin's Press

First published in Great Britain 1993 by
THE MACMILLAN PRESS LTD
Houndmills, Basingstoke, Hampshire RG21 2XS
and London
Companies and representatives
throughout the world

A catalogue record for this book is available
from the British Library.

ISBN 0-333-52346-6

Printed in Great Britain by
Antony Rowe Ltd
Chippenham, Wiltshire

First published in the United States of America 1993 by
Scholarly and Reference Division,
ST. MARTIN'S PRESS, INC.,
175 Fifth Avenue,
New York, N.Y. 10010

ISBN 0-312-08994-5

Library of Congress Cataloging-in-Publication Data
Featherstone, Kevin.
The United States and the European Community in the 1990s / Kevin
Featherstone and Roy H. Ginsberg.
p.   cm.
Includes index.
ISBN 0-312-08994-5
1. United States—Foreign economic relations—European Economic
Community countries.   2. European Economic Community countries-
-Foreign economic relations—United States.   3. United States-
-Relations—European Economic Community countries.   4. European
Economic Community Countries—Relations—United States.   5. n-us e.
I. Ginsberg, Roy H.   II. Title.
HF1456.5.E825F4   1993
337.7304—dc20
92-32753
CIP

To Kirsten and Monica Jane, and to Nina

Contents

Contents

List of Figures

List of Tables

List of Abbreviations

ACP	African, Caribbean, and Pacific countries of Lomé convention
ASA	American Soybean Association
CDU	Christian Democratic Union (Germany)
CMEA	Council for Mutual Economic Assistance (also known as COMECON)
COCOM	Co-ordinating Committee
COPA	Committee of Professional Agricultural Organisations
CSCE	Conference on Security and Cooperation in Europe
EBRD	European Bank for Reconstruction and Development
EDC	European Defence Community
EEC	European Economic Community
EFTA	European Free Trade Area
EIB	European Investment Bank
EMS	European Monetary System
EMU	Economic and Monetary Union
EPC	European Political Cooperation
ERP	European Recovery Program
EURATOM	European Atomic Energy Community
FAO	Food and Agriculture Organization
GATT	General Agreement on Tariffs and Trade
GDP	Gross Domestic Product
GNP	Gross National Product
G5	Group of Five
G7	Group of Seven
IAEA	International Atomic Energy Agency
IBRD	International Bank for Reconstruction and Development
ILO	International Labour Organisation
IMF	International Monetary Fund
INF	Intermediate-range Nuclear Forces
MBB	Messerschmitt–Bolkow–Blohm
MFN	Most-favoured-nation treatment
MTN	Multilateral trade negotiations
NAFTA	North American Free Trade Area

NATO	North Atlantic Treaty Organisation
NGFI	Non-Grain Feed Ingredients
OECD	Organisation for Economic Cooperation and Development
OEEC	Organisation for European Economic Cooperation
OPEC	Organisation of Petroleum Exporting Countries
PLO	Palestinian Liberation Organisation
SEA	Single European Act
UNCTAD	United Nations Conference on Trade and Development
USTR	United States Trade Representative
VRA	Voluntary Restraint Agreement
WEU	Western European Union

Preface

This book has a very broad scope: the political, economic and social dimensions of the relations between the United States and the European Community (EC) in recent times. The basic theme is of the changing nature of their interdependence and the need to adapt the management of their bilateral relations to it. The book, therefore, has both an analytical and a policy dimension: it offers a detailed empirical investigation of their interdependence and it considers the policy consequences for both sides which result from their shared sensitivity. It recognises that their bilateral relations have changed significantly over distinct stages since 1945 and it looks forward to how their ties might develop in the new circumstances of the post-cold-war era.

Studying the broad panorama of US–EC interdependence is a daunting task. Yet it has seemed to be a very necessary one, given the few studies which exist on this subject. Much attention has been paid to military issues in transatlantic relations in the post-war period. In the new conditions of the 1990s, it is essential to take a wider approach and to acknowledge the increasing importance of the European Community in transatlantic links.

By this stage it should be clear what the book is not about. It is not a study of how policy is made, either in the US or in the EC. Nor is it primarily concerned with the history of this policy, on either side, though it does make reference to it at various stages to illustrate changing patterns in their interdependence. These other subjects are very worthy of investigation. Indeed, there is a need for a number of new studies on different aspects of US–EC relations: this is but an introduction to their varied forms of interdependence.

The authors came to this project from diverse backgrounds. They believe that this has greatly enriched their work. Collaboration has meant a clash of different cultures, values, and perceptions and the need to resolve the academic and political differences which have inevitably arisen. Both authors grew up when the cold war dominated perceptions of international relations; both have had to break free from the '*idées fixes*' associated with that period. The combination of the two perspectives, drawn from either side of the Atlantic, has strengthened this bilateral study: it has incorporated views from both directions.

The research for a book of this kind has meant that the authors have accumulated a number of personal debts. Research has taken place on both sides of the Atlantic. Several practitioners kindly gave interviews to one or both of the authors: Sir Roy Denman; Robert Schaetzel; Joseph Greenwald; George Vest; Sam Gejdenson; and André Pierre. Other specialists offered valuable help with information: Glennon Harrison and Bill Cooper (Congressional Research Service); Nancy Bullock, John Glennon, Robert Pollard, Joyce Rabens (US State Department); Adrian Basora (US National Security Council); Cesira Klayman (EC delegation, Washington); Judith Koucky, Sally Marks (US National Archives); James Taylor (US Department of Labor); Lutz Gobel (Council of the EC Secretariat); and Robert Petersen (European Parliament).

Individual chapters have been read and commented upon by Steven Brams, Leah Haus, Larry Mead and Sarah Steinmetz (New York University); Glenda Rosenthal (Columbia); Robert Keohane (Harvard); Henry R. Nau (The George Washington University); Pat Garland (US State Department); Christopher Hill (LSE); and Emil Kirchner (Essex). Others gave general comments: Karl Cerny (Georgetown); Lily Feldman (the American Institute for Contemporary German Studies); and Mike Smith (Coventry, UK). Both authors are grateful to each of them; they have no responsibility for any weaknesses that remain.

Roy Ginsberg would like to express his personal thanks to the Office of the Dean, Skidmore College, and the Faculty Development Committee for financial support of the project. Christine DeLucia gave invaluable secretarial support, and Kevin Callahan was a very efficient research assistant.

Kevin Featherstone would like to record his personal gratitude to the Nuffield Foundation (London) for the award of a grant to support the research; to the University of Minnesota and New York University for the use of their research facilities; and to the University of Bradford for similar support. Several research assistants offered invaluable help: Adrian Pritchard, Lori Marso, and Rosemary Clay collected material for Chapter 3. Grace Hudson (Bradford) helped with library searches. Ele Cosgrove (Bradford) gave highly efficient secretarial support.

In addition, both authors would like to record their gratitude to Tim Farmiloe and Clare Wace, together with their colleagues, at Macmillan, the originating publishers, for their support and understanding.

Finally, the preparation of this book imposed a number of burdens on those closest to us – Kirsten and Monica Jane, and Nina – who responded with love, support and tolerance. Appropriately, the book is dedicated to them, with our love and gratitude.

KEVIN FEATHERSTONE
ROY H. GINSBERG

Section One

The New Context of United States–European Community Relations

1 Introduction

The United States and the European Community (EC) have arrived at a new juncture in the history of their partnership. Within their own domain, the United States and the EC are profoundly interdependent. Bilateral trade and investment, and the sales generated by investment, top $1 trillion annually and provide 6 million European and American jobs. Bilateral relations are also distinguished by political components: collective self-defence through the North Atlantic Treaty Organisation and similar commitments to political pluralism and market economics. At the same time, relations are often marked by contrasting positions on many major international and bilateral issues. Overall, the partnership is of immense value to both Americans and Europeans; yet in the 1990s, the United States and the EC have reached a new plateau in their bilateral relationship. No longer is the United States a hegemon with the EC orbiting in its sphere. Best described as a post-hegemonic and complex interdependent relationship, the US and EC have entered the 1990s on a much more equal basis with important implications for the future of their international relations. Yet, at large, US–EC relations remain captive to the vicissitudes of the international order, although some would argue that those relations have helped to recast the cold war order into the present post-cold-war one. Relations could be reformed to accommodate change – if a convergence of interests exists both among the EC member governments towards the United States and between the EC itself and the United States – or they could remain transfixed by the spectre of change, with the two sides unable to reach a new *modus vivendi*. As the United States and the EC now engage in wholesale rethinking of their common interests in a world far different from that of forty or even four years ago, appropriate adjustments must be made.

Over the past decade, there has been a disquieting dearth of literature on US–EC relations. There is a pressing need for several new volumes on the subject given its ever-widening complexity and the recent epic changes within and around the North Atlantic. This book represents but one attempt to put substance into the study of US–EC relations. In so doing it

3

- aims to establish the interdependence that exists between the US and EC in the 1990s;
- seeks to indicate how their shared dependence constrains the actions one or the other might take; and
- considers how far the current management of US–EC relations may be at variance with the reality of their changed conditions and the consequences of this disjunction.

The book has both an analytical and a policy dimension. It confronts the problem of how to analyse such a complex set of relations as those which exist between the US and the EC. It takes as its main theoretical foundation the concept of interdependence to help paint the overall picture. To establish their mutual dependence, the book highlights the interactions that link the US and the EC. The analysis focuses on the political, economic and social aspects of US–EC interdependence. However, while the concept of interdependence helps us to establish the broad panorama of interactions, the harmony or disharmony that results from specific US or EC policies must be explained in other terms.

The policy dimension of this book highlights the dilemma on the current agenda of US and EC decision-makers, i.e. to assess the impact on their bilateral relations of the changed global and transatlantic conditions of the 1980s and 1990s, and to make the necessary strategic changes. The two dimensions – analytical and policy – are intertwined. The 'policy problem' has, to some extent, also been an 'analytic problem,' i.e. how to understand the nature and evolution of US–EC relations.

Because of the type of political system the EC represents, the analysis covers both the European national governments and the common EC institutions. A study of the relations existing between the US administration and the EC institutions must necessarily take into account the diverse national foundations of the Community. The book surveys how these relations have developed since the 1950s, but also considers how they might change in the 1990s. This book focuses on the analysis of, and the implications which arise from, US–EC interdependence. It is not a history of US–EC relations, it does not chronicle the history of US and EC policies towards one another and it is not a study of how policy is made in either the US or the EC. These matters deserve careful study, but they fall outside the book's thematic purview.

The most important condition that the US and EC share in the present international system is their mutual dependence. Understanding this mutual dependence clarifies both their current world roles and the strategic choices they face. Both the US and the EC have to grapple with the constraints of interdependence. Interdependence limits their choices, but it does not predetermine harmony or disharmony in their relations. Interdependence has to be 'managed' by political leaders in an environment over which they have limited control. Policy dilemmas are both complex and delicate, and require regular review.

Before undertaking detailed analyses of contemporary US–EC interactions, it is necessary to consider the position of both parties in the international system. The discussion begins with how the US and the EC are responding to current international changes. It argues that the magnitude of the policy adjustments that are currently required can be fully gauged only by understanding how their relations have evolved since the 1950s. These changes are reviewed by distinguishing between three historical periods. This further clarifies the need for policy adjustments by both the US and the EC. The type of adjustments to be made depend ultimately on how US–EC relations are understood: that is, there is a problem of analysis. This chapter defines the problem and outlines how this book aims to confront it. The structure of the book is thus governed by both the analytical and the policy dimensions, and conclusions on each are drawn in Chapter 6.

CURRENT INTERNATIONAL CHANGES

The United States and the EC must adjust to the changing distribution of world power in order to maintain influence and pursue their interests. Within the span of a few months at the end of the 1980s, the two cold war-era allies responded in unison to epic change in Eastern Europe: the collapse of the Soviet power grip over former satellites, German reunification and the rise of potentially new liberal regimes. Ironically, the same two allies were brought together five decades earlier not over the collapse of Soviet power in Eastern Europe but over its rise.

By deferring to EC leadership in the co-ordination of Western aid to the struggling states of Eastern Europe beginning in 1989, the United States gave long-denied recognition to the EC as an important player in the international arena. Such a convergence of policy views towards the East is remarkable when one considers that, prior to 1989, quite divergent views on the appropriate Western response to the Soviet bloc eluded transatlantic agreement. Eastern European states are now being engaged by the EC in the practices of political and economic liberalism and EC aid is tied to moves towards democratic practices and market economics. For them, the EC serves as a model for political reconciliation and economic rebirth through regional integration. This reflects the long road the Western European states themselves have travelled: that road led from fascism, international hatreds, regional disintegration and economic decline in the 1930s–40s to political pluralism, regional integration and economic rebirth in the 1950s–60s.

The speed of German reunification – and the widespread European acceptance of it – occurred in part because of the prior existence of the EC. The EC provided the framework for the rise of West Germany as a new state and its acceptance by the other Europeans as stable, pluralist, prosperous and co-operative. Thus anchored, West Germany, by word and deed, opened the way for reunification with the East. A reunified Germany ensconced in a deepening community of democratic states, which relaunched its own quest for economic unification in 1987, sent ripples of change across the Atlantic. Those ripples produced a tidal wave by December 1991 when the EC states – at their historic Maastricht Summit – agreed to further expand the purview of the EC into new areas of co-operation.

In the 1990s, the EC has become an economic and political superpower in its own right. The quest to complete the internal market has been complemented by an important, though oft-neglected, political co-operation dimension: the expansion in depth and breadth of EC foreign policy actions rooted in treaty law and habits of co-operation developed through European Political Co-operation (EPC). It has become a pole of attraction for neighbouring states from Sweden to Turkey. Change in Eastern Europe catapulted the EC onto a much higher level of political leadership than had been attained hitherto and elevated the political will to complete much of the '1992 programme' on time. By the early 1990s, the west of Europe – rich, stable, democratic, reinvigorated, and committed to realising the completion of the single market – is providing leadership and incentives for democratic change in the east of Europe – clearly unstable, underdeveloped, disunified and torn in some areas by ethnic strife. Indeed the EC appeared in 1991 as a bastion of stability admid chronic change against the backdrop of the formal dissolution of the Soviet Union by year's end. This has led some observers to predict that the EC of the 1990s will itself become the institutional structure of Europe rather than form a part of that structure.

Yet EC involvement in international relations was not limited to the former Soviet bloc. An attempt to upgrade the level and quality of EC relations with the United States and the European responses to Iraq's invasion of Kuwait and civil war in Yugoslavia meant that the EC could not remain aloof from the pressures of international inter-dependence as it entered the 1990s. In response to the '1992 pro-gramme,' the pace of German reunification and developments in Eastern Europe, the Bush Administration in 1989 began to quickly change the course of US foreign policy towards the EC from one of ambivalence (1970s–80s) to one of co-operation – a move not seriously attempted since the Kennedy administration. Out of this new and pragmatic recognition, the EC and the United States in-creased the frequency and level of their periodic bilateral meetings and expanded the content of co-operation into new areas – moves that were embodied in the November 1990 'Transatlantic Declara-tion' (see Appendix 2).

The ink was barely dry on this declaration when on 29 November 1990 the United Nations Security Council authorised the UN member states to use 'all necessary means' to uphold the previous Security Council resolutions demanding Iraqi withdrawal from Kuwait if Iraq did not withdraw by 15 January 1991. The EC had imposed full economic sanctions against Iraq two days in advance of the United Nations sanctions (of 6 August 1990) and some of its members committed naval, air and ground support to the anti-Iraq forces in Operation Desert Shield (August 9) and in Operation Desert Storm (16 January 1991). The gravity of the Iraqi threat to European interests pointed to the need for the Europeans to begin to deal with security threats outside the NATO area. At the time, some argued that the EC's shortcomings were made painfully clear by the inappli-cability of the Rome Treaty and EPC to the foreign security needs of the EC members and by the lack of political will in using the gravity of the occasion to overcome institutional constraints. Still others argued that the Europeans appeared weak because of the lack of unison within the Western European Union (WEU) as to the appropriate military response beyond co-ordination and consulta-tion. The European response to the Iraqi invasion threw an unex-pected light on the opening of the December 1990 intergovernmental conference of EC leaders in Rome. The future of the EC as a security actor was left to negotiations among the members, with implications not only for the future of Europe but for EC relations with the United States. That future was decided, at least for the next few years, at Maastricht in December 1991, when the EC leaders agreed to formalise links between the EC and the WEU aimed at giving the EC the potential capability to take co-ordinated military action outside the NATO area. A much more difficult decision – whether or not to constitutionally incorporate collective self-defence into the EC – was postponed until the EC's next intergovernmental conference on political union planned for 1996. In the meantime, it remains to be seen if the formalised EC–WEU link will result in an activated military arm of the EC.

No sooner had the EC tried to digest the implications of the end of the Gulf War and the liberation of Kuwait (28 February 1991) for its future security needs than the Dutch Council Presidency was thrown into the imbroglio of the civil conflict in Yugoslavia after the 25 June declarations of Croatian and Slovenian independence and the Serbian attack on Croatia which followed. Intent to not again be charged with lack of resolve, the EC quickly found itself deeply engaged in active mediation and in the dispatch of ceasefire monitors, but no consensus was to be found among its members to dispatch military forces. The EC's multiple attempts to engineer a ceasefire, its sponsorship of a peace conference involving the belligerents, and the downing by Serbian forces of one of its helicopters – with all five EC monitors killed – all point to the extraordinary efforts of the EC to stop the civil war short of military intervention.

The United States too had to adjust to international changes in the early 1990s with important implications for US–EC relations. The Bush administration challenged the EC to be a partner of the United States in the redevelopment of Latin America – mirroring the US support of EC aid efforts in Eastern Europe. The new US attitude towards the EC also reflected the realities of a post-cold-war multipolar international order. The United States, as one of several major powers with different kinds of strengths, must work with and enlist the support of these other powers, such as the EC, to manage economic as well as other spheres of international relations.

US leadership of the UN-sanctioned forces organised to liberate Kuwait from Iraq had potentially adverse implications for US–EC relations. Liberation highlighted American military strength, resolve and leadership and again pointed to – depending on one's interpretation – the EC's treaty constraints on military action or the EC's inability to break through those constraints and act militarily on the basis of intergovernmental action. Just at a time when the EC's international influence appeared to be on the ascendancy, US leadership of the anti-Iraq forces, including British and French troops, highlighted the military strength of the United States and the disunity of the EC states on a matter of vital interest to their security. Modest, token, passive or no military support was offered by other EC member states. A more upbeat, confident United States helped to reverse years of self-doubt, with implications for attitudes towards the EC. Although the EC itself was not directly relevant to the actual liberation of Kuwait, it did play an active diplomatic and economic role on behalf of Kuwait and the frontline states during the crisis. Previous conventional US skepticism toward the EC, given its response to the crisis, returned to some foreign policy circles in Washington and appeared for a short while to reverse the improved US attitude toward the EC. However, as it turned out, the United States continued its course of improved relations with the EC. Despite the imbalance between US and European military capabilities and global political leadership, the United States recognised that the EC will be an important and indispensable, though underutilised and underdeveloped, international partner.

The Bush administration supported the EC's mediating role in the Yugoslav crisis. The EC was well situated geographically, commercially, financially and politically to exercise leadership over the crisis. The United States was less well situated to provide a leading role, given its geographical distance, cautious political will, and meager resources at a time of massive internal and external indebtedness. Indeed, if the EC failed to lead the antagonists to a peaceful resolution then the US would have lost nothing and UN mediators would step in. As it turned out, EC mediation did not end the crisis and the introduction of UN peacekeepers was a likely scenario at the beginning of 1992. Again, the EC, despite all of its best civilian efforts, found that its overall effort was hamstrung by institutional constraints and internal divisions over the appropriateness of an EC military presence in Yugoslavia.

Despite the limits to the EC's military power – as shown by the Gulf Crisis – or by the constraints on its peacemaking – as shown by the Yugoslav situation, the civilian influence and power of the EC will be enhanced in a post-cold-war world: economic, financial, and political power will be more readily usable and widely effective relative to military power in a growing number of areas in international relations, e.g. in rebuilding the Polish, Lebanese and Cambodian economies, destroying or rebuilding the GATT, aiding the liberalisation process in the former Soviet Union, or helping to manage the international monetary system after the EC achieves the final stage of EMU. Although still a military superpower, the United States will have to adjust to the influence of other power centres in the world – e.g., the EC and Japan – who have at their disposal sizeable resources to influence political developments. Even if the EC and Japan were yet neither able nor willing to act with resolve in all areas of international affairs, their potential to help influence international relations in the very near future cannot be readily dismissed. In the fluid current of post-cold-war international politics, the United States and the EC must adjust to the changing distribution of world power not only to pursue their own interests but to help maintain a semblance of world order.

THE US AND THE EC IN THE INTERNATIONAL SYSTEM

The international politics and international political literature is rich with alternative perspectives which attempt to describe and explain relations among states and how those relations shift from period to period, but none focus on the US–EC relationship. Most theorists would agree to the importance of international politics to US–EC relations; however, none have undertaken an in-depth and systematic study of how the international system affects the course of US–EC relations, and vice versa.[1]

The genesis of US–EC relations drew much less from domestic sources than from the current of bipolar/cold war international politics, although international economic co-operation at the Bretton Woods conference in 1944 (to establish a new world economic order) predated the advent of the cold war. Both sides needed a military, political and economic partnership in order to contain Soviet communism and bolster a liberal world political economy. Since the United States had a preponderance of the world's material resources at the time, the EC was placed in a junior position in the partnership. The future EC states lined up behind, and took the lead from, the United States in

– the implementation of the Marshall Plan through the OEEC in 1948;

- the Berlin Crisis of 1948;
- the establishment of the GATT in 1948;
- the creation of the West German state in 1949; and
- the defence of South Korea in 1950.

The United States, overcoming an isolationist political culture, provided the future EC states with the ultimate guarantee – military security with the establishment of NATO in 1949. The United States played a critical role in helping to convince sceptical Europeans of the virtues of the Schuman Plan, resulting in the establishment of the ECSC in 1951.

From the European side, the structure of the international system of the late 1940s and 1950s dictated that the cues be taken from the Americans. There was little room for EC manoeuvre on the international stage because the hierarchical distribution of power was too tightly sealed. In addition, the EC itself was preoccupied with internal economic integration and had not yet developed a mechanism for foreign policy co-operation. The Soviet invasion of Hungary in 1956 was a brutal reminder of how the EC states were dependent on the American nuclear deterrent. From the American side, the threat from the Soviet Union forced actions to bolster the economic and physical security of Western Europe. If Soviet pressures had not existed in the period then the US relationship with Western Europe would have taken on a very different form.

The status quo of the EC dependent upon the United States was not acceptable in the long run. The strong opposition of the United States to the Anglo-French and Israeli intervention in Egypt in 1956 threw into clear light the division of world power into two preeminent blocs. The Western Europeans saw a superpower condominium in clear relief. The United States was not willing to go to war with the Soviets should they have intervened on the side of Egypt – as was possible – nor was the United States prepared to intervene on the side of Hungary during the Soviet–Warsaw Pact intervention that had occurred during the Suez Crisis. Strong pressure from the United States forced the British, French and Israelis to desist and withdraw from Egypt. The Soviets and Americans were seen to co-operate when they permitted a UN peacekeeping operation to enter Egypt. What shocked the West Europeans was the pressure of the United States on the British and French relative to that placed on the Soviets over Hungary. The net effect was a re-evaluation of British foreign policy, gradually leading away from the close link with the United

States and towards application for membership in the EC as well as the development of a fundamental rift in US–European relations. Like the Suez Crisis but with heavier stakes, the Cuban Missile Crisis again showed the dependence of the EC on the superpowers and its relative isolation in a world crisis situation.

Indeed, as the cold war began to thaw in the 1960s and 1970s and the international system moved from a bipolar to a multipolar configuration, US–EC relations began to take on a different hue. The factors that began to dilute the influence of the superpowers over the international system were as follows:

– the rise of China as an international power;
– a three-fold jump in the number of new states due to decolonisation;
– the economic reconstruction of the EC and Japan into economic superpowers each in its their own right;
– the proliferation of nuclear weapons;
– the expansion of international trade and economic interdependence;
– the advent of East–West detente; and
– the rise of influential non-state actors on the world scene, e.g., the PLO and OPEC.

In the cold war multipolar international system, US–Soviet *détente* remained touch-and-go and the world was still divided militarily and dangerously into two fairly hostile camps. However, neither bloc was monolithic. Cracks began to appear in the Atlantic Alliance with, e.g., French withdrawal from the military command structure of NATO, European opposition to US involvement in the Vietnam War and the unilateral action of the United States to break with the gold standard and fixed exchange rates by 1973. The extent of US hegemony in Europe greatly diminished as the EC developed more independently with, e.g., completion of the customs union (1968), establishment of EPC (1970), EMS (1979), foreign policy actions in the Middle East and in East Europe (1970s–80s), and enlargement (1970s–80s). Just as the bipolar world order was being pried open by systemic change, the EC was taking steps more and more independent of the United States as the United States buckled under multiple domestic economic pressures and international responsibilities. Involvement in the Vietnam War weighed down the energies and financial resources of the United States and exposed its limitations to allies and foes alike. As the EC questioned the role of the US in its security and the future of a bipolar cold war world order, it slowly began to assert its own interests in international affairs.

Cracks appeared in the Soviet bloc in the 1960s–70s with the invasion of Czechoslovakia and the rumblings for more liberalism in the satellite states. The effects of the Soviet invasion of Afghanistan and Soviet interference in the domestic affairs of Poland further isolated USSR internationally and pointed to a weakening position. By the 1980s the Soviet Union had weakened under economic mismanagement, popular disaffection and decades of brutal dictatorship. Its limitations, too, were exposed to the outside world. By the late 1980s, it was clear that the cold war was finally being put to rest with the Soviet withdrawal from Eastern Europe and the quickness of German reunification.

The post-cold-war international system, in which there are multiple poles and different kinds of power minus the cold war, presents new challenges to US–EC relations. If the US–EC partnership was largely a product of cold war bipolarity, then what can be said about that partnership in the succeeding era? The pressures of coping with the rise of nationalism in Eastern Europe, the collapse of the old Soviet Union, the pressing need to push for peace in the Middle East, the future of the international trade and monetary order, and the demands of the developing world looming over the horizon all impinge on the US and EC and require common approaches. Thus the international system of the 1990s, while drastically transformed, poses no less significant challenges to US–EC relations.

BILATERAL RELATIONS ACROSS
THREE HISTORICAL PERIODS

Three historical periods are identified in this section and are used as guideposts throughout the book: hegemonic (1945–circa 65); hegemonic decline (1966–circa 85); and post-hegemony (circa 1986 and after). This exercise shows (a) how interdependence has grown from its asymmetric form in the cold war to its complex form in the post-cold-war international system and (b) how policy and behavioural adjustments have lagged far behind historical change.

The basis for a close political, military and economic alliance between the US and EC states was established during the hegemonic period when the Soviet Union took hostile actions in Eastern Europe and the ensuing cold war forced the Europeans to accept American leadership and protection. The decisions taken in the late 1940s and early 1950s to create transatlantic and European institutions to strengthen the overall position of the western world moulded US–EC relations for the next four decades. Both sides needed one another for protection, although the future EC states were obviously more dependent on the United States than was the reverse. Keohane defines hegemony as the power of a state to control access to raw materials, sources of capital and markets; to maintain a large market for imports; and to possess the advantages in the production of goods with high value added yielding relatively high wages and profits (Keohane, 1984: 33). In other words, a hegemon has a preponderance of material resources and is stronger than any other power. The international profile of the United States and its relationship with the EC states during the 1945–65 period fits this definition of hegemony; this section will show how this hegemony affected US–EC relations.

During the period of hegemonic decline, the EC developed into an economic superpower in its own right with the capability to make its economic and diplomatic weight felt in civilian international relations. After the mid-1960s, US domination of the world political economy was challenged by the economic recovery and increasing unity of the EC (and Japan), with interdependence replacing hegemony (Keohane, 1984: 9). With the relative decline of the United States *vis-à-vis* the EC in nonmilitary matters, vestiges of American hegemony in US–EC relations appeared anachronistic. Either there were initiatives to break the vault of cold-war-era ties between the two that were unsuccessful (the US-sponsored Grand Design in 1962 and the Year of Europe in 1973) or there were no attempts to adjust bilateral policies at all (EC offered no initiatives due to its embyronic political development in earlier years and to the continuation of major differences among members on the formulation of a common 'US policy'). US–EC relations were caught in a time-warp. The hegemon tried to hold on to its outdated prerogatives in an increasingly interdependent (as opposed to dependent) world, while the former client did not initiate a new, more rounded relationship with its former patron but instead moved toward greater relative economic and foreign policy independence from it.

Then, by the late 1980s, the time-warp finally cracked with the epic changes in Europe, both East and West, the end of the cold war, the EC's potential to shape the future architecture of the continent, and the growing US acceptance of the EC as a real and potential world leader. It has been argued that hegemony is neither a necessary nor sufficient condition for the emergence of co-operative relationships: international co-operation can take place without it (Keohane, 1984: 31). The end of US economic and political hegemony over the EC ushered in a period of working co-operation between them which began in the mid-1980s (in the response to the Single European Act) and accelerated by the end of the decade (in the response of the US and EC to the collapse of the cold war). The current post-hegemonic period, then, refers to the opening up of a more symmetric interdependent relationship between the United States and the EC, although in defence the Europeans are likely to remain more dependent on the United States than the converse for some years to come. In 1947 the United States launched the largest peacetime unilateral transfer of resources to help rebuild Western Europe. In 1989 the United States and the EC were in far different positions. The EC led the West in the largest transfer of resources from one region to another since the days of the Marshall Plan. As the US and EC enter the post-hegemonic era in their bilateral relationship, they are again on the threshold of momumental change. Indeed, the demise of the cold war is as much a historic turning point in their relations as was its dawn.

In the immediate years ahead, key policy decisions will be taken both separately and together that will shape bilateral relations for decades to come, much as the key policy decisions taken in the late 1940s shaped relations that lasted until the 1980s. Key decisions to accommodate change is one problem, but perhaps what is more fundamental is the question: will decisions that need to be made actually be made, given the difficulties of reaching agreement, be it at the EC level or at the US–EC level? The decisions of the late 1940s that shaped bilateral relations for so long were taken against the backdrop of the most calamitous war in the history of humanity and its offspring, the cold war, so there was a sense of urgency behind transatlantic co-operation. The developments of the late 1980s and early 1990s are no less epic, but decision-makers are not dealing with the effects of world war. It will be more difficult for the US and the EC in global peacetime to adjust to change, but no less critical for the future shape of US–EC and international relations. Indeed, the current period of post-hegemonic stability – whereby no one power has the resources or will to dominate the international order – will define international relations well into the future. Hegemonic leadership is unlikely to be renewed in this century, by the US or any other state: hegemonic powers have, historically, emerged only after world wars.

During peacetime, weaker states have tended to gain on the hegemon rather than vice versa. The central problem of the world political economy is how to organise co-operation without hegemony (Keohane, 1984: 9).

HEGEMONY

Hegemonic leadership can help to create a pattern of order (Keohane, 1984: 44). The hegemon provides its partners with leadership in return for deferrence but it cannot make and enforce either without accepting a degree of consent from other sovereign states. Hegemony and sovereignty are not alternatives but are symbiotically related (Keohane, 1984: 46). With its resources and internal political will, and the decline in relative power of other former great powers at the war's end, the United States eventually led an acquiescent Western Europe out of the rubble of the Second World War into post-war reconstruction. The US both benefited from, and paid some of the costs of, rebuilding the emerging EC: both sides were willing to co-operate in the construction of a new post-war international system. The Americans and the Western Europeans needed one another.

Indeed, today's US–EC relationship harks back to the dawn of the cold war, when the United States took part in supporting the idea of Europe-wide co-operation. The 1947 Truman Doctrine's commitment to offering military assistance to states under communist pressure was designed to contain communism and was a precursor to the economic commitment to rebuild Europe. On 5 June 1947, at a speech at Harvard University, Secretary of State George C. Marshall offered massive aid to revive the war-torn economies of the European powers. Marshall, like State Department policy adviser George F. Kennan, recognised that aid must be extended to Germany despite the misgivings many would have who had previously suffered at German hands. Containment of Soviet power – and future German power – by pressing for a faster pace of European economic recovery was foremost in the minds of the US architects of the Marshall Plan. Marshall's offer led a year later to Congressional enactment of the European Economic Co-operation Act. That law created the European Recovery Program (ERP), which extended $13.3 billion ($60 billion in today's dollars) in aid between 1948–51. In its first year,

ERP aid accounted for 10 per cent of the federal budget and 2 per cent of the GNP of the United States.[2]

The United States was interested in encouraging co-operation among the Europeans as a first step toward a process of unity. A united Europe would heal old wounds and be better able to stand up to Soviet pressure and become a partner of the United States in the post-war international economic order. One string was tied to Marshall Aid. Rather than dictate the specific projects eligible for Marshall Aid, the United States insisted that the Europeans would have to organise themselves to co-ordinate proposals concerning aid allocation. What followed in 1948 was the Organisation for European Economic Co-operation (OEEC), the first post-war intergovernmental organisation of former belligerent states. Although the OEEC itself did not go on to provide the blueprint for a united Europe, as anticipated by the United States, it was a necessary and symbolic step toward the creation of the Federal Republic of Germany in 1949 and the Schuman Plan that followed in 1950. Today's European Community is the heir to the Schuman Plan.

Although the precise role of the United States in supporting Europe-wide co-operation is being debated, subscribers either to the conventional wisdom[3] or to a revisionist perspective[4] agree on one point. The outcome of the developments and negotiations in the late 1940s, involving American and European leaders, resulted in a totally new and beneficial relationship among the European powers. A brief comparison of the contending perspectives on the genesis of the EC and the role of the US in that genesis yields insight into the current debate about the future of those relations. Conventional (and more liberal) thought points to the endurance of bilateral relations based on mutual advantages, whereas revisionist thought points to ambivalance in those relations.[5] In the conventional wisdom, the United States:

- was instrumental in saving West Germany from starvation and, with other parts of Western Europe, from economic collapse and Soviet control through the Marshall Plan;
- was a critical force in integrating West Germany into the Western European fold through the OEEC and the ECSC, despite doubting neighbours;
- played a critical role in pressing both France and West Germany, with help from Jean Monnet, to accept co-operation with one

another, which helped to clear the obstacles to Franco-German reconciliation enshrined in the Schuman Plan; and
– pursued policies encouraging integration which fed on the ideas and actions of indigenous federalists from Count Coudenhove-Kalergi in the 1920s to Jean Monnet in the 1940s.

According to historians who specialise in Monnet's relationship with key American decision-makers of the era, Monnet's connections with figures such as Secretary of State Dean Acheson and the American High Commissioner in Germany John 'Jack' McCloy helped the United States to play a key and effective role in making the Schuman Plan a reality.[6] US interventions, through diplomacy, discussion, negotiation, prodding, promises and pressure, helped to bridge French and German positions, enabling the former protagonists to sign the Paris Treaty – the constitution of the ECSC – in 1950. Indeed, there is no doubt that the Americans wanted the Schuman Plan to become a reality, so they were willing to work with the French and Germans to help it along.

The Americans applied pressure on the French to accept German rearmament as a complement to the Schuman Plan and a necessary corollary to the Korean War. Even though the Schuman Plan (largely inspired by Monnet) was a French product, French hostility towards Germany persisted and thus it was no easy task for the Americans to help move French views. The French proposed the Pleven Plan (a European army with a small role for Germany) as a first step toward finding a security complement to the Schuman Plan. Although imperfect, it sent signals that France was moving in the direction of a broader acceptance of West Germany and its rearmament.

The Americans applied pressure on the Germans to accept the Schuman Plan in exchange for promises of German equality in the emerging security structure of Western Europe. The Germans did not approve of the French links between the Pleven and Schuman Plans, but were pressed by the Americans to take a more favorable view of the latter. McCloy, with input from Monnet, helped contribute to the process of understanding necessary to forge German acceptance of the Schuman Plan.

In sum, subscribers to conventional thought maintain that the Marshall and Schuman Plans represented the marriage of an American vision with an indigenous European movement. The Americans envisaged a united Europe to reverse the dangers of disunity in the face of the Soviet threat and the uncertainty concerning Germany's future. The Europeans, particularly Robert Schuman and Konrad Adenauer, pressed by the federalists, envisaged new forms of regional co-operation (from the intergovernmental to the federal models), given the alternatives of war and Soviet control. Conventionalists tend to emphasise US leadership rather than US self-interest in finding a place for a rearmed Germany in a uniting Europe to fend off the communists and to build a market within which to trade. They also attribute the early thrust behind European integration to American leadership and sacrifice, given the costs of aid and the monetary and commercial concessions given to the Europeans as they began to construct what is now the EC.

The revisionist perspective, elaborated chiefly by Alan Milward and John Palmer (and generally supported by realist theorists) seeks to dispel 'myths' about the economic conditions that 'necessitated' Marshall Aid and the precise roles of the United States, the European federalists and the major European states in the events that led up to the creation of the European Coal and Steel Community in 1951. They charge that:

- the United States had a 'free hand' in determining the rules and operating policies of the various post-war international institutions;
- there was no real economic crisis in 1947 that required massive aid to stave off political collapse;
- the European federalists were unable to translate their ideas through public support into action; and
- the French and Germans through the Paris Treaty (ECSC) – not the Americans through the Organisation of Economic Cooperation and Development (OEEC) – worked out their own peace treaty leading to integration based on a European approach. The OEEC was too closely tied to American aid and ideas about how the Europeans should organise themselves.

William Clayton, Assistant Secretary of State for Economic Affairs, reported in 1947 that 'Europe is steadily deteriorating . . . millions of people in the cities are slowly starving.'[7] Despite urgent calls from the State Department, revisionists maintain that these calls exaggerated the impending economic collapse of Western Europe in 1947 to gain public and congressional support for the political objectives of the Marshall Plan. These objectives were to quiet the domestic neo-isolationists, contain Soviet power by uniting Western Europe, encourage political pluralism, rebuild markets with which to trade, and garner a new, though junior, partner in the post-war international order. Nau, however, has argued that the dependence of US export trade on Western Europe was less significant than the domestic choices the US government made in lending support to the European idea (Nau, 1990). By showing that European economic stability was closely tied to US security, the government would receive support for an unprecedented and costly initiative (Milward, 1984: 5).

Palmer maintains that the history of US relations with the future EC states in the late 1940s has been written within an ideological framework determined by the academics and political advocates of 'Pax Americana.' The EC experience of that Pax Americana has been interpreted through the perspective of the cold war ideology manufactured by the United States rather than by the EC states (Palmer, 1987: 30–31). For generations, Europeans have been taught to believe that the enormous US military presence in Europe was primarily for the European rather than the American good and that without it Western Europe's political existence would have been jeopardized. US involvement was presented as a commitment of 'selflessness and generousity unparalleled in modern history' (Palmer, 1987: 31). The war devastated Europe, resulting in its dependence on the United States first through Lend Lease, then through the Marshall Plan. To many Europeans in the late 1940s there were only two options: accept domination by the United States or conquest by Russia (Palmer, 1987: 11).

Milward maintains that Western Europe enjoyed the speed and success of the economic recovery with high profit, investment and employment levels in most countries. Economic recovery from the war was uneven, but by no means did that indicate that all of Western Europe was near collapse. The crisis of 1947 was not a crisis in production but an acute shortage of dollars brought about by the fast pace at which production had revived. The European countries' payments deficit limited their ability to buy food and capital goods from the United States. Aid enabled the Europeans to cover deficits with the dollar area and continue the recovery that had begun earlier (Milward, 1984: 6–7).

Revisionists maintain that the US objective was to unite Western Europe through a British-led OEEC, first as a free trade area and later by a political union. Yet the OEEC was too contrived by the United States to serve as the appropriate springboard for unity. The British were not at all interested in European free trade and in making a commitment, much less a leadership one, to European political unity, and the French were not interested in the OEEC. They felt the American stamp on the OEEC very strongly and were not interested in the idea of free trade in general, and competition with Germany in particular, in advance of their own economic revitalisation programme. There were limits on the OEEC. Through it, the United States tried to forge regional co-operation through the politically charged issue of how to allocate Marshall Aid. Besides stating that the OEEC was reduced to a low level of political importance, Milward concludes that Marshall Aid was not important enough to give the United States sufficient leverage to reconstruct Western Europe 'according to its own wishes' (Milward, 1984: 469). 'The Europeans succeeded in finding the correct prescription to forge a peace treaty (the Paris Treaty) in which each of the former enemies could find key national interests satisfied. The Americans had much less to do with the creation of the ECSC than is accepted by conventional wisdom' (Milward, 1984: 471).

Ultimately, it would take a European creation, the ECSC, to make peace and establish institutions designed to promote trade liberalisation. Trade liberalisation ended up being less politically divisive than economic aid allocation. The French were able to overcome their fears of trade with Germany when it became clear that they had to accept and live with West German statehood and succeeded in negotiating with Germany terms in the Paris Treaty that were favourable to French interests. What then emerged in the Schuman Plan and later the ECSC was the construction of an institutionalised pattern of economic interdependence which both served the separate national interests of the countries concerned and laid the basis of a successful reconstruction and durable peace. The pillar of reconstruction was the ECSC, not the ERP and the OEEC (Milward, 1984: 469). Milward continues:

> When all credit is accorded to the persistence with which American policy strove to promote German recovery, its success still depended on the creation of a framework acceptable to the European[s]. . . . The Europeans made their own peace settlement in place of the major peace settlement that never came . . . [and] created an alternative pattern of reconstruction . . . (1984: 472)

The revisionist explanation leaves much to be desired. It fails to consider that American self-interests coincided with European self-interests at a time of economic and political uncertainty for all Western Europe. It fails to appreciate the dire economic hardship (widespread undernourishment bordering on starvation and massive dislocation) and potential for political instability given the uncertainty of Germany's future and the certainty of massive Soviet power perched so close by. It fails to appreciate the flexibility in the American approach for European integration and the US commitment to the notion that integration would bring enduring peace, with or without the American imprint. Revisionist thought fails to grasp the symbolism of American monetary and political support for German independence and European unity.

Michael Hogan studies the role of the United States in the early stages of integration, through the eyes neither of starry-eyed federalists and visionary Atlanticists nor of the hard-nosed unidimensional revisionists, but through a more balanced approach. He systematically argues the key role played by the United States in building European co-operation. Hogan concludes as follows:

- the United States was not trying to dictate integration as much as it was helping to rebuild the European market based on its own liberal model to promote growth, counter communism and bring Western Europe into a liberal, multilateral world economic order.
- US policy-makers were sincere in their conviction that unification promised the best future, though they viewed integration as a gradual process to make the Europeans self-supporting, harness West Germany to the cause of European recovery and security, and lay the groundwork for further unity.
- Through their aid and support for an integrated market, and their last-minute intervention in the Franco-German negotiations, the Americans had played a part in creating the conditions under which the Schuman Plan could succeed.
- US policy-makers were prepared to sacrifice certain US commercial and financial interests to achieve integration, albeit of an indigenous (and regulated) form.
- The Marshall Plan must be judged as one of the most successful peacetime foreign policies launched by the United States in this century: economically, as a program to control inflation, revive trade, industrial reorganisation, and production; politically, as a program to promote stability, resolve the German problem, and contain the USSR. The success was due to the US emphasis on self-help. As its leverage was not absolute, the new era was neither solely the result of American initiative nor fully linked with American thinking.[8]

Conceding that Milward's revisionism is a healthy corrective to earlier American paeans of the Marshall Plan, Hogan nonetheless goes on to fault Milward for denigrating the American contribution and leading to conclusions almost as unbalanced as those Milward seeks to refute. According to Hogan:

- The payments crisis portended a serious crisis in production that would come with the collapse of the critical dollar imports.
- The Marshall Plan was the 'crucial margin' that made European self-help possible. It faciliated essential imports, eased production bottlenecks, encouraged higher rates of capital formation, and helped to suppress inflation, all of which led to gains in productivity, to improvements in trade, and to an era of social peace and prosperity more durable than any other in modern European history.
- Although the Marshall Plan projected US power into Western Europe on a scale far greater than ever before, it did so to protect what policy-makers regarded as important economic and strategic assets and in a way that was far less heavy-handed than examples of US military intervention in various parts of the world since then. The Marshall Plan was a reasonable defence of US interests. US and European interests were largely complementary.
- The principle of self-help, to which the Americans generally adhered, gave the Europeans a good deal of control over their own destinies and leverage over the US. US leaders needed their allies as much as their allies needed them.[9]

Hogan's thesis bridges conventional and revisionist interpretations and helps to shed light on US actions in the early history of European recovery and integration. That understanding is absolutely germane to the study of US–EC relations. Where the two interpretations overlap is in their appreciation of the ultimate effect of the various attempts at integration – the peace structure and the permanent reconciliation – which is the lasting accomplishment of the work of key European and American leaders.

The Truman Administration recognised that proactive policies were needed to affirm Western values – at a time when such values were threatened by repressive forces from Czechoslovakia to Korea – which led the US Government to support further European co-operation. Commitment to the defence of Western Europe in the form of the 1949 North Atlantic Treaty Organisation (NATO) signalled American determination to keep Western Europe free from

Soviet domination and indeed just predated the US support for the Schuman Plan. The importance of NATO for US–EC relations is that it bridged previous American rhetoric in favour of European unity with a firm security commitment to defend that unity. From then on, the United States would be a 'European' power.

By the mid-1950s, the momentum for integration was fuelled by a more exclusively indigenous European movement, which responded to the collapse of the European Defence Community (EDC) in 1954. The EDC project created strains in US–European relations because the Eisenhower administration was concerned that EDC might undermine NATO. When Eisenhower was convinced that EDC was not designed to undermine NATO, US support for EDC was given. However, in retrospect, the EDC project showed that differences existed over 'Atlanticist' and 'Europeanist' views on the defence of Europe. By the time the European Economic Community (EEC) and the European Atomic Energy Community (EURATOM) Treaties were signed in 1957, direct American influence in the construction of the European project was greatly reduced. What the Americans failed to fathom in the early post-war era is that Europe's quest for unity was in part a response to preponderant American power – however benevolent it might have been. Unity would enable the Europeans to regain their pre-war international posture, deter Soviet aggression, and become less dependent on the United States. Future US–EC foreign and trade policy disputes would be symptomatic of their different perceptions of the goals of early post-war integration.

During the early post-war years, the EC members had little choice but to co-operate with the United States until they completed the post-war reconstruction process and learned to live in the shadow of the Soviet Union. What differences did exist were papered over to hold together the economic and military alliance at the zenith of the cold war. With the exceptions of a breakdown in European-American trust over the 1956 Suez Crisis and the 1962 Chicken War, both sides co-operated as allies and partners in the cold war. The allies (a) built up the new liberal world trade order embodied by the General Agreement on Tariffs and Trade and negotiated tariffs down from their pre-war heights, (b) expanded international trade, (c) built up such international financial institutions as the World Bank and the International Monetary Fund and (d) formed a defensive military alliance that provided them with the assurance of collective security within which economic development could occur.

The legacy of the early post-war period for today's US–EC relations is that during these years the institutions, practices and procedures managing transatlantic relations were established. The United States (rather than any European member) assumed NATO's supreme allied command. The United States accepted the costs to its trade interests of European economic integration, but then had second thoughts about those costs as the EC emerged as an economic powerhouse and commercial competitor just a few years later. The US had seen European unity as part of its plan to contain the spread of Soviet power, but when the EC states sought to adopt and sustain a policy of Ostpolitik – despite the Soviet invasions of Czechoslovakia (1968) and Afghanistan (1979) and Soviet actions in Angola and Poland in the 1970s–80s – the United States disapproved. As the US and EC travelled from the early post-war era to the present, bilateral institutions, practices and procedures remained the same, throwing relations into a tumult in the period of hegemonic decline. This period, which we now discuss, provided a difficult but necessary transitional phase between hegemony and post-hegemony.

HEGEMONIC DECLINE

The United States had 'less preponderant power' in this period than in the previous one and was less willing to defend its interests in terms complementary to those of Europe; indeed, the Europeans were less inclined to defer to US interests (Keohane, 1984: 49). The tenor of relations began to change significantly during this period when the EC began to 'draw level with and then to overtake the US as the leading world trading power' (Palmer, 1987: 138). US hegemonial attitudes and patterns of behaviour persisted because they were hard to break, but the rise of EC independence *vis-à-vis* the United States began to usher in a much more symmetric US–EC interdependent relationship.

The EC had developed into a core of rich states so attractive to its neighbours that membership and the number of associated states would each eventually double by the 1980s. West Germany had become the EC's economic driving engine and a model of political stability and democratic government. During the 1960s, the EC had eliminated internal tariffs, completed a number of important integration policies, and survived a French institutional challenge. By the 1970s it had begun to strike out on its own in international affairs by developing coherent policies towards the Mediterranean Basin,

Eastern Europe, the Middle East and the Third World. The Europeans were beginning to question the marriage of convenience they entered into with the United States two decades earlier.

The war with North Vietnam preoccupied Americans to the chagrin of the Europeans, deeply dividing the two sides because of widespread European opposition to the war. European despair over the war and the war's weakening effect on American political and economic power helped to spur the EC states into adopting their own procedures for foreign policy co-operation in 1970. The EC states were not intent on breaking their economic partnership and military alliance with the United States. They were, however, emboldened by their own economic success and more unified in facing the prospect of a weakened, less reliable, internally divided United States. Out of this looming crisis in European confidence in the United States, the EC states began to sketch out their own group style of diplomacy and foreign policy interests. Recognising that the possibilities for international influence grew exponentially when the members spoke with one voice, the number and variety of EC foreign policy actions expanded by the mid-1970s. Indeed, a politics of scale was at work as EC states came to realise the cost-savings of working as a unit to influence international politics – when and if national interests converged to permit such action – over working separately (Ginsberg, 1989a). The jump in EC foreign policy actions in the 1970s was also spurred by the accession of the United Kingdom, Ireland and Denmark in 1973 (Ginsberg, 1989a).

Just before US involvement in Vietnam grew deeper, the Kennedy administration had challenged the EC to a 'Grand Design' whereby the two sides would become equal partners in managing mutual interests. Not prepared at that time to accept the challenge, the quest for symmetry would not be seriously revisited by the partners and accepted by the EC itself until the second year of the Bush Administration in 1990. The Vietnam War, US support for Israel and American concerns about closer East–West ties in Europe – at the expense of NATO – eroded the cohesion between the US and EC and gave the Europeans reasons to form alternative policies. Although alternative foreign policies were put forth by the EC in the 1970s, a unified EC policy towards the United States continued to be elusive. There was no European consensus on an EC 'US policy'. There is still none today. Members have yet to come to grips with how to provide for their own security outside NATO. The Europeans have yet to resolve the question of whether their unity can be achieved with or without the United States playing an active security and political role.

In the 1960s the United States ran large payments deficits owing to economic problems at home, massive aid given to allies, the defence of South Vietnam, European accumulation of dollar holdings and a gold drain on the dollar. The US payments crisis coupled with an expanding trade deficit led the Nixon administration in the early 1970s to unilaterally strengthen the dollar and combat domestic recession. It abruptly suspended gold payments for dollars and abandoned fixed exchange rates between the major currencies, leaving them to float freely in response to market forces. The effect on the Europeans was, again, catalytic. Recognising their vulnerability to American action, the Europeans were spurred to increase their own monetary co-operation, which led gradually to the European Monetary System in 1979 and EMU in the 1990s. The 1979 step towards further monetary cohesion and partial autonomy from the United States was taken in response to the 'irresponsible and increasing unilateralism of the Americans in financial matters' (Palmer, 1987: 11). Recognising the damage done to relations with the EC by cavalier and unilateral actions, and the rise of an independent European political power in the world, the Nixon Administration tried in vain to revive US–European relations in 1973 in a policy initiative called 'The Year of Europe'. By then, the Europeans rebuffed the Americans for their impetuous rediscovery, which said much about the views of the former patron and its clients. Foreign policy disputes gathered speed with the divergence of views on how to fashion relations with the Soviet bloc and respond to the Israeli–Palestinian dispute.

Trade disputes rose to the top of the bilateral agenda in the 1970s because (a) the Americans were less disposed to accept the negative effects of EC policies on their exports, (b) trade deficits and export markets were redefined as national (economic) security concerns and (c) the spectre of a Soviet threat to Western Europe diminished, exposing commercial disputes between the highly interdependent partners. In the past, the framework of the defence alliance (NATO) and the pressing need to co-operate in the face of the Soviet threat helped to patch up trade squabbles. In global peacetime, even allies would be exposed to commercial rivalry of the most vicious sort given their high stakes in mutual dependence.

All was not fractious during the hegemonic decline period, however. Despite the rise in trade and foreign policy disputes, the two sides managed the world's largest two-way trade and investment partnership. Throughout the period, indeed, most of the flow of trade and investment went untouched by disputes. Trade squabbles were blown out of proportion as interdependence increased mutual policy sensitivities, as well as the political weight of domestic producers in policy decision-making at the national level. The two sides continued to negotiate in GATT to reduce international tariffs. They co-operated to form the International Energy Agency (minus France) in 1974, help finalise the Helsinki Accords of the Conference on Security and Co-operation in Europe (CSCE) in 1975, and help end the Israeli occupation of the Sinai peninsula in 1979.

What is significant about the hegemonic decline period is that the two sides had to adjust to their new relative roles in the international system. The adjustment process was very slow. Part of the problem of adjustment was that the United States continued to respond to the EC in terms of a patron–client relationship or indeed would ignore the EC and maintain bilateral ties with the individual members even when the EC itself had authority. American policy flip-flopped between ignoring or discounting the Europeans and overpowering them with calls for cooperation. The EC for its part cried out for recognition of its interests but failed to develop a coherent policy towards the United States. Lack of an EC 'US policy' contrasted sharply with the development of well-formed EC policies towards Eastern Europe, the EFTA states, the Mediterranean Basin, Africa, South-East Asia and Central America.

In sum, the capabilities and relative power bases of the two partners changed over the course of the hegemonic decline period, but the structure and distribution of labour (in defence and economic policy leadership) remained ensconced in early post-war hegemonic practices. The EC had to cope with schizophrenic US policies that ranged from sudden neglect to hostility to overzealous rediscovery and with the politics of America's relative decline. The United States had to cope with the EC's inability to forge a common policy towards the US, opposition to US interests, ingratitude for an unequal sharing of the burden of NATO defence, the growth pains of integration and the uncertainty of Europe's relative ascendancy. Each partner went through significant internal and external changes which were not addressed in the structure of their bilateral relations. Policy adjustments to accommodate change and manage both the growth in interdependence and the divisions over foreign policy issues were not seriously contemplated during the hegemonic decline period.

POST-HEGEMONY

In the period of hegemonic decline, US economic and political hegemony *vis-à-vis* the EC declined but was not fully eliminated, especially in the minds of the Americans. In the present period of bilateral relations, the US has largely ceased to behave as a political and economic hegemon *vis-à-vis* the EC in response to an acceptance of its own limitations, the rise in EC abilities and influence, and the changes in Europe and the broader international system that occurred in the mid-to-late 1980s. Vestiges of the cold war lingered on into the 1980s because, despite the advent of Ostpolitik and détente, the world from the Atlantic to the Urals was still divided into two military, political and economic camps. The ending of the cold war, establishment of a more peaceful military, political and economic order in Europe, the emergence of nascent liberal regimes in Eastern Europe and the climate of co-operation between the United States and the Soviet Union brought about a shift from a cold-war to a post-cold-war international order. Keohane has argued that under the international conditions of the late 1980s, international co-operation can take place without hegemony because (a) there will be no more hegemons in the twentieth century; (b) world politics is not a constant state of war; and (c) states do have complementary interests (Keohane 1984: 183). Keohane's contentions, when applied to the development of post-hegemonic US–EC relations, will be revisited in subsequent chapters.

The impact of the post-cold-war world order on the US–EC relationship has been catalytic. Now that both sides accept the end to the cold war and the need to rethink the military and political ties that once bound them together to face the common enemy, the whole gamut of US–EC relations has been thrown open to question and to change. That adjustment has taken the form of the post-hegemonic period in US–EC relations which is now in its infancy.

Developments in the 1980s triggered a new phase in US–EC relations, owing first to the relaunching of the EC with the passage and implementation of the Single European Act and the progress of European Political Co-operation (EPC) and second to the democratic revolutions in Eastern Europe. Whereas in the period of hegemonic decline, US and EC views diverged sharply when it came to the correct common western response to relations with the East, during the present era the two sides' positions have become more balanced.

From the EC perspective, the cold war in Europe began to end when the EC adopted West Germany's policy of Ostpolitik as its own during the hegemonic decline period in the 1970s (although the EC refused to recognise CMEA and domestically the CDU continued to attack Brandt's and Schmidt's Ostpolitik). Gorbachev's policies in Eastern Europe complemented the EC's long-standing policies there and so the EC view of Eastern Europe was not such a radical change from that of the past. From the US perspective, the cold war did not end in the 1970s but in the late 1980s with Gorbachev's policies of glasnost and perestroika, new thinking in foreign policy, and withdrawal from Eastern Europe (though the INF Treaty of 1987 was a harbinger of what was to come later in the decade).

So long as the superpowers remained divided, there were limits to how far Ostpolitik could move the continent toward more unity and peace under EC leadership. The United States had historically opposed EC Ostpolitik when unlinked to hostile Soviet actions in areas of the world outside Europe. The retreat of Soviet power in Eastern Europe that began in 1989 left Ostpolitik to serve as a springboard for further EC leadership and action in Eastern Europe. The United States did not have the policy in place, geographic location, extensive relative experience in dealing with the Eastern European states, and the will and resources to take the lead in managing change across the old European divide. The EC did.

Not only did the EC emerge as a proven structure of peace for the democratising states of Eastern Europe and as a new home for the former East Germany in 1989–90, but it was already making headway with plans to relaunch the common market. The Single European Act of 1987 also triggered negotiations for monetary and political union in late 1990 and throughout 1991 as well. The two epic changes across Europe – the '1992 project' in the West and the retreat of Soviet power in the East – unleashed the EC from the constraints of the cold war. The challenge of change in Eastern Europe drove home to Western Europe the need to strengthen the EC internal market by completing it. Thus what started out as two distinct political phenomena have been partially linked: both halves of Europe seek peace, freedom and economic security. The EC has of necessity rallied to the challenge by offering a wide range of economic, financial, trade and political incentives for the reforming states of Eastern Europe. Aid is tied to democratic reform and market liberalisation. Thus the EC is using the incentives it has to help induce the kinds of changes it desires.

How did these European developments affect US–EC relations? The United States government had begun to review relations with the EC before the retreat of the Soviet empire because of the expected impact of the '1992 project' and the accelerated development of EPC on US interests, although the review was affected by the Soviet retreat from Eastern Europe. The consensus that emerged in the United States by the end of the first year of the Bush administration was that there would be no 'Fortress Europe' and that the United States would stand to benefit from the completed common market if preparatory measures were taken. Thus a new US 'EC policy' emerged. The United States began to reach out to the EC as a partner in dealing with the uncertainties of a post-cold-war European order. Responsive to the democratic revolutions in Eastern Europe and to how the collapse of Soviet power would affect NATO, the Bush administration made overtures to the EC to improve institutional and political relations. Thus, in part, the new US policy was as much a response to the growing economic and political strength of the EC, emboldened by the Single European Act, as it was to the retreat of Soviet power in Eastern Europe and the rise of new, potentially liberal, independent regimes. The new US 'EC policy' would recognise the hard facts: if the United States was to have influence with the Europeans, it could not be seen to oppose further unification. Thus, it would be best for the United States to work with the EC to develop a relationship in which the responsibilities and burdens of managing global western interests would be more evenly shared. The shift in tone reversed decades of indecision over the appropriate response of the United States towards the EC as an independent foreign policy actor.

The role of the EC in Eastern Europe on behalf of the United States and the other advanced developed states bodes well for the rise of a more symmetrical and effective relationship between the United States and the EC. The retreat of the former Soviet Union from Eastern Europe eliminated a major source of division in US–EC relations: how to deal with the Soviet bloc. With consensus on the EC's role in the emerging new Europe, and given the agreement of the US and EC Council Presidencies to changes in 1990 to upgrade relations and widen co-operation, there is evidence to suggest that the long-awaited policy adjustment in US–EC relations may be beginning to happen. The challenge to US–EC relations in the 1990s is to exploit the 'peace dividend' in constructive ways. Without the Soviet threat, some ask, what is left to link the US with the EC beyond trade?

Whereas in the earlier periods, the US and EC had asymmetric or, at best, mixed forms of interdependence, during the current period complex interdependence has emerged as the chief concept and principle of US–EC relations.

THE NEED FOR POLICY ADJUSTMENT

Although the Transatlantic Declaration of November 1990 brought under one rubric decisions made over the previous twelve months to expand areas of co-operation and hold more frequent meetings at higher political levels, the document was more cosmetic than substantive. The question of a US–EC treaty to manage the world's largest interdependent relationship and mutual interests in areas outside Europe was put on hold for five reasons. First, the Europeans were considering negotiations to draft a new treaty on political union that would govern foreign and security policies, so that a treaty with the United States was at best premature. Second, the Europeans were also preoccupied with internal negotiations leading up to another draft treaty on economic and monetary union. Third, the Europeans were rushing to enact before 1 January 1993 the directives necessary to unify the common market as envisaged by the Single European Act. Fourth, some of the Europeans, the French in particular, were loath to forge new contractual links with the United States at a moment in European history when the EC was perched to lead a reuniting Europe. Fifth, after having taken the original initiative, sections within the Bush administration retreated from more ambitious and binding commitments, preferring instead a weaker 'declaration' to a 'treaty'.

To return to an earlier point, the original structure and function of US–EC relations have been bypassed by epic European and international changes. Uncertainties remain as to how – indeed, if – bilateral relations will be reworked to account for change. The economic and military security of the two sides is at stake. The work of the analytical thinker and the policy-maker requires a blueprint and a vision to help set out a framework for re-establishing relations on the basis of the politics of the post-cold-war period.

The EC's dilemma is how to manage its political and economic relations with the United States in the context of its own enhanced integration and of major changes in the external internation: vironment. It is affected by international developments in bot economic and security spheres. Economically, the completion of the single market and moves towards EMU change the agenda of its external relations. Moreover, protectionist disputes closely involve the EC and threaten the liberal international trading order. Militarily, the EC after Maastricht is gradually developing a defence responsibility, but how European governments see the future of NATO remains unclear. The EC faces instability on its doorstep in Eastern Europe, with the collapse of communism, the fragility of the new Commonwealth of Independent States among the former Soviet republics and civil war in Yugoslavia. European interests also need defending further afield, beyond the NATO area (e.g., in Kuwait). The EC seems less clear now than for some time as to what it wants from the United States, and Western European interests in economics, politics and security have become a complex mosiac.

The US dilemma is to maintain its interests in a rapidly changing Europe. The Bush administration hopes that, whatever new security structure emerges in Europe in the 1990s, there will be an appropriate place for the United States and NATO. The United States is a member of NATO but will never become a member of the EC. Until there is an institutional link between the US and EC, the United States will want to retain its influence in Europe through NATO. Through NATO as it now exists, the United States may remain militarily (as opposed to economically) more powerful than the EC states.

The two have deep stakes in one another's economies, given the existence of complex interdependence. During the cold war, some trade and other disputes were intentionally subdued or ignored owing to the imperatives of allied co-operation in the face of the Soviet threat. Now that the cold war is gone, a 'no-holds-barred' approach to dispute settlement could occur unless a reinvigorated political content is given to US–EC economic relations.

The collapse of Soviet power in Europe could boost or harm relations, depending on the extent to which both sides can agree on how to shape their future relationship. Relations could be boosted if a new security partnership is based on equality. Equality in a security partnership could come only if the EC states themselves can incorporate defence into their emerging political union. Even then, there is no guarantee that the EC states, once they have developed a defence alliance, will work with the United States in the pursuit of common interests globally.

The end of the Soviet threat to Western Europe has also eliminated the most divisive political issue in US–EC relations: how to deal with the Soviet bloc. The consensus which emerged in 1989–90 in Brussels and Washington was to work together to help the process of democratisation and the opening up of centrally planned economies to market economies. Yet without the Soviet threat, many ask what will bind the US and EC together politically. The future of NATO, the CSCE, WEU and the EC has dominated transatlantic dialogue, leaving the future shape of US–EC political relations subject to change for some time to come.

To sum up, the movement from hegemonic decline to post-hegemony marks a moment of truth for the United States and the EC. A much more symmetrical relationship emerged as the United States began to accept and support the EC as a partner and as the EC accepted and appreciated that recognition. The new tenor of relations was long overdue given the tensions and disputes that have increased since the early 1970s. But this flirtation may be short-lived if the two sides cannot come to terms with the appropriate mechanisms necessary to forge co-operation in areas of the world where joint responses may be needed to promote mutual interests. New institutional structures may be needed to bridge the post-cold-war Atlantic divide but are very difficult to construct in peacetime. However, if the will to work together by those in the highest levels of decision-making on both sides is carried out and sustained by their successors then informal modes of co-operation may work in lieu of new institutional structures.

THE ANALYTICAL PROBLEM

Readers of the literature on contemporary international relations will find few explanatory concepts pertaining to US–EC relations. The dearth of helpful literature is in stark contrast to the massive economic interdependence between the United States and the EC. Table 1.1 lists selected English language historical and policy books published in the 1980s relevant to US–EC relations by approach, author, date of publication and summary or thesis. A rating of low, medium or high is given for each book in terms of the extent to which the US–EC relationship is directly covered. The table shows that books on the Atlantic Alliance and NATO dominate the literature on US–European relations, with only low to medium coverage of

TABLE 1.1 *Selected policy and historical books relevant to US–EC relations in the 1980s*

Approach	Author	Topic	Summary or thesis	US–EC relations
Strategic security	Barnet (1983)	Atlantic Alliance	Chronicle of the Alliance with emphasis on the erosion of members' domestic consensuses for the Alliance.	Low
	Langer (1986)	Atlantic Alliance	Intra-alliance irritation over out-of-area issues and East–West relations has caused a crisis of cohesion.	Low
	Calleo (1987)	Atlantic Alliance	US failure to come to terms with economic weakness while it exaggerates the importance of military factors.	Medium
	Palmer (1987)	Atlantic Alliance	Problem of a post-Atlantic world with the US in decline and the EC unable to speak with one voice; divergent defense interests mean Alliance is crumbling.	Medium
	Kaplan (1988)	NATO	Chronicle of US–NATO relations.	Low
	Gill (1989)	Atlantic Alliance	Unprecedented strategic challenges will face the Alliance in the 1990s; 'Atlanticist world' is an anachronistic label.	Low
	Lepgold (1990)	Atlantic Alliance	US will be show to adapt to change; West Europe began to act in ways that made NATO obsolescent long before 1989.	Low

continued on page 36

TABLE 1.1 *continued*

Approach	Author	Topic	Summary or thesis	US–EC relations
	Lucas (1990)	Atlantic Alliance	European *détente* in the 1980s became a driving force and the most important arena for the reformation of East–West.	Medium
State-to-state	Harrison (1981)	French–US relations	Continuity in French disaffection for the Alliance predates de Gaulle; suggests a more co-operative French approach.	Medium
	Bull (1986)	UK–US relations	Analysis of history, defence and economic relations.	Medium
	Ninkovich (1988)	FRG–US relations	Chronicle of bilateral diplomatic relations.	Low
	Hanrieder (1989)	FRG–US relations	German security and welfare remain linked to international circumstances that have shaped German history.	Low
Public attitudes	Inglehart (1990)	Changes in political culture	Changes in political culture produce shifts in post-materialism which have diverse ramifications.	Low
Political economy	Woolcock (1985)	US–EC trade policies	US–EC policies are of central importance to global trade; differences over industrial/trade policies increase overall strain; political/security ties help minimise trade disputes.	High
	Tsoukalis (1986)	US–European trade relations	Divergent economic policies have increased; post-war international structures are inadequate to resolve problems.	High

Palmer (1987)	US–European trade relations	Relationship is decaying owing to global changes and bifurcating evolution of US/European geopolitics/trade/defence conflicts.	Medium
Baldwin (1988)	US–EC trade relations	Global trade system requires active support of US and EC; unresolved trade disputes weaken an already strained system.	High
Gill (1989)	US–European economic relations	Transatlantic system is undergoing a crisis of hegemony involving shift away from consensus behind Atlanticism.	Medium
Bilateral relations Freedman (1983)	US–European relations	Covers US/European views of Atlanticism; security policies/interests; economic interdependence, trade–monetary relations.	High
Smith (1987)	European–US relations	Relations couple continuity and change with recurrent uncertainty; events may outstrip capacities to adjust.	High
Ginsberg (1989)	US–EC political relations	EC actions are more independent yet 'US' policy is elusive; US–EC policy is uneven. Both struggle to adjust to change.	High

US–EC relations, followed by books on relations between individual European countries and the United States with a mixture of coverage.[10] It is not that these studies are at fault for not directly examining US–EC relations; indeed, they do not purport to do this. However, the net effect for the student of US–EC relations is a bibliography of books dealing with US–European relations from traditional perspectives in which US–EC relations *per se* tend to be lost or sidestepped. Books on political economy capture most of the scholarly work on US–EC relations, but they too are limited because they underemphasise the political and security dimensions of US–EC relations and instead cover trade, economic, and monetary relations at the expense of a broader fusion. Only one book deals with EC foreign policy actions in general, and EC foreign policy actions *vis-à-vis* the United States in particular (Ginsberg). Two other books deal more generally with US–European relations (Freedman, Smith).

In addition to the small number of works on US–EC relations, few conceptual books directly touch those relations. The dearth of conceptual work is a function of the broader literature on the EC itself and the simple fact that such a body does not lend itself to traditional foreign policy studies. The literature has been captive to the EC's own ups and downs. After two decades of richly descriptive studies on integration that followed the EC's own early years, the search for conceptual explanations of policy behavior was derailed in the 1970s. This was when the EC fell short of the full-blown economic and political union predicted by ambitious integration theories put forth by leading American thinkers. Many dismissed the EC in one fell swoop, either writing it off as secondary in political importance to its member governments or subsuming the politics of the EC to those of the international system. Still others either tried to squeeze the enormous complexity of the EC into largely unconnected atheoretical case studies or found established international relations concepts inadequate. Academic neglect of the EC was in part a reaction to the divided EC response to the oil cartel in 1973–4. Yet had pre-1973 EC-watchers continued to examine the EC that grew out of that low point in regional integration, they would have witnessed a resurgence of EC institutional and policy growth.

Realisation that the EC itself was becoming more complex and diverse made publication of grand conceptual works – in the vein of Ernst Hass, Leon Lindberg, Stuart Scheingold and others – problematic. In retrospect, mass abandonment of scholarly interest by leading Americans theorists beyond the early 1970s was too abrupt, leaving theory to lag far behind the key policy developments of the 1980s–90s, especially in such areas as foreign and monetary policies, enlargement, internal market, and institutional reform.

Part of the problem of conceptualising about US–EC relations stems from the EC's unique status as an unorthodox international actor, a status that defies traditional political science theory. First, without understanding the EC as a foreign policy actor, it is impossible to begin to construct a theoretical understanding of US–EC relations. Second, the study of the EC has fallen through the cracks of the traditional political science subfields of comparative and international politics. This indeed may be one of the main reasons why the study of the EC has suffered in the United States. Conversely, in Europe the study of the EC has been more continuous, although the Europeans produce more case studies than they do conceptual or theoretical studies. Case studies have served to deepen knowledge of the EC but – when they are not linked to concepts for understanding the broader EC – they fail to widen overall knowledge. The task is to marry the explanations that derive from American conceptual enterprise on the EC of the 1960s (offering breadth) with the European case studies of the 1970s–80s (offering depth).

Integration theories of the 1950s–60s failed to predict impediments to European integration, but produced a body of thought rich in explanation and description that is yet to be repeated in any subsequent collection of ideas on the EC. Realist, neo-realist, neo-mercantilist, liberal and post-hegemonic streams of thought that dominated the international relations literature during the 1970s–80s failed miserably to capture the dynamics behind the EC itself (Nau, 1979). After all, despite the gloomiest forecast for European integration and the rosiest forecast for the resurgence of national power, EC member governments have agreed to common positions requiring sacrifices of their interests. The rise of the EC's civilian influence in and away from Europe defies realist logic; and the relationship between the United States and the EC can no longer be accounted for in terms of hegemony. Interdependence theory of the 1970s–80s placed the EC's existence in the broader international political economy. This approach was useful to a point, but failed to explain the dynamics of internal EC politics that produced joint actions rooted not in global interdependence but in the internal dynamics of the customs union (Ginsberg, 1989a).

Academics who analyse US–EC relations cannot, however, begin to aid policy-makers and legislators with the description and explanation of changing relations (the task we define for ourselves) until they have developed and tested their own explanatory concepts. It falls not to the policy-maker and legislator, who hops, skips and jumps from crisis to crisis without the benefit of a guiding framework, but to the academic to study the partners and their ties as they are, not as they were, and to argue the need for adjustment, outline how best this might be made, and provide the new concepts that will aid the policy adjustment process.

The authors argue that there is a need for students of US–EC relations to have an analytic framework (subject of course to rigorous testing). There are several key concepts in the literature on the theory of international politics (linkage politics, neo-functionalism, regimes, interdependence, and international system to name a few) that could apply to the US–EC relationship but are either compartmentalised to the point of not being very helpful or are simply not applied to or tested in the domain of US–EC relations.

The complexity of the US–EC relationship necessitates a broad-based framework. This should embrace the different spheres of political activity affecting the relationship (e.g., domestic, European, bilateral) while focusing on its most important components. The US–EC environment is one of profound interdependence, but the concept of interdependence lacks specificity: relationships produce varied outcomes with little predictability. The breadth of the concept covers the complexity and range of US–EC relations; the analytic problem is to investigate empirically its most important characteristics.

The analytical problem is also a policy problem. Policy review cannot move ahead without a deeper analysis of the determinants of bilateral relations. The search for a suitable framework of tested concepts to describe and explain US–EC relations is the ultimate foundation for empirical understanding of those relations in the policy sphere.

ORGANISATION OF THE BOOK

In Section One, 'The New Context of United States–European Community Relations', the main problems that practitioners and scholars encounter in managing and studying bilateral relations are set out in the first two chapters. The effect of the changes in Europe and in the international order on US–EC relations have been outlined in this first chapter. Chapter 2 draws from the theoretical literature on international politics key concepts relevant to the study of US–EC relations. The concept of complex interdependence is then related more closely to US–EC relations and incorporated into a working analytic framework. Section Two, 'Empirical Analysis of US–EC Interdependence', shows in Chapters 3–5 how US–EC relations stretch across a wide number of dimensions and are profoundly interdependent. Chapter 3 applies the concept of complex interdependence to US–EC political relations. It does so by examining linkage processes, patterns of behaviour, and foreign policy actions to portray the intensity of their relations and the mutual sensitivites that result from them. Chapter 4 applies the concept of complex interdependence to US–EC economic relations. It describes and explains the multilateral and bilateral fora and processes of economic relations and uses indicators of economic relations, such as investment flows and trade-related employment data, to substantiate the existence of complex interdependence. The chapter inventories trade disputes and traces their resolution since 1962. Chapter 5 examines the strength of the social foundations which underpin the US–EC relationship. It considers changes in political culture, public policy traditions and public attitudes and asks: are the two sides growing closer together or drawing apart? Chapter 6 forms Section Three, 'Research and Policy Implications', and draws conclusions about the conceptual framework provided by 'complex interdependence' and suggests future lines of research. It also suggests policy adjustments in US–EC relations in light of the weight of evidence provided in earlier chapters.

In reality, the subject of each chapter could stand on its own as a separate book, given all the critical and interrelated components of US–EC relations. The authors have risked breadth over depth, giving the reader a panoramic view of US–EC relations.

When all is told, the story of US–EC relations should reveal a unique partnership that is struggling in the 1990s to adapt to epic change. Table 1.2 captures the complexity of those relations. Key aspects of bilateral relations (and their corresponding coverage in the book by chapter) are identified. For each aspect, there are centripetal forces which tend to cement bonds (because of mutual need, commonly held values) and centrifugal forces which tend to pull away from those bonds (because of the costs of mutual dependence and differences in political culture, state policies and security needs). The tug

TABLE 1.2 *Centripetal and centrifugal forces in US–EC relations: the balance sheet**

Aspect of the relationship and related chapters in book	Centripetal forces	Centrifugal forces
Culture (Chapter 5)	Common Judeo-Christian heritage (from which certain commonly held values and beliefs derive).	Different political cultures (e.g. over the relationship between state, society and the individual).
Historical experiences (Chapters 1, 5)	Wartime and post-war cohesion (which produced a unity of purpose in defeating the Nazi menace and containing Soviet power); ethnic ties.	Passage of wartime–post-war generation leaves young people with no memory of Second World War, the cold war and the origins of the Atlantic Alliance; growing population of US citizens of Asian/African descent relative to those of European descent reduces intensity of Euro-American ethnic ties.
Political and economic systems (Chapters 3, 4)	Pluralist democracies; advanced developed, mixed capitalist economies; mutual commitments to human rights, democratic practices at home and abroad.	Different and conflicting, views/policies on social welfare/state intervention in economy with implications for bilateral trade; nature of pluralist political systems provides opportunities for producers to lobby for protectionist action, in turn upsetting bilateral balance.
Interdependence (Chapters 1, 2, 4, 5)	Mutually symmetric trade and investment relationship; increasing evidence of a more symmetric political interdependence.	Asymmetric monetary interdependence (due to dollar's continuing global role) and asymmetric security interdependence (due to US military strength relative to the individual EC states and US nuclear umbrella through NATO.
International trade (Chapters 3, 4)	Common stakes in a fluid multilateral world trade order; together the two constitute 53 per cent of total world trade.	Politicisation of world trade has led to rise.in area and number of US–EC conflict; differences over use of export subsidies/credits to garner larger shares of third country markets.

Bilateral trade (Chapter 4)	Heavy dependence on each other's markets; the US and EC are each other's largest single markets.	Acute commercial rivalry in each other's market; disputes over scope/level of state aid to industry, NTBs.
Bilateral investment (Chapter 4)	Heavy dependence on each other's markets; the US and EC are each other's largest investment partners (US foreign direct investment in EC is $503 billion; EC foreign direct investment in the US is $325 billion).	Some restrictions on access to each other's service markets.
Foreign policy (Chapters 3, 6)	Mutual interests in maintaining the security of the Western countries and in co-operating to reach common objectives.	Broad discord over policies toward the various regions of the world (Middle East, Central America) and international issues (strategic trade, anti-terrorism); lack of mechanism outside NATO to coordinate policy.
Strategic security (Chapters 1, 3, 6)	Collective self-defence through NATO; as EC becomes more politically unified – with the possibility of its own or associated (WEU) security dimension – a US–EC security relationship could emerge to replace 'US hegemony' with equality.	Decline of the specter of a Soviet invasion – NATO's *raison d'être* – reduces the urgency behind the need for common defense and changes the original politico-security framework that enshrouded, and put into broader perspective, US–EC commercial relations.
International system (Chapters 1, 6)	Members of a group of two dozen like-minded states in an international system of 150 other states, many hostile to West.	Changes in the international system complicate bilateral ties, ease each side's relations with other partners, reduce US influence over EC, and provides room and incentive for EC to forge its own global interests.

*This table is based in part on a previous work, Ginsberg (1989b).

between these contending forces means that US–EC relations are not static, that the balance struck between these forces in the past is not certain to continue in the future, and that management of relations to maintain balance seems commonsensical, given mutual interests.[11] Indeed, the weight of the evidence provided in the chapters ahead points to several serious strains. Yet, at the same time, enduring links point to the continuation of very dense, mutually beneficial relations between highly interdependent partners. US–EC relations will not be revived by 1950s-style Atlanticist idealism, but by pragmatic adjustments to meet challenge and change for bilateral as well as global benefit. The book aims to bring the complex and changing US–EC relationship to a much higher level of analytical and policy understanding.

NOTES

1. See Keohane (1984), Kennedy (1987), Gilpin (1987), Calleo (1987); also Nau (1990) and Nye (1990). Although most of these scholars do not explicitly address US–EC relations, their concepts of international politics produce very diverse explanations of where the US and EC fit into the international order.
2. Frank Loy, 'Marshall Plan for European Recovery is 40 Years Old', *Europe*, June 1987, p. 16.
3. The conventional wisdom perspective dominates the literature on US–EC relations. Many officials of the ERP era, academic writers, and historians or former practitioners associated with the Council for Jean Monnet Studies in the United States write that US aid saved Western Europe from economic collapse and Soviet hegemony. Richard Mayne wrote that Marshall aid '. . . saved Europeans from imminent economic ruin' (Mayne: 107). Roger Morgan wrote about how, after an exceptionally bad winter, European recovery from the devastation of the war was held back in spring 1947 and how American action was needed to remedy a catastrophic economic situation.
4. The revisionist perspective is largely captured by Milward (1984). Revisionist historians have questioned the value of the ERP to the European recovery effort and view the Marshall Plan as a product of US national self-interest and nothing more.
5. According to Milward, 'it is small wonder that from the conception of the EC, its relationship with the United States has been so ambivalent' (Milward) (1984: 502).
6. At a conference on 'Jean Monnet and the Americans', held at Hyde Park in October 1990, the Council for Jean Monnet Studies sponsored papers (leading to a book) on the key links between Monnet and the Americans from the ERP to the ECSC.

7. As quoted in 'The Marshall Plan: Doing Well by Doing Good', *The Economist*, 15 June 1991, pp. 30–1.
8. Hogan (1989).
9. The preceding section is based on the conclusion in Hogan, (1989: 427–45).
10. Studies on the Atlantic Alliance, while very important in their own domain, subsume the relevance of US–EC relations to the strategic alliance as if the former were less critical than the latter. Relations between individual EC states and the United States, while also critical in their own domain, tend to glide over US–EC relations or give them parenthetical attention as if the two sets of relationships were ships passing each other at night.
11. Roy H. Ginsberg (1989b: 257). There was a time in the early post-war era when the centrifugal forces were either non-existent or underplayed for the sake of broader amity. After post-war reconstruction, when the glow of Allied victory and any urgency beyond containment of communism receded, centrifugal forces challenged the assumptions behind the centripetal forces and the depth of commitment beyond trade and investment flows. Centrifugal forces produced petty differences that threatened broader ties. The existence of the relationship now depends on a balance struck between those contending forces. Domestic and international pressures that work against transatlantic accord must not be underestimated. The centrifugal forces have grown in number and substance since the 1960s as the US, the EC and the surrounding international system have changed. A gradual transition in the EC's American relationship has been at work since the 1970s, causing inevitable frictions in the bilateral relationship. Whether the triumph of centripetal over centrifugal forces will continue remains the most critical question facing bilateral relations today.

REFERENCES

Baldwin, Robert E., Hamilton, Core B. and Safir, André (eds) (1988) *Issues in US–EC Trade Relations* (Chicago: University of Chicago Press).

Barnet, Richard J. (1983) *The Alliance: America, Europe, and Japan* (New York: Simon and Schuster).

Bull, Hedly and Louis, William R. (1986) *The Special Relationship: Anglo-American Relations Since 1945* (Oxford: Clarendon).

Calleo, David (1987) *Beyond American Hegemony: The Future of the Western Alliance* (New York: Basic).

Freedman, Lawrence (ed.) (1983) *The Troubled Alliance: Atlantic Relations in the 1980s* (New York: St Martin's).

Gill, Stephen (ed.) (1989) *Atlantic Relations: Beyond the Reagan Era* (New York: St Martin's).

Gilpin, Robert (1987) *The Political Economy of International Relation* (Princeton: Princeton University Press).

Ginsberg, Roy H. (1989a) *Foreign Policy Actions of the European Community: The Politics of Scale* (Boulder: Lynne Rienner).

Ginsberg, Roy H. (1989b) 'United States-European Community Relations', in Juliet Lodge (ed.) *The European Community and the Challenge of the Future* (New York: St Martin's).

Hanrieder, Wolfram F. (1989) *Germany, America, Europe* (New Haven: Yale University Press).

Harrison, Martin M. (1981) *The Reluctant Ally: France and Atlantic Security* (Baltimore: Johns Hopkins University Press).

Hogan, Michael J. (1987) *The Marshall Plan: America, Britain, and the Reconstruction of Western Europe, 1947–52* (Cambridge: Cambridge University Press).

Inglehart, Ronald (1990) *Cultural Shifts in Advanced Industrial Society* (Princeton: Princeton University Press).

Kaplan, Lawrence S. (1988) *NATO and the United States: The Enduring Alliance* (Boston: Twayne).

Kennedy, P. (1987) *The Rise and Fall of the Great Power: Economic Change and Military Conflict from 1500 to 2000* (New York: Vintage).

Keohane, Robert O. (1984) *After Hegemony: Cooperation and Discord in the World Political Economy* (Princeton: Princeton University Press).

Langer, Peter H. (1986) *Transatlantic Discord and NATO's Crisis of Cohesion* (Washington: Pergamon–Brassey's).

Lepgold, Joseph (1990) *The Declining Hegemon: The United States and European Defense, 1960–90* (New York: Greenwood, 1990).

Lucas, Michael R. (1990) *The Western Alliance After INF* (Boulder: Lynne Rienner).

Milward, Alan S. (1984) *The Reconstruction of Western Europe, 1945–51* (Berkeley: University of California Press).

Nau, Henry R. (1979) 'From Integration to Interdependence: Gains, Losses, and Continuing Gaps', *International Organization*, vol. 33, no. 1 (winter) pp. 119–47.

Nau, Henry R. (1990) *The Myth of American Decline* (New York: Oxford University Press).

Ninkovich, Frank A. (1988) *Germany and the United States* (Boston: Twayne).

Nye, Joseph S., Jr. (1990) *Bound to Lead: The Changing Nature of American Power* (New York: Basic).

Palmer, John (1987) *Europe Without America?: The Crisis in Atlantic Relations* (Oxford: Oxford University Press).

Smith, Michael, *Western Europe and the United States: The Uncertain Alliance* (London: Allen and Unwin).

Tsoukalis, Loukas (ed.) (1986) *Europe, America, and the World Economy* (Oxford: Blackwell).

Wallace, Helen, Wallace, William, and Well, Carole (eds) (1977) *Policy-Making in the European Communities* (New York: Wiley).

Woolcock, Stephen, Hart, Jeffrey, and Van der Ven, Hens (1985) *Interdependence in the Post-Multilateral Era* (Lanham: University Press).

2 A Framework for Analysis

How are we to understand the US–EC relationship? What are the positions of the United States and of the European Community in the contemporary international system? What kind of relationship do they have with each other? The answers to these questions should have both theoretical and empirical components. A framework for empirical analysis needs to be based on a clear theoretical foundation.

The purpose of this chapter is to justify the choice of 'interdependence' as the guiding concept for the empirical analysis which follows in the rest of the book (see especially Chapters 3–5). The aim is to provide a framework which applies 'interdependence' to US–EC relations, while taking account of the position of both in the international system. The framework is purposely broadly set, to establish the overall context of US–EC relations. It forms the theoretical basis for the particular empirical investigations presented here, though it also, in some respects, extends beyond them. The concept of interdependence necessarily encompasses domestic, bilateral, and international dimensions. The later empirical analyses focus mainly on the bilateral dimension.

The relevance of the concept of interdependence is outlined here by reference to alternative approaches in international relations, involving a critique of a wide-ranging theoretical literature. In order to highlight the essential features of the framework, however, and allow non-specialist readers to go directly to the empirical and policy chapters, a summary of the analytical framework is provided at the outset.

A FRAMEWORK FOR ANALYSIS: SUMMARY

The analysis of this study will be based on a careful combination of different theoretical approaches. This is justified by the complexity of the subject, and by the current lack of consensus among scholars of International Relations in general and of the European Community in particular. Both of these reasons limit the scope for parsimony in the analysis of US–EC relations. A comprehensive account must begin by recognising the varied nature of this relationship.

A framework should highlight the actors involved in the relationship, allowing for subsequent discussion of their relative power

47

and capabilities (the 'structure' of the international system to Waltz, 1986). Such an evaluation should be made across different policy spheres ('issue-areas' to Keohane, 1986). The analysis should also distinguish the processes that link the major actors involved in the relationship (Keohane and Nye, 1987: 745). The relationship can also be assessed by reference to the actual policies pursued by the actors. This should allow for actors changing their interests and objectives, but not making decisions on the basis of perfect information (Keohane, 1986: 193). Such distinctions follow those suggested by Keohane, who advocated a synthesis of existing theories (1986: 193–4).

There are four interlocking environments relevant to the present analysis. The first is that of the EC, which is an aggregation of actors operating through diverse channels. A distinction remains between EC and national government policies and actions in relation to a third party such as the US. The second environment is that of the bilateral interactions between the EC and the US. The third environment is the US foreign policy-making process, within which policy towards the EC is elaborated. Finally, there is the wider world environment in so far as it impinges on the US–EC relationship. It is the combination of these four environments which underpins US–EC relations. This chapter will consider each in turn. Figure 2.1 incorporates these environments into the analytical framework developed here.

The US–EC relationship involves several *distinct policy spheres*. Even before the EC was established the United States and the European countries had created a security alliance under NATO. Defence issues continue to be considered within this framework; by contrast, it was only after the passage of the Single European Act that the EC began to discuss the 'political and economic aspects' of security.[1] For these reasons, relatively less attention is given to the military–security dimension in the present study. The two policy spheres which form the *main focus* for the present study are those involving *politics* and *economics* (see Chapters 3 and 4). It is in these areas that the US–EC nexus takes on its greatest significance in the international system. The connection between US–EC relations and the wider international system was discussed in Chapter 1. Separate examination is made of the relevance of *social* and *cultural* factors affecting US–EC relations in Chapter 5, which considers the political relevance of culture, socialisation and policy learning. The *actors* involved in the US–EC relationship are many and varied. The *processes* of transatlantic relations reflect *multiple channels* of contact and, presumably, of influence between these actors. This is suggested

The US political system	US–EC linkages	The EC political system
Types of actors: Political leaders: administration, Congress. Bureaucratic staff: administration, Congress. Non-governmental actors: e.g. policy institutes, lobby organisations, press.	*Types of actors* Economic: multinational firms; trade finance and investment bodies. Political: multiple, as listed under two systems; no joint US–EC organisation; officials of NATO, international regimes. Other, non-state actors.	*Types of actors* *European* Political leaders in Council, Commission, Parliament. Bureaucratic staff: EC institutions, as above. Non-governmental actors: e.g. parties, lobby organisations. *National* Political leaders: government, parliament. Bureaucratic staff: government. Non-governmental actors: e.g. parties, lobby organisations, press.
Types of relationship: Formal: federalism, separation of powers. Policy process: open, diversified, decentralised.	*Types of relationship* Economic transactions (trade investment); political: multiple channels but no joint US–EC organisation *per se*, regular high-level meetings (involving EC institutions and national governments), security co-ordination via NATO, US–EPC foreign policy co-ordination; co-operation via international regimes. Social and cultural exchanges.	*Types of relationship* Hybrid structures: combines federal (neo-functional) elements and intergovernmentalism, involving both European and national levels.
	Agenda Multiple issues; no consistent hierarchy; no threat of military force.	
Interests (of government actors): Varied (no consistent hierarchy): rational, but based on imperfect information.		*Interests* (of EC, national institutional actors): loosely defined: varied (no consistent hierarchy); rational, but based on imperfect information.

FIGURE 2.1 *US–EC Relations: the Analytical framework.* The characteristics of the international system are its dynamics increased multipolarity; and that US–EC relations are more affected by outside pressures.

by the literature on linkage politics, interdependence, and the contemporary international system (see the section 'Bilateral US–EC Relations' below). Both the US and the EC can be identified as highly differentiated political systems, reminiscent of the descriptions of structural functionalism (Almond and Powell, 1966). Within the EC there are actors at the Community, national and sub-national levels. US foreign policy actors operate within a 'cocoon' comprising the administration, Congress, and a variety of non-governmental organisations (Nau, 1990). Straddling the bilateral relationship are bodies operating within distinct spheres. Economically, multinational enterprises, finance and investment networks, and organisations fostering co-operation (OECD) and various 'international regimes' (GATT) can be highlighted (see Chapter 4). Save for NATO, much less formalised are the political structures (processes) of transatlantic relations. Agreements, summits, and frequent intergovernmental contacts are important here (see Chapter 3).

The outlines of the analytical framework to be followed are portrayed in Table 2.1. It incorporates contributions drawn from a diverse literature – all too often left in distinct compartments – which is surveyed in the rest of this chapter. It follows the lead given by Keohane in his 'modified structural research programme', and thus has a general liberal orientation (1986: 193–4). It is a broad, multi-dimensional analysis. It covers different spheres of activity and of policy. It assumes that international relations have a dynamic quality, changing in response to new conditions. It recognises the importance of pressures in the domestic political environment affecting external actions. Extending Keohane's prospectus, it also identifies the EC as a unique entity in international politics: an aggregation of domestic and regional actors, but also one capable of producing decisions binding on its members. The internal processes of the EC in the 1990s are seen here as being best understood by a revised neo-functional theory (see the next section in this chapter). National governments remain very important, but the EC places member-governments in a special environment. Allowance is made for a variety of non-state actors and for multiple channels linking each of the major actors. It gives special attention to the processes (interactions) in different policy spheres, linking the major actors. Such interactions involve formal institutions, regular patterns of behaviour and flows of information.

Such aspects go beyond traditional realist assumptions, but these must be a matter for empirical investigation rather than a-priori assumptions. For similar reasons, it is posited that the power and capability of any actor is conditional upon the particular policy sphere involved. Whatever their limitations in establishing a general framework, it is recognised that political realism and neo-mercantilism, nevertheless, offer a means by which the actual policies and also the relative power of the major actors involved in the US–EC relationship might be evaluated. The analysis of subsequent chapters examines the US–EC relationship through the lens of this revised 'structural' framework (Keohane, 1986).

The conceptual framework applied to US–EC relations must take account of the evolution of these relations. The relevance of 'interdependence' is much greater – indeed, it is crucial – to an understanding of US–EC relations in the 1990s than it was in the 1950s. As argued in Chapter 1, US–EC relations can be distinguished over three periods: hegemony (c. 1945–65), decline of hegemony (c. 1966–85); and post-hegemony (since c. 1986). The interdependence framework developed here refers most directly to the 1980s and 1990s. Other tools – in particular, realism and 'hegemony' – are more relevant to the 1950s. The dynamism in international relations ought not to be neglected.

The rationale behind the analytical framework posited here is more fully discussed in the subsequent sections of this chapter. Several qualifications must be made in advance of this critique. A number of different approaches are considered: whether they be understood as 'perspectives', 'models', 'pre-theories' or 'theories'. Any survey must be selective. It is important to emphasise that the different approaches are not being evaluated in general but rather with specific reference to the US–EC relationship. The critique focuses, in turn, on the EC as a political system, on the US–EC bilateral relationship and on the domestic–external dimension of US politics.

THE EC AS A POLITICAL SYSTEM

The European Community is a *sui-generis* structure in the contemporary international system. As a political actor on the world stage it is inadequately accounted for by the existing scholarship of International Relations. Moreover, the literature on the European Community exhibits little consensus on its political operation. In placing the EC in the international system it is necessary to distinguish between the national spheres of political activity and that of the

Community. The EC is not a single actor operating in an undifferentiated environment: any study of its bilateral relations with the US must thus recognise its internal complexity.

The institutional structure of the EC is portrayed in Figure 2.2. The EC is a hybrid, based on two separate notions of power and representation which can be termed intergovernmentalism and federalism (Nugent, 1989; Lodge, 1989). The Council of Ministers, composed of national government ministers, and the summit meetings of the European Council, comprising the heads of government (president in the case of France), best represent the intergovernmentalist character of the EC. The European Parliament, the world's first directly elected international assembly, best represents the federal dimension. Straddling these two dimensions are the Commission and the Court of Justice. The Court, based in Luxembourg, adjudicates on EC laws which take precedence over national legislation. It is not to be confused with the European Court of Human Rights in Strasbourg, which is not an EC institution.[2] The Commission, the administrative and executive agency of the EC based in Brussels, is the only body formally entitled to propose new legislation. The Commission is appointed by the national governments. The limits to representation and accountability inherent in this hybrid structure have prompted criticism of the EC's 'democratic deficit.'[3] EC legislation is passed according to several processes, which differ according to policy sector. The final outcome is determined by the Council and (with some exceptions) the Parliament, though the relative power of each varies according to the provisions governing the particular policy sector involved. The power of the European Parliament varies between, *inter alia*, the co-decision procedure (e.g. internal market policies), the co-operation procedure (e.g. social security), the assent procedure (e.g. external agreements, the accession of new members) and the consultation procedure (delivering opinions) (Millar, 1991). The EC has been compared to a federalist structure and an intergovernmental organisation. In reality, it is both, though the exact mix has varied over time. In the current period of reform, the EC seems set to become increasingly supranational and federal.

The supranational character of the EC was significantly enhanced by the agreements reached at the December 1991 European Council meeting in Maastricht. Major changes were agreed covering economic and monetary union, social policy and foreign policy. A three-stage plan to achieve Economic and Monetary Union (EMU) before the end of the century will involve a single EC currency and a

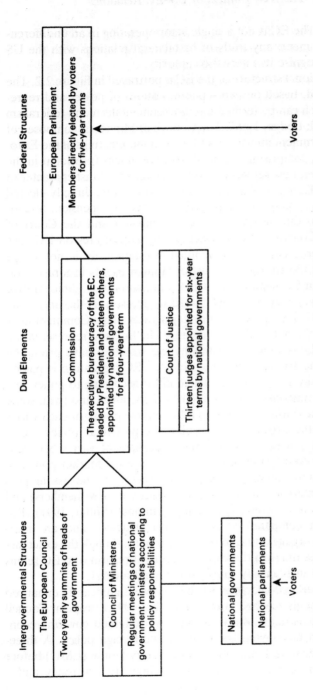

FIGURE 2.2. *Institutional structure of the European Community: a hybrid.* This is a simplified sketch designed to emphasise the dual character of representation in the EC institutional structure. Further details are available in Lodge (1989) and Nugent (1989). Other institutions also exist: the Economic and Social Committee (which gives its opinion on EC policies), the European Investment Bank (which offers loans and guarantees to promote economic development within the EC) and the Court of Auditors (which produces annual audits and reports on EC finances). In the context of the present study, these institutions are of lesser importance.

European central bank. The pace of these changes will depend on how closely national economies meet the specified convergence criteria. However, the final phase of EMU is due to begin by 1 January 1999 at the latest, with a single currency established at least between a group of EC member-states before the end of the century. All EC governments, except the UK, also agreed at Maastricht to commit themselves to fulfilling the aims of the EC Social Charter approved in December 1989. These provisions will establish EC-level agreements across a whole range of employment and social policies.

In external relations, the EC has long operated in a unique and differentiated manner. In external trade negotiations the Commission is the key actor, having executive authority initially mandated by the Council of Ministers. For agreements with other states and the accession of new members, each of the three main institutions – Council, Commission, Parliament – are involved, with the latter now having a right of veto. For more general foreign policy matters – under 'European Political Co-operation' (EPC) – national representatives in the Council are the key actors. The 1991 Maastricht agreements further enhanced EC co-operation in this regard. One of the fundamental objectives of the EC now is to seek the implementation of a common foreign and security policy, including eventually the framing of a common defence policy (see Chapter 3).

The EC's ability to act in this sphere in the recent past has been well documented elsewhere (cf. Ginsberg, 1989; Ifestos, 1987). Neo-functional explanations (discussed below) saw the EC being forced to act externally in response to the stimuli from outside governments affected by EC trading policies: a process termed 'externalisation' (Schmitter, 1969). Ginsberg (1989) identified an additional explanatory concept of EC foreign policy activity: a European interests model. This is based on the 'internal dynamic' of the EC and represents a synthesis of different theoretical explanations. It helps 'to better understand why the EC acts in foreign affairs on its own accord, independent of external pressures to act' promoting its own regional interests (1989: 35). Again both explanations illustrate the need to adopt a broad-based conception of the EC as a political actor.

The power of national governments within the EC political system is very important, but the Community is more than what others have called an 'intergovernmentalist' entity. Intergovernmentalism applied to the EC sees 'governments carefully aggregating domestic positions at the national level', and 'holding the gates between the Commission and their domestic politics' (Wallace *et al.*, 1977). The conception is inspired by a realist approach (see next section). 'Intergovernmentalism' appears to be an outdated description, particularly after the adoption of the Single European Act by the EC and its current moves on Economic and Monetary Union and Political Union. The national political systems are much more open to wider EC activities than this conception implies. An accurate understanding of the pressures behind the adoption of the Single European Act (SEA), for example, would recognise the significance of the part played by the European Parliament, the Commission, outside pro-integrationist lobbies, and business leaders. Individual national governments entered a new terrain of debate: for some of them, this was against their initial instincts (e.g. Britain). In important respects, what appeared to be a 'neo-functionalist' integrative process came into play, beyond the explanatory confines of realism or of inter-governmentalism. To assert that it was still national governments that had to bargain over the SEA would be to neglect a full explanation as to how such matters arrived on the EC's agenda in the first place (but for a realist interpretation, see Moravcsik, 1991).

'Neo-functionalism', as a theory of regional integration developed in the 1950s by Ernst Haas, now seems more appropriate to the EC than it did in the 1970s (Haas, 1958). Keohane and Hoffmann (1989) agree that the Single European Act has revived the supranational style of decision-making that was lost after 1966. 'Yet', they argue, 'this style is supranationality without supranational institutions: the Commission is not a supranational entity in the sense of being an authoritative decision-maker above the nation-state, nor has loyalty been transferred from the nation-state to it' (1989: 13). They are certainly correct to note the variation of decision-making styles that can stem from the EC's political structures, particularly given that the latter have gone through periods of change. A similar point was noted by Rosenthal in her review of the 1968–71 period when she commented that there 'are many different processes of decision making in the EC so there is not just one method but many different methods of influencing decisions' (1975: 135).

Crucial to the neo-functionalist interpretation was the view that integration would proceed on the basis of 'spillover' from one policy sector to another (Haas, 1958, 1968). Keohane and Hoffman (1989) have reviewed the concept of spillover in the light of recent experience. They contend that

[handwritten marginalia: Spillover - one policy leads to another]

successful spillover requires prior programmatic agreement among governments, expressed in an intergovernmental bargain. Such a bargain is clearly important in accounting for the Single European Act. Without the turnaround of French economic policy in 1983 and the decision by the British Government to accept treaty amendment in order to institutionalise deregulation, no consensus would have been reached on a program to dismantle barriers within Europe. (p. 29)

Thus 'spillover' is revived, but intergovernmentalism is not completely dead. The evolutionary nature of the EC is rightly recognised. Yet Keohane and Hoffman may have gone too far to accommodate intergovernmentalism: 'spillover' did not occur earlier because of national government resistance, but neither was there the same 'extragovernmental' pressure for further integration in the 1970s as became apparent in the 1980s. Although it is outside the purview of this study, the key question which needs careful research is how and why the change in governmental and non-governmental opinion occurred between the 1970s and the 1980s.

What kind of political system does the EC have? Haas, the father of 'neo-functionalism', declared in 1975 that regional integration theory had become 'a component of a larger analytical framework' of interdependence, constituting a special case of the latter. There is much to commend such a statement, but its dismissal of neo-functionalism was premature, and it offers little help to understanding the specific nature of the EC's political structures. As Nau (1979) noted, studies of interdependence often lack the analytic and theoretical rigour of regional integration theory. Keohane and Hoffman suggest that the Community be viewed as 'a set of complex overlapping networks, in which a supranational style of decision-making, characterised by compromises upgrading common interests, can under favourable conditions lead to the pooling of sovereignty' (1989: 3). This seems to be an accurate reflection of what has actually happened in recent years, while the concept of 'networks' acknowledges the ambiguous and evolving character of the EC's political structures. It is important, also, to note their recognition that the EC can upgrade common interests, a process which extends beyond the narrow confines of power politics as posited by realists and at least some champions of intergovernmentalism.

In sum, any explanation of the EC as a political system needs to recognise four basic dimensions. The first dimension is the ideas and values, and the motivations and interests which have supported integration and led to the adoption of particular policies. The political actors involved in the integration process follow different values and motivations: for some these extend beyond the narrow conceptions of power politics and 'lowest-common-denominator' bargaining outcomes.

The second dimension is the different spheres or 'levels' of activity of the EC. That is, it is necessary to understand how its various parts operate in relation to each other. Beyond the formal institutions are the cross-national party groupings (e.g. the Socialist Group in the European Parliament) and lobby organisations (e.g. the Committee of Professional Agricultural Organisations (COPA)) exerting their own policy influence. Moreover, in addition to the 'supranational' EC institutions, individual national and, increasingly, sub-national, administrations and organisations have become involved in EC processes.

The third dimension of the EC as a political system is the balance of power existing within it. The EC's dual structure of accountability (intergovernmental and federal) gives it an ambiguous and flexible character. Yet the EC integration process, especially after the Single European Act, indicates that national government power and responsibility have been constrained. A narrow focus on them would be misleading, omitting other important actors and interactions, and inadequately accounting for the policy agendas and reactions of national governments themselves.

The final dimension in an explanation of the EC is that it should take account of the EC's dynamic quality, the evolving nature of the integration process. Ultimately, it must account for key changes in the EC's development, contrasting, for example, the 1965 crisis prompted by de Gaulle and the adoption of the Single European Act in the 1980s. To account for the history of integration is beyond the current task, but it helps to highlight the breadth of the perspective needed.

Added together, these are four demanding requirements of any explanation of the EC's political system. Progress seems most likely on the basis of conceiving of the EC as an entity operating in a highly interdependent world, whose internal dynamics in the 1990s approximate to an amended neo-functionalist formulation. The EC's actors, motivations, interactions and locus of power extend beyond an intergovernmentalist interpretation. Externally, different EC actions can be understood by a range of approaches that extend beyond realism to include a regional integration or an interdependence logic (Ginsberg, 1989). Internally, the EC system may well equate to 'organisational networks' as recently suggested by Keohane and Hoffman, as this conception has a broad-based, open and dynamic character which also recognises the operational ambiguities of the Community (1989). Thus, to understand the role of the EC, a synthesis is necessary of explanations covering its internal processes (a revised neo-functionalism) and external actions (e.g. regional integration and interdependence). The analytical framework pursued here recognises this.

BILATERAL US–EC RELATIONS

There are two major alternative approaches to understanding US–EC relations in the contemporary world. Both are drawn from the scholarship of International Relations. Although they have achieved much prominence, neither has been applied to a comprehensive study of the US–EC relationship. The first approach is to try to combine realism and neo-mercantilism; the second is to identify the bilateral relationship as a case study in interdependence. The two approaches differ in their focus: the first places prime emphasis on the role of nation-states, while the second identifies a variety of actors relevant to the relationship. 'Interdependence' is a concept applied most readily to the international system as a whole. In part, it highlights the scope for co-operation via international regimes, based on shared interests. By contrast, realism and neo-mercantilism portray the world as conflictual, as nations seek to increase their power and wealth. The two approaches have important contrasts: they are separate dramas, with distinct actors and plots, written in different languages.

Yet from these differences there may be a potential compatibility between the two approaches. In having distinct concerns, they may not contradict one another (Keohane, 1986). To some extent, they refer to different features of the same world. This does not mean that they are equally valid either in general or in particular cases. In order to determine their applicability to US–EC relations, it is necessary to consider each in turn.

(a) Political Realism and Neo-mercantilism

Political realism focuses on nation-states, and their power and security interests. This immediately suggests its limitations with respect to studying US–EC relations. As already noted, the EC is not equivalent to a nation-state and it is *sui generis* in the contemporary world. Moreover, the agenda of US–EC relations has involved political and economic issues more than traditional questions of security. Thus, whatever its other applications, political realism as traditionally conceived offers an incomplete guide to US–EC relations.

Political realism has different concerns. Morgenthau, in a classic realist statement, described a world 'whose moving force is the aspiration for power of sovereign nations' (1948). The concepts of power, rationality, national interest and the balance of power were central to his framework. More recently Waltz (1979) has offered a 'neo-realist' formulation. He accepts the need to place national actions in the context of a theory of the international system as a whole, but he argues that 'states are the units whose interactions form the structure of international political systems' and that 'they will long remain so' (Waltz in Keohane, 1986: 90). International relations are 'decentralised and anarchic', in contrast to domestic politics which have a common governmental structure. Waltz doubts whether it is possible to combine domestic and international politics into one theory (in Keohane 1986: 340). Both Morgenthau and Waltz dismiss the role of international organisations. To Morgenthau, nations participate in such bodies in order to strive for power. For Waltz, international organisations either behave as new states (he cites the medieval papacy as an example) or they remain so weak that the power of the individual states within them shines through (in Keohane, 1986: 81).

In sum, there are a number of reasons why both realist and neo-realist formulations are inadequate when faced with the complexities of US–EC relations. These can be set down as follows:

(i) There are *a greater variety of actors* involved in this relationship than any brand of realism acknowledges. It would not be helpful to begin research with rigid, preconceived notions of the relative power of these actors. The type of actor varies: most notably, the EC itself has a unique internal political structure with different levels of power and modes of decision-making. There are, in addition, numerous non-governmental actors operating within the US–EC environment.

(ii) The actors relevant to US–EC relations pursue *a variety of interests*, even as individual units. Change within the EC, for example, has been critically affected by Community-level factors distinct from the nation-states. Also, actors within successive US administrations have given different priorities to security and economic issues in the context of relations with Western Europe (e.g. Kennedy as opposed to Nixon). Traditional distinctions between 'high' and 'low' politics have become increasingly blurred (e.g. the political and economic aspects of security).

(iii) The agenda of US relations with the EC institutions – of fundamental importance to the political and economic relations of the Western World – has had little direct relationship to security issues. Moreover, security issues have zero-sum outcomes. Yet, zero-sum struggles for power cannot be comfortably transposed to the non-security arena: many political and economic issues involve the potential for collective gain, as Nye (1990) has noted. Western economic management is such an arena.

(iv) The realist perspective neglects the *complex and sensitive linkages* which underpin US–EC relations. Neither the US nor the EC is an autonomous political actor: an accurate account of their external relations would conceive of them as highly differentiated, penetrated and constrained systems. The linkages existing between them transmit profound and reciprocal effects (see the discussion of 'complex interdependence' below).

The parsimony of political realism is attractive. While its narrowness offers an incomplete framework for studying US–EC relations, its interpretation of actors' interests does provide a relevant basis on which to evaluate actual policies and performances over time. Political realism also offers a distinctive (and, usually, skeptical) view of the scope for US–EC co-operation in the contemporary world.

Of central concern to political realists (and, indeed, neo-mercantilists) is the nature and effect of hegemonic power in international relations. Some recent realist studies have suggested that the end of the cold war increases the danger of crisis and war in Europe, east and west. Both US and Soviet hegemony has declined. Hitherto, a balanced, bipolar nuclear world maintained peace, which overcame a historic fractricidal tendency on the part of each of the European nations (Mearsheimer, 1990). Other works inspired by realism (and neo-mercantilism) have charted the decline of US hegemony. Kennedy (1987), in a broad historical survey, saw cyclical trends in hegemonic leadership and the relative decline of the US because of its failure to balance its economic position with that of its military strength. Similarly, Calleo (1987) describes the failure of the US to come to terms with its economic weakness, while it exaggerates the importance of military factors. Nau has offered a different interpretation, arguing that suggestions of US decline are a myth: it is a matter of how it asserts its policy choices and priorities (1990).

Whether or not the US and/or the EC are hegemonic powers is a question which extends well beyond their bilateral relations. One or the other may be a hegemon *vis-à-vis* third parties, but they are not in a position of over-arching dominance in their bilateral relationship. The US does not stand in the same hegemonic relationship to Western Europe in the 1990s as it did in the late 1940s and in the 1950s (the 'hegemonic period' elaborated in the previous chapter). In addition, no one suggests that the EC dominates the US. Yet, the US has not lost all of its hegemony in the world; rather it increasingly varies by region and policy sphere (Nye, 1990). For its part, the EC acts as a hegemon to some degree in its relations with Eastern Europe, the Mediterranean basin and the ACP states. The relevance of 'hegemony' is thus to be judged empirically in relation to particular conditions. In the 1990s, it seems less relevant to the bilateral US–EC relationship.

While the complexity and sensitivity of US–EC relations go beyond a realist perspective, the relevance of neo-mercantilism deserves separate consideration, given its focus on the economic sphere. In truth, recent realist literature has given considerable attention to economic trends (cf. Gilpin, 1987), blurring the distinction between it and neo-mercantilism. In such cases, they can be considered as part of the same category. Not surprisingly, some limitations that apply to neo-mercantilism are similar to those of realism.

Mercantilism developed as a historical explanation for the external economic policies of national governments. In a classic work by Heckscher first published in 1934, mercantilism 'deals with the economic policy of the time between the Middle Ages and the age of *laissez-faire*' (1955: 20). Viner sets down common mercantilist assumptions: the pursuit of wealth and power are seen as being intimately connected; indeed, they are complementary goals (1958: 286 in Gilpin, 1987: 32). Today, neo-mercantilism suggests that Western countries will pursue external economic policies 'that advance their security goals and preserve their national autonomy' (Haus, 1991: 166). Gilpin has referred to benign and malevolent mercantilism and, more generally, to economic nationalism (1987: 404).

Gilpin believes that the decline of US hegemony 'has seriously undermined the stable political framework that sustained the expansion of a liberal world economy in the post-war era' (1987: 351). Consequently, the US and its economic partners find themselves in a situation in which they have a strong incentive to co-operate and co-ordinate their policies in order to resolve the supply and demand problems, but they also have a strong incentive 'to cheat and to attempt to solve their own domestic problems at the expense of the others' (1987: 360). Gilpin thus disputes the scope for co-operation or pluralist management in the post-American hegemony era as advanced by Keohane (1984). Instead he paints a worrying picture of increasing fragmentation and instability in the global political economy, as a result of trends towards economic nationalism, regionalism and sectoral protectionism. Without a hegemon the best that can be expected is 'some form of benign mercantilism' involving some national protectionism intended to safeguard certain values and interests (Gilpin 1987: 404). In trade relations, governments will increasingly pursue bilateralism and conditional reciprocity (1987: 401).

As with other approaches considered here, the relevance of neo-mercantilism to US–EC relations is to be judged in terms of both the structure (and processes) of the relationship as well the actual policies pursued by the actors involved. Among studies in the neo-mercantilist genre, Gilpin's work is the most relevant to US–EC relations. The controversies and sensitivities arising in US–EC economic relations will be discussed in Chapter 4 (on trade and investment) and Chapter 5 (on the domestic contexts).

In general, neo-mercantilism suffers from some of the limitations of realism. In so far as it focuses on the primary role of national governments, it neglects the distinctive role of the EC and of other important actors such as multinational corporations. Gilpin does endeavour to incorporate both. Yet his description of the EC descending into 'a loose federation of twelve states' (1987: 375) was quickly shown to be outdated. To give greater recognition to the role played by the EC might disturb some neo-mercantilist assumptions as to the operation of national economic interests. As members of the EC, national governments have interpreted their interests in being part of the Community in a broadly based manner. National interests have been calculated to take account of political and social gains, as well as different economic advantages. The EC is not a purely economic exercise, but even in this sphere interests take varied forms.[4]

The advantage of an approach based on political realism and neo-mercantilism is the relative clarity and parsimony of its explanation. It can be applied to the US–EC relationship and tested by empirical evidence, such as with trade disputes. As a framework for analysis it appears to have limitations, but its interpretation of current policy trends deserves careful attention. Given the difference in focus, it might also be combined with notions of interdependence, as suggested by Keohane (1986). The concept of interdependence is the reverse image of realism and neo-mercantilism: it has a broad systemic coverage, but lacks specificity when applied to particular cases. As a general framework for analysis it does, however, appear as a more accurate account of the contemporary US–EC linkage.

(b) The Complexity of Interdependence

In a system of international interdependence there are distinctive interactions between various types of actors. The United States and the European Community, for example, represent two very different international actors. Rosenau has suggested not only that the international system should be conceived of in horizontal terms – the relations between states – but also that the vertical relationships between international, national and local politics should be incorporated (1969). These vertical relationships exhibit 'linkage politics'. The boundaries of individual nation–state systems are regularly transcended by various types of political actors: subnational, transnational and supranational. Undifferentiated environments should not be assumed at either the domestic or the international level. Indeed, the international system is highly differentiated, not only in terms of the 'levels' of politics, but also according to the intensity of co-operation, the types of actors and the nature of the issues involved.

Rosenau has recognised a variety of types of actors operating in the international system. Scholars must 'break free' from the 'conceptual jail' of conceiving of world politics in a state-centric fashion. Other forms of (non-state) political activity are becoming important and it is an analytic distraction to think of hierarchies. At the close of the twentieth century we are witnessing, he argues, a fundamental transition to a 'post-international politics'. This is because 'More and more of the interactions that sustain world politics unfold without the direct involvement of nations or states' (1990: 6). Though this adds untold complexity, analysts do need to keep an open mind as to the types of political actors identified as relevant.

Rosenau's conception of 'interdependence' has been distinctive. He has consistently focused on interactive effects within the international system: for example, the external repercussions emanating from political activity in one political system. 'Political adaptation' is a key aspect to this notion of interdependence. This conception follows that of Russett (1963) who referred to 'responsiveness' being necessary before suggesting that 'two nations are affected by each others' actions' (1963: 97). The focus is on interactions and their consequences for the actors involved. Hassner has also emphasised the effect of interdependence on the interactions between actors (1975). Yet, more generally, it must be noted that Rosenau provides no single formulation of 'interdependence' and his conception remains somewhat loose as a consequence.

The concept of interdependence was notably refined by Robert Keohane and Joseph Nye in their book *Power and Interdependence* in 1977. They examined the relationship between political power and economic interdependence (Keohane 1989a: 412). They saw 'dependence' as a state of being determined, or significantly affected by, external forces. 'Interdependence' they understood as a state of mutual dependence, in which there are reciprocal effects among nations. Keohane and Nye contrasted the basic assumptions of realism with what they described as another ideal model: '*complex interdependence*'. Complex interdependence has three main characteristics. Firstly, there are multiple channels of various types which connect societies. Secondly, the agenda of international relations consist of multiple issues that are arranged neither in a clear nor a consistent hierarchy. Finally, military force is not used by governments towards other governments within an interdependent region, though it might be *vis-à-vis* outside countries. Moreover, these three characteristics give rise to distinctive political processes (1977: 29–36). There are four elements to these processes: linkage strategies ('linkages by strong states will be more difficult to make since force will be ineffective': 1977: 37), agenda setting (how issues come to receive sustained attention by high officials), transnational and transgovernmental relations, and the role of international organisations.

The concept of 'complex interdependence' represents a significant step forward. It is a useful model with which the present world can be compared. Yet Keohane and Nye have created confusion over the extent to which they believe 'complex interdependence' describes the current world.[5]

Any conception of interdependence in the present world needs to be a highly differentiated one. The extent of interdependence clearly varies from one policy sector to another, be it security, trade, finance or energy. Some linkage between sectors may be established in a bargaining situation by one or more of the actors involved. 'Creating and resisting linkages between issues where one is less or more vulnerable becomes part of the (international) power game', as Nye has noted more recently (1990b). The critical focus for any study of interdependence must be on interactions and their consequences for the actors involved. This follows the lead of Rosenau, as well as Keohane and Nye. Interdependence involves repercussions or 'reciprocal effects'; the autonomy of actors is reduced and choices are constrained. Interdependence affects, and is itself affected by, policy choices on the part of the actors involved. Differences are likely with respect to the types of actors involved, the extent of 'reciprocal effects', the type of power relationships existing and the levels of policy autonomy available.

Keohane and Nye have distinguished between 'interconnectedness' and 'interdependence' (Keohane and Nye, 1977). The latter exists when interactions (transactions) involve 'significantly costly effects' (1977: 9). The effects result from the transactions themselves and they vary according to type. They use an economic illustration of this point: 'a country that imports all of its oil is likely to be more dependent' on a continued flow than is an importer of purely luxury goods (1977: 9). Transactions have both costs and benefits, producing symmetrical or assymetrical outcomes. They do not limit the term 'interdependence' only to relationships which are mutually beneficial: costs may exceed benefits. There will, though, always be costs, 'since interdependence restricts autonomy' (1977: 9). Interdependence exists when the costs of the transactions ('interactions' is preferred here) are actually or potentially significant. Further differentiation can be drawn between 'sensitivity' and 'vulnerability' in a nation's response to external pressures (1977: 12–13; and see here Chapter 3, note 6).

Interdependence is a general concept drawing together economic as well as political aspects. The concept is inherently multi-dimensional. Yet the manifestations of interdependence are likely to take distinct forms: interdependence is likely to produce 'political' and 'economic' expressions which can be distinguished. Moreover, an interdependent relationship may have a stronger economic dimension, than a political or security one.

From even a cursory examination, it would seem that US–EC relations in the 1990s may come close to the Keohane–Nye conception of 'complex interdependence'. The relationship appears to display a profound level of interdependence, albeit one varying across policy sectors. Curiously, Keohane and Nye (1977, 1987) gave the relationship very little attention. Yet the US–EC relationship meets most of their conditions. The use of force by either party against the other is unthinkable. Multiple channels do clearly connect US and EC actors. The agenda of US–EC relations is composed of multiple issues, though whether they are arranged in a clear, consistent hierarchy or not is arguable. The relative importance of different sets of issues as reflected in the attention given to them by political leaders has fluctuated over time in response to varied pressures. In any event, the one condition that potentially separates US–EC relations from the Keohane and Nye model of 'complex interdependence' is that of a policy hierarchy. In addition, the various political processes they associate with their model would, in principle, seem relevant to the study of transatlantic relations.

The present study seeks to determine the extent to which US–EC relations approximate to the model of 'complex interdependence' outlined by Keohane and Nye. This will involve the identification of relevant actors and processes, as well as evidence of policy constraint resulting from interdependence. The shortfall in this perspective is that, as currently formulated, it lacks parsimony. Applying it to particular relationships is difficult because it lacks specificity. 'Interdependence' is a concept most readily applied at the level of the international system; there are empirical problems in adapting it to the micro-level of individual state policy or action. This point will be pursued further in relation to political interactions in Chapter 3.

The concept of interdependence need not be seen as totally incompatible with some realist precepts. Keohane has advocated 'a multidimensional approach to world politics that incorporates several analytical frameworks or research programmes' (1986: 191). Indeed, he has identified a potential synthesis between realism and interdependence for similar reasons. The Keohane and Nye formulation of interdependence is said to draw upon 'structural realism' (Keohane 1986: 160). As a counterpoint to this, Keohane suggests a 'modified structural research programme' based on three assumptions (1986: 193–4). This would recognise that while states remain the principal actors in world politics, also important are non-state actors, intergovernmental organisations (not 'international organisations'), and transnational and transgovernmental relations. Secondly, actors are assumed to behave rationally (as under realism), but not to have perfect information or unchanging preferences and objectives. Finally, the assumption that the pursuit of power constitutes an overriding interest for states is rejected. Instead, the definition of interests varies according to different conditions. Moreover, state power is not necessarily fungible across issue areas.

The present study of US–EC relations will follow this lead. It adopts a broad, multidimensional analysis. It recognises the importance of pressures in the domestic political environment to external actions. In addition, it also identifies the EC as a unique entity in international politics: an aggregation of domestic and regional actors, but also one capable of producing binding, unitary decisions. A wider perspective is also incorporated: apart from the political and economic dimensions, account is also taken of social factors such as culture, socialisation and policy learning. Keohane and Nye have themselves highlighted the importance of interactions and learning (1987: 751). Moreover, the approach adopted here recognises a utility in empirically testing realist assumptions on policy interests and the scope for cooperation (as suggested by Keohane's 'structural realism').

Systems of interdependence may also possess organised structures or procedures linking international actors which reflect and reinforce their mutual sensitivity. That is, their importance to the operation of interdependence lies in what they communicate: their policy content and effects. In their overtly political form such structures or procedures can include common institutions, treaties and alliances, extensive and frequent meetings, as well as 'international regimes'.

Chapter 3 will explore the political dynamics of interdependence in more detail, but it is appropriate here to refer briefly to the concept of 'international regimes' as it has developed from a wider, theoretical literature. International regimes have come to play a prominent part in the relations between Western nations. A generally accepted definition of international regimes is that they are

> sets of implicit or explicit principles, norms, rules and decision-making procedures around which actors' expectations converge in a given area of international relations. Principles are beliefs of fact, causation, and rectitude. Norms are standards of behaviour defined in terms of rights and obligations. Rules are specific prescriptions or proscriptions for action. Decision-making procedures are prevailing practices for making and implementing collective choice. (Krasner, 1983: 2)

Important to such regimes is the degree to which they produce policy agreements which are accepted and which thus represent a constraint of choice upon the actors involved. In this manner, regimes reflect interdependence.

The concept has been widely discussed. Keohane and Nye (1977, 1987) noted that interdependence might be affected by such regimes: for example, the old Bretton Woods international monetary system. Keohane (1984) addressed the question of why institutionalised international co-operation persists as US hegemony declines. He argued that co-operation is possible without hegemonic leadership, if international regimes have been established (1984: 32). When 'shared interests are sufficiently important and other key conditions are met, co-operation can emerge and regimes can be created without hegemony' (1984: 50). Keohane distinguished 'co-operation' from 'harmony' as well as from 'discord'. Keohane considered regimes in a variety of contexts – monetary, trade, oil – yet he gave little direct attention to transatlantic co-operation.[6]

Unfortunately, the standard definitions of an international regime remain loose, and this makes empirical classification difficult. At most the EC itself might be regarded as a distinct variant of an 'international regime'; but it is of a stronger form than other regimes.[7] EC institutions have economic responsibilities which do directly impinge upon transactions and the structure of the economy. Legal sovereignty has been transferred to EC institutions. Moreover, attitudes and interests have been affected. Each of these points go beyond conventional understandings of a regime. As William Wallace has noted, the EC is less than a federation, but more than a regime (Wallace *et al.*, 1983).

The relevance of the concept of an 'international regime' to the environment of US–EC relations is a broader and distinct question. The role of organisations such as the GATT, the IMF and the OECD can be compared to international regimes (see Appendix 1). Yet, many regimes extend beyond the transatlantic arena. Moreover, the Krasner definition of an international regime cited earlier seems so general that it might even be applied to the totality of US–EC relations. This could cause confusion.

In adopting interdependence as the guiding concept for the analysis of US–EC relations, separate consideration needs to be given to the position of the US in the international system. While the internal complexity of the EC as a political system is easily recognized, an interdependence perspective also suggests that the US should not be viewed as a single, undifferentiated actor in the international system. This question is discussed below.

THE US IN THE INTERNATIONAL SYSTEM

The US is hardly a single, unified actor in the international system. A study of its external relations should not begin by discounting its internal complexity. It is arguable that even Presidential action should not be understood in terms of one individual, given the complexity of the executive branch and the separation of powers. In any event, although the president remains as one of the most important political actors in the international system, there are other actors, linkages and sensitivities shaping the nation's external relations, not only in the political sphere but also in the security, economic and social fields as well.

The present study is not concerned so much with how policy is established domestically, as with its international aims and effects. Nevertheless, both policy and behaviour are affected by the character of this environment. In his now classic study of the causes of foreign policy action (over Cuba) Allison has testified to the importance of differentiating the domestic arena (1971). Foreign policy studies often assume that

> governmental behaviour can be most satisfactorily understood by analogy with the purposive acts of individuals. In many cases this is a fruitful assumption . . . But this simplification – like all simplifications – obscures as well as reveals. In particular, it obscures the persistently neglected field of bureaucracy: the maker of government policy is not one calculating decision-maker but is rather a conglomerate of large organisations and political actions. What this fact implies . . . concern[s] the basic categories and assumptions with which we approach events. (1971: 3)

Moreover, policy is not only made by organisational or bureaucratic actors within the official government process; there is also a wider domestic environment of relevance. Recently, Nau (1990) has argued that foreign policies are to be understood as a matter of choice: not simply by individual governments acting alone, but rather in response to policy ideas advanced within

> the cocoon of nongovernmental organisations that surrounds domestic bureaucratic and international institutional decision-making processes. Ideas compete in this cocoon to shape social views. These views then permeate, through political coalitions and

elections, more immediate policymaking processes at both the domestic and international level to influence choices about national purpose and economic efficiency. This larger consensus in the cocoon of nongovernmental organisations enables highly pluralistic, democratic policymaking institutions to work. (1990: 7)

The reader does not have to accept Nau's 'choice-oriented perspective' in its entirety, in order to share his recognition of the relevance of this wider domestic environment.

From an international relations standpoint, then, the US is to be understood as a highly differentiated and open political system composed of a variety of relevant actors. 'US foreign relations' refers here to the whole panoply of external relations involving actors within this domestic system. In addition, however, it is not simply a matter of different types of actors, but also the variety and extent of linkages (or channels, networks) and of sensitivities (or 'constraints' to Keohane and Nye).

CONCLUSION

This chapter has argued that the interactions between the US and the EC are best understood via the concept of interdependence. Both the US and the EC are to be seen as complex and open political systems. In particular, the EC is a *sui generis* entity in the current international system. US–EC relations are affected by different types of actors, multiple channels of contact and influence, and high levels of mutual sensitivity to each other's actions. The nature of their interdependence will vary across a range of policy spheres.

The concept of interdependence establishes the overall perspective. Yet, within this perspective, a more accurate understanding may be possible by accomodating the knowledge gained from other approaches in International Relations. In particular, the policies and interests pursued by key political actors can be assessed empirically according to the precepts of realism and neo-mercantilism. 'Interdependence' lacks parsimony and specificity; realism and neo-mercantilism may be straitjackets cut off from important features of the US–EC relationship.

The emphasis placed here on the concept of interdependence is prompted by the circumstances of US–EC relations in the 1980s and 1990s. Theoretical understanding follows changes in the international system. In the period of US hegemony over the West (c. 1945–65), realist assumptions had a special relevance. The cold war focused scholarly attention on the security-based politics of the NATO alliance. For its part, the European integration process was still at an early stage: neo-functionalism reflected the concern with its internal creation. Later, in parallel to the decline of US hegemony, the EC became more assertive externally. With US–Soviet détente, economics became more important: multidimensional sensitivities were apparent. The position of the EC in the international system and the extent of economic interpenetration between nations (*inter alia*) now suggest the relevance of 'interdependence' to US–EC relations. The concept embraces more of the complexity of diverse channels, issues, and power capabilities associated with the current international system.

The analyses in Section Two of the book follow the framework elaborated here. Their empirical concerns are guided by the concept of interdependence. The discussion also assesses the relevance of interdependence to the historical development of US–EC relations.

Concepts and theory help to clarify and direct a framework for empirical analysis. The interactions between the US and the EC need to be distinguished and placed in context: the trees must be placed in the forest. Conceptual clarity also deepens the understanding of policy issues and alternatives (see Chapter 6). The kind of theoretical reflection offered here is thus not an academic distraction: rather, in its sharpest form, it is the ultimate foundation for empirical understanding.

NOTES

1. At the December 1991 Maastricht EC Council ('Summit') meeting, new arrangements for defence co-operation, involving the West European Union, were agreed. See Chapter 3, and The *Financial Times*, 12 December 1991.
2. The European Court of Human Rights is associated with the Council of Europe, an international organisation which also has its headquarters in Strasbourg. The Council of Europe is a much looser form of organisation, which seeks to foster co-operation between European nations. It is not based on supranationalism or a transfer of sovereignty. The Council of Europe was established in 1949 by ten European nations. (In 1991 it had 25 members, plus several Eastern European states with special guest status.) Its establishment thus pre-dated the ECSC and the EEC. It

represented an early effort to promote European integration: its institutional weakness meant that the UK was prepared to participate in it, but the Council failed to meet the aspirations of continental nations who wished to build a closer union. Some have envisaged the Council playing a more important role after the collapse of communism in Eastern Europe.

3. The discussions on political union at Maastricht were, in part, intended to resolve the 'democratic deficit'. In reality, only modest changes to the powers of the European Parliament were agreed.

4. Neo-mercantilist assumptions might be usefully incorporated into a 'game theory' of US–EC economic relations (Brams, 1991). This would require a model to be created simulating the strategic interplay between all major actors. To be accurate, the model would need to be complex and diversified to account for the role of various actors and for differences between policy sectors. Such a model is beyond the scope of the present study. In any event, in following such a methodology, the results can depend on the theoretical model used, the structural parameters assumed, and the set of strategies selected. The scope for a successful and acceptable application of a game-theoretic model may thus be limited.

5. In 1987 Keohane and Nye admonished some of their critics by stating that they had never claimed that 'complex interdependence' was an accurate description of the present world. Yet, in 1989, for example, Keohane and Hoffman were declaring that 'Boundaries are difficult to draw in a world of complex interdependence . . .' (1989: 6), which seemed to suggest the reverse. This question is essentially an empirical one: the formulation of Keohane and Nye recognised this.

6. This is surprising given the exceptional intensity of this co-operation. True, Western co-operation has certainly extended beyond the transatlantic region, but it is here that much of its impulse and sustenance has occurred. Moreover, the rise of the European Community raises important questions for the evolution of transatlantic co-operation. In *After Hegemony* (1984), Keohane's references to either the EC or NATO were few and superficial, however.

7. Somewhat confusingly, Keohane and Hoffman have compared the present EC to an international regime (1989: 9, 33).

REFERENCES

Almond, G. and Powell, G. B. (1966) *Comparative Politics: A Developmental Approach* (Boston: Little, Brown).

Allison, G. (1971) *Essence of Decision: Explaining the Cuban Missile Crisis* (Boston: Little, Brown).

Baldwin, R. E., Hamilton, C. B. and Sapir, A. (eds) (1988) *Issues in US–EC Trade Relations* (Chicago: University of Chicago Press).

Brams, S. J. (1991) 'Game Theory and Multilateral Negotiations: The Single European Act and the Uruguay Round', Paper presented at Conference of

International Institute for Applied Systems Analysis; Laxenburg, Austria, 1–2 July.

Calleo, D. (1987) *Beyond American Hegemony: The Future of the Western Alliance* (New York: Basic).

Gilpin, R. (1987) *The Political Economy of International Relations* (Princeton: Princeton University Press).

Ginsberg, R. H. (1989) *Foreign Policy Actions of the European Community: The Politics of Scale* (Boulder: Rienner).

Haas, E. B. (1958, revised 1968) *The Uniting of Europe: Political, Social and Economic Forces* (Stanford: Stanford University Press).

Haas, E. B. (1975) *The Obsolescence of Regional Integration Theory* (Berkeley: University of California Press).

Hassner, P. (1975) 'Dominant States and Vulnerable Societies: The East–West Case', in L. Lindberg, Alford, R., Crouch, C. and Offe, C., *Stress and Contradiction in Modern Capitalism* (Lexington, Mass.: Lexington Books).

Haus, L. (1991) 'The East European Countries and GATT: the Role of Realism, Mercantilism, and Regime Theory in Explaining East–West Trade Negotiations', *International Organization*, vol. 45, no. 2 (spring).

Heckscher, E. F. (1955) *Mercantilism* (2 vols) (London: Allen and Unwin).

Ifestos, P. (1987) *European Political Co-operation: Towards a Framework of Supranational Diplomacy?* (Aldershot, UK: Avebury/Gower).

Jones, R. J. B. (1986) *Conflict and Control in the World Economy: Contemporary Economic Realism and Neo-Mercantilism* (Atlantic Highlands, N.J.: Humanities Press International).

Kennedy, P. (1987) *The Rise and Fall of the Great Powers: Economic Change and Military Conflict from 1500 to 2000* (New York: Vintage).

Keohane, R. (1984) *After Hegemony: Co-operation and Discord in the World Political Economy* (Princeton: Princeton University Press).

Keohane, R. (1986) *Neorealism and its Critics* (New York: Columbia University Press).

Keohane, R. (1989a) 'A Personal Intellectual History', in Kruzel and Rosenau (1989).

Keohane, R. (1989b) *International Institutions and State Power: Essays in International Relations Theory* (Boulder: Westview).

Keohane, R. and Hoffman, S. (1989) *European Community Politics and Institutional Change*, Working Paper Series no. 25 (Center for European Studies, Harvard University).

Keohane, R. and Nye, J. S., (1977, revised 1987) *Power and Interdependence* (Boston: Little, Brown).

Keohane, R. and Nye, J. S. (1987) 'Power and Interdependence Revisited', *International Organization*, vol. 41, no. 4 (autumn).

Krasner, S. (1983) *International Regimes* (Ithaca, N.Y.: Cornell University Press).

Kruzel, J. and Rosenau, J. N. (eds) (1989) *Journeys Through Politics: Autobiographical Reflections of Thirty-Four Academic Travelers* (Lexington, Mass.: Lexington Books).

Lodge, J., (ed) (1989) *The European Community and the Challenge of the Future* (London: Pinter).

Mearsheimer, J. J. (1990) 'Back to the Future: Instability in Europe after the Cold War', *International Security*, vol. 15, no. 1.

Millar, D. (1991) 'Draft Treaty on European Union: Synopsis of Section on Political Union' (Edinburgh: Europa Institute).

Moravcsik, A. (1991) 'Negotiating the Single European Act: National Interests and Conventional Statecraft in the European Community', *International Organization*, vol. 45, no. 1 (winter).

Morgenthau, H. (1948) *Politics Among Nations* (New York: Knopf).

Nau, H. (1979) 'From Integration to Interdependence: Gains, Losses, and Continuing Gaps', *International Organization*, 33, 1, Winter.

Nau, H. (1989) 'US Domestic Economic Policy and Postwar International Economic Performance: Ideas, Interests and Politics', Paper delivered to Annual Meeting of the American Political Science Association, Atlanta.

Nau, H. (1990) *The Myth of America's Decline: Leading the World Economy into the 1990s* (New York: Oxford University Press).

Nugent, N. (1989) *The Government and Politics of the European Community* (London: Macmillan).

Nye, J. S. (1990a) *Bound to Lead: The Changing Nature of American Power* (New York: Basic).

Nye, J. S. (1990b) 'The Transformation of American Power', *The Aspen Institute Quarterly* (winter).

Rosenau, J. N. (1969) *Linkage Politics: Essays on the Convergence of National and International Systems* (New York: Free Press).

Rosenau, J. N. (1980) *The Scientific Study of Foreign Policy: Essays on the Analysis of World Politics* (London: Pinter).

Rosenau, J. N. (1981) *The Study of Political Adaptation* (London: Pinter).

Rosenau, J. N. (1984) 'A Pre-Theory Revisited: World Politics in an Era of Cascading Interdependence', *International Studies Quarterly*, vol. 28, pp. 245–305.

Rosenau, J. N. (1990) *Turbulence in World Politics: A Theory of Change and Continuity* (Princeton: Princeton University Press).

Rosenthal, G. (1975) *The Men Behind the Decisions* (London: Lexington Books).

Russett, B. (1963) *Community and Contention: Britain and America in the Twentieth Century* (Cambridge, Mass.: MIT Press).

Schmitter, P. (1969) 'Three Neofunctional Hypotheses about International Integration', *International Organization*, (winter) pp. 161–6.

Viner, J. (1958) *The Long View and the Short: Studies in Economic Theory and Policy* (New York: Free Press).

Wallace, H., Wallace, W., and Webb, C. (eds) (1977; 1983), *Policy-Making in the European Community* (London: Wiley).

Waltz, K. N. (1979), *Theory of International Politics* (Reading, Mass.: Addison-Wesley).

Waltz, K. N. (1986) in Keohane (1986).

Section Two

Empirical Analysis of US–EC Interdependence

3 The Political Dimension

INTRODUCTION

What is the nature of the political relationship that exists between the US and the EC? Chapter 2 argued that while particular aspects of US–EC relations might be understood in terms of realist theory, the totality of their interactions is best studied via the concept of interdependence. This chapter applies this framework to the political relations between the US and the EC. It focuses on the interactions, rather than on either the US or the EC as separate actors in the international system. Their interactions illustrate their interdependence.

Before this, some clarification of the concept of interdependence is necessary. The ultimate effect of interdependence is to limit the political choices available to individual actors. The latter sacrifice, willingly or unwillingly, some degree of their autonomy. Interdependence affects the interactions between actors: yet there is scope for both harmony and disharmony between them (Keohane and Nye, 1977: 10). Interdependence is the more intense when it impinges upon significant and sensitive policy matters.

The empirical study of interdependence should not focus on policy constraints and outcomes alone, however. The operation of interdependence can also be gauged in terms of policy processes and behaviour. That is, interdependence is in part manifested by actors participating in linkage processes, within which they display regular patterns of behaviour. Processes are the channels within which actors interact: they are distinct from the actors themselves; they are the links between them (Waltz, 1979). Patterns of behaviour are exhibited by actors: they involve different types of contact and meetings, for example, concerned with matters of mutual sensitivity. Yet processes and behaviour are distinct from the policy effects that might be evident. Processes and behaviour are significant: they indicate how relations between actors have changed in the contemporary international system. Interdependence implies an intensity of relations reflected in processes and behaviour. Taking part in the 'game' is important, as well as the results.

A highly intense economic linkage may coexist with a political relationship which is loosely organised. Indeed, the US–EC relationship has traditionally been of this form, in part following the

77

character of the EC itself. The manifestations of interdependence can vary between sectors, along with its recognition, acceptance and organisation. To understand the totality of interdependent relations a broad perspective is needed.

The actors involved in US–EC relations are many and varied: (a) governmental (e.g. foreign ministers, ambassadors, bureaucrats); (b) non-governmental (e.g. multinational corporations, think-tanks); (c) individual (e.g. legislators, corporate heads, journalists); (d) institutional (e.g. European Parliament, US Congress, European Council of Ministers). Actors operate at different levels: domestic (national), regional (EC-level) and international (affecting both the US and the EC), within and beyond formal institutions. A full account of their role would be an enormous task.

Parsimony is necessary. In order to gauge the major contours of US–EC political relations, this chapter proceeds by examining, in turn, linkage processes, patterns of behaviour, and mutual policy sensitivities. This allows attention to be given to important and varied elements of the mosaic: institutional structures, leadership interactions and foreign policy issues. The analysis will cover the EC at the level of both national governments and Community institutions. The interactions of both with the US are placed here in the context of US–EC interdependence. This dual focus indicates how far US–European ties have grown beyond traditional realist notions of government-to-government relations. Indeed, this overview seeks to show that a comprehensive understanding of US–EC political relations must be based on the concept of interdependence.

PROCESSES

The processes of US–EC relations reflect the fact that they are part of a broader set of transatlantic relations. Thus, the processes are neither coterminous with the US–EC linkage nor limited to its specific policy agenda. It is important to place US–EC relations in this context: they are part of a more complex whole, which testifies to a wider interdependence.

Several distinctions can be drawn. The term 'transatlantic relations' here incorporates all multilateral ties across different sectors – military (e.g. NATO, CSCE); economic (e.g. OECD, Western economic summits), trade (e.g. GATT, UN commodity agreements, US–EC meetings), energy (e.g. IEA) and monetary (e.g. IMF, the

World Bank) – involving the countries and institutions of North America and Western Europe. An inventory of these various organisations and fora, as they relate to US–EC relations, is given in Appendix 1. 'US–European relations' covers all the bilateral and multilateral ties linking the US alone to Europe (EC and non-EC). 'US–EC relations' refers to the US and EC institutions and member-states. The dividing line between US–EC and US–European relations has become blurred, however, given the increasing breadth and importance of the EC's role (Ginsberg, 1989b).

Membership of the EC has had a discernable impact upon the relations the EC national governments have with the US administration. In many policy areas the administration cannot deal with the national governments alone: the EC intrudes into the agenda of their discussions. In some policy sectors (e.g. trade) the US administration is required to recognise the pre-eminent negotiating role the EC Commission has as compared with any individual national government in the EC. In external trade negotiations the EC Commission acts on behalf of the Community as whole, on the basis of a mandate agreed with the Council of Ministers. The Commission has many other treaty powers that affect external relations, which are independent of the Council of Ministers (e.g. import relief, competition policy, diplomatic representation). While in such instances the EC Commission might be thought to be acting 'above' the level of the EC national governments, in other areas it acts 'alongside' some or all of them as a fringe participant in international fora (such as the Group of Seven (G7) economic meetings or at the Conference on Security and Co-operation in Europe). In yet other areas, the EC Commission has traditionally played little or no role (e.g. security policy). Added to this complexity is the role of the EC Council of Ministers. The increasing importance of EC foreign policy co-ordination (under 'European Political Cooperation') has encouraged the US administration to engage in close working relations with this process. Moreover, the government holding the presidency ('chairmanship') of the EC Council also attends the G7 World Economic Summits, alongside the EC Commission president (if the presidency is held by a non-G7 government, then this necessitates an extra participant at the G7 summit meeting). The varied responsibilities given to the EC Commission and Council has thus created a highly complex political structure in Western Europe for the US administration to relate to.

The US has been obliged to recognise the dual level of political activity in the EC. In its long-term relations with the various EC national governments, various trends can be briefly distinguished. At first, a 'special relationship' between the US and Britain developed under Roosevelt and Churchill, but after the death of Roosevelt this partnership was never to be the same again. Howard has described the warm relations between Kennedy and Macmillan, and Reagan and Thatcher, as no more than 'Indian summers' set against an inexorable decline resulting from Britain's weakness (Louis and Bull, 1986: 389). Nevertheless, Howard notes the high level of contacts that have grown up between government officials: in the armed forces, the intelligence services and the civilian bureaucracy. Indeed, 'The links between the two intelligence communities obviously constitute the most enduring if the least publicised aspect of the "Special Relationship"' (Louis and Bull, 1986: 389). US pre-eminence (if not hegemony) changed the character of the special relationship with Britain, but the level of interactions increased.

The strategic position, and later the economic strength, of West Germany heightened its importance to Washington to such an extent that this bilateral relationship had by the 1980s become at least as significant and intense as the Anglo-American linkage. As Hanrieder has written, 'America and Europe' became the long-term dual pillars of West German foreign policy: 'Since the establishment of the Federal Republic, its security has depended on NATO and through it on the United States and American national security policies' (1989: 29). This security dependence continued at least until German reunification in 1990, though West German economic growth gradually gave Bonn a greater political leverage within the Western alliance. To some in the US, West Germany by the mid-1970s had become Washington's most important European partner (Bergsten: 1976).

The position of France has, of course, been somewhat different. Hassner and Roper have contrasted the British and French approaches to relations with Washington:

> as a rule, [the UK] has refrained from expressing its real preferences when they clashed with the supreme imperative: that of being in agreement with the United States. For France, on the contrary, the supreme imperative has long seemed to lie precisely in being seen to differ from the Americans. (Hassner and Roper, 1990: 11)

Cerny has differentiated the French position from that of West Germany: French policies have been much less determined by the structure of the international system than have those of Bonn (Cerny, 1980: 2). Harrison has explained that the position of France as a 'reluctant ally' stemmed from its perception of an 'unrewarding Atlantic experience after 1949' which was compounded by 'a particularly profound estrangement from the United States and NATO' after the Suez debacle in 1956 (Harrison, 1981: 7). In the 1980s relations did improve, however: anti-American sentiments among the French public lessened greatly (see Chapter 5) and President Mitterrand was more receptive to Western coordination (adopting a 'non-Gaullist' position, for example, over the 1990–1 Gulf crisis). Yet Washington's relations with Paris continue to be less intimate and more conditional than those it enjoys with London or Bonn.

To the US administration, its relations with London, Bonn and Paris have consistently been more important than its links with the other Western European capitals. It has clearly differentiated its relations accordingly. The other EC national governments, with the possible exception of Italy, have had significantly less intense relations with the US. (This contrast is confirmed later by a detailed empirical analysis of transatlantic political interactions, when patterns of behaviour are examined.) The administration's bilateral relations with the EC national governments have thus fluctuated and varied in the post-war period. In both directions, a crucial determinant of these relations has been the differing perceptions of security interests and the desired course for East–West diplomacy. US–EC relations have been affected by these attitudes.

Historically, the bilateral political relationship that has existed between the US administration and the EC institutions has been slow to develop, has exhibited little formal character, and in general has been of a lesser intensity than that involving Washington and the major European governments. This is, in part, a reflection of the ambiguity faced by the US administration in responding to the emergence of two separate levels of political activity in Western Europe: the European and the national. It is also a result, though, of the US placing prime emphasis on security matters: a sphere in which the European national governments have remained the key actors. For much of the past, successive US administrations have thus placed more importance on their political relations with the various EC national governments than on those they have had with Brussels.

In the late 1980s, however, new developments in Europe forced the US administration to rethink its approach to the EC. The initiation of the Single European Act not only produced an economic challenge to US interests but also gave some enhancement to the EC's foreign policy co-ordination within the European Political Co-operation (EPC) process.[1] The Community was becoming a more important actor in world affairs when liberalisation in Eastern Europe produced a spate of revolutions in 1989–90 which changed the European situation profoundly. Gorbachev was not yet the Soviet leader when the EC's single market programme was being drawn up. Now Europe, Eastern and Western, warranted close attention in Washington. The result was that the US administration and the EC agreed to the 'Transatlantic Declaration' which upgraded and ex-panded their bilateral contacts.

It is important to distinguish the political links between the US and the EC institutions. Apart from the interactions between the US administration and national government representatives and officials related to EC policy matters, the direct contacts involving the US and the EC institutions can be divided into five categories:

(a) the contacts and meetings between the EC Commission and the US administration;
(b) the role of the EC Commission delegation in Washington and the US mission to the EC in Brussels;
(c) the meetings and visits held between the European Parliament and the US Congress;
(d) the meetings between the EC Council and US presidencies;
(e) the relationship established between the 'European Political Co-operation' process and the US administration.

In general, these relationships have shown significant change over the course of the EC's development.

The scope and frequency of the contacts and meetings between the EC Commission and the US administration have varied since 1958. Initially, they were relatively few in number and irregular. In the early 1970s a practice of six-monthly meetings was begun involving senior administration representatives and members of the Com-mission. These complemented the individual visits made by repre-sentatives of both sides. In the 1970s and 1980s, EC Commission Presidents made irregular visits to Washington: Ortoli visited once (1973), Jenkins on three occasions (1977, 1978, 1980) and Thorn twice (1981, 1983). Delors has made several official visits to Washing-ton since he first met Reagan there in April 1985. President Ford met Ortoli in Brussels in 1975 during a NATO visit, while President

Carter was the first holder of his office to visit the Commission headquarters in January 1976 (and again in 1978). Somewhat symbolically, President Reagan never visited the Commission (though he did deliver a speech to the European Parliament on 8 May 1985). Reflecting a downturn in US–EC relations, under Reagan in 1983 the biannual Commission–administration meetings were reduced to an annual basis, due in part to the belief that both sides had extensive contact in other fora and by other means. This remained the practice until 1990. In its first year of office, however, the Bush administration had already signalled its new approach towards the EC. Bush himself met Commission President Delors in Brussels at the end of May 1989 and again in Washington in June 1989. By February 1990 new arrangements for US–EC meetings had been agreed (these are discussed at the end of this section).

Within the Commission, the primary responsibility for EC–US relations rests with Directorate-General I (External Relations). The role of the individual Commissioners heading the D–G can be significant. Sir Christopher Soames, in charge of External Relations from 1973 to 1977, helped give a higher profile to US–EC relations. More recently, the replacement of Willy de Clerq by Frans Andriessen in the same post in 1989 is said to have been welcomed in Washington and to have contributed to an improvement in relations. More specialist contact was maintained on an *ad hoc* basis from the 1980s onwards by the consultations between D–G I and the Commission's forward studies office and the US State Department's Policy Planning Office, which have also involved representatives from the EC national governments.

On a continuing basis, relations between the US administration and the EC Commission are handled by the work of the Commission's delegation in Washington. The work of the delegation is distinct from that of the embassies of the EC national governments, and its responsibilities vary according to the competence of the EC Commission in particular policy sectors. So far, the heads of the delegation have included two former prime ministers, Jens Otto Krag (1974–6) and Andreas van Agt (1989–), though the latter was the first holder of his post to be formally accredited to the White House (rather than to the State Department) with the rank of ambassador. Performing a similar, reciprocal role is the US mission to the EC, based in Brussels. For much of the period prior to the Bush administration, many of the heads of the US mission were middle-rank diplomats. President Bush's appointment of Thomas M. T. Niles to this post in 1989 was seen as indicating the increased importance of the office.

The work of both the EC delegation and the US mission are primarily concerned with information, representation and lobbying. Their scope is widely set: the EC delegation deals with both the administration and Congress, while the US mission has contact with each of the EC institutions. Both offices act as a channel of communication with their home authorities; in some cases, contact between the two offices can influence the outcome of difficult bilateral negotiations.[2] To varying degrees, both offices face relatively open and permeable institutions: the departments of the administration and groups within Congress; and the members and staff of the Commission and other EC institutions. In this situation, the role of personalities and their contacts can play an important role in working relations. As in other instances, however, the impact of 'embassies' on policy is limited: the more important exchanges are the direct contacts between the home authorities on both sides.

Other EC institutions have their own meetings with Washington. Most notably, special delegations of the US Congress and of the European Parliament have exchanged visits since 1972, which last several days, to discuss matters of mutual concern. These are now well-established on a biannual basis, with meetings typically being held in Europe each January and in the US each June. When they are held in Europe, they usually take place in the country whose government currently holds the EC presidency. The meetings involve, on average, 26 Members of the European Parliament and approximately 15 members of the House of Representatives (not the Senate). When the meetings are held in the US, the EP delegation typically meets members of the US Administration in Washington, and the actual joint EP–Congress session is held in the home state of one of the members of the US delegation. As a separate group, the members of the EP delegation meet three or four times per year to prepare for the bilateral sessions. The agendas for the bilateral meetings vary, but they have broadened in scope in recent years to cover wider international issues, such as those arising from the dramatic changes in Eastern Europe. The agenda for the Lisbon meeting in January 1992, for example, covered general international issues (the new world order, the Soviet Union, Yugoslavia, drugs and terrorism), developments in the US and the EC (the creation of North American Free Trade Area and of the European Economic Area, the aftermath of the Maastricht EC Summit), and bilateral relations (transatlantic security co-operation, trade disputes). The prime purpose of these joint meetings is to increase bilateral understanding and to enhance expertise, and to thereby help in resolving disputes. As such they serve to break down barriers of insularity, opening up one system to the other. Overall, however, they remain supplementary to other linkages and their specific policy impact, while difficult to judge, is probably modest.

Finally, the European Political Cooperation (EPC) process, by which the EC governments seek to co-ordinate their foreign policies, contains special provisions of relevance to US–EC relations. EPC developed gradually after 1970, initially as a process separate from other EC mechanisms (Ifestos, 1987; Pijpers *et al.*, 1988; Allen *et al.*, 1982; Lodge, 1989). The context in which EPC was initiated owed much to changing European perceptions of the international system.

Inadvertently, the US acted as a partial stimulus to EPC. The European recognition of 'the perceived decline of American hege-mony in the Western world' and the disappearance of US nuclear superiority over the Soviet Union meant that European interests 'could no longer be based solely on the Atlantic Alliance' (Ifestos, 1987: 176, 137). In addition, in the Vietnam era there was pressure in Europe to distinguish its interests from those of the US, while in-stances of unilateral action by the US also provoked a reaction (e.g. the 1971 dollar crisis).

After having neglected its relations with the EC institutions, the Nixon administration launched its 'Year of Europe' initiative in 1973, seeking to redirect the development of EC foreign policy activity back to an Atlantic-based centre (Ginsberg, 1989b). Anticipating the potential challenge of EPC to US leadership of the Western Alliance, Kissinger insisted that the US should be consulted on EC foreign policy actions or declarations before they were taken or made. In a speech in London in December 1973 he declared that,

I would be less than frank, were I to conceal our uneasiness about some of the recent practices of the European Community in the political field. To present the decisions of a unifying Europe to us as *faits accomplis*, not subject to effective discussion, is alien to the tradition of US–European relations . . . the attitude of the uni-fying Europe . . . seems to attempt to elevate refusal to consult into a principle defining European identity. (Ifestos, 1987: 181)

The dispute about US–EC consultation complicated the parallel discussions of the EC on a 'declaration of principles' to govern its relations with the US. Consultations between Chancellor Brandt and President Nixon, and among EC governments themselves, prior to a meeting of EC foreign ministers in Gymnich in West Germany in June 1974, produced a compromise.

The 'Gymnich formula' announced by Hans Dietrich Genscher, the West German Foreign Minister, recognised that

> . . . in elaborating common [EC] positions on foreign policy, there arises the question of consultations with allied or friendly countries. . . . We decided on a pragmatic approach in each individual case which means that the country holding the (EC) presidency will be authorised by the other . . . partners to hold consultations on behalf of [all EC governments]. In practice, therefore, if any member of the EC raises within the framework of EPC the question of informing and consulting any ally or a friendly state, the [EC ministers] will discuss the matter and, upon reaching agreement, authorise the [EC] presidency to proceed on that basis. The Ministers trust that this gentleman's agreement will also lead to smooth and pragmatic consultations with the United States which will take into account the interests of both sides. (Ifestos, 1987: 182–3)

This *modus vivendi* gave an imprecise definition to US– EC consultations. Nevertheless, the formula seemed to work to the general satisfaction of both sides (Rummel in Pijpers et al., 1988: 137). The State Department established the practice of regularly consulting the Presidency of the EPC (the national government currently holding the chair of EC meetings) at the start of its six-month term of office. Rummel notes, though, the one-way traffic in these arrangements: 'the EPC Presidency is not expected to be regularly kept abreast with the US foreign policy making process' (Rummel, 1988: 137).

Set against this background, co-operation among the EC national embassies in Washington to co-ordinate on EPC and other matters (as they affect the US) developed with more intensity than in any other non-member state capital (Taylor, 1979). Meetings of EC ambassadors and deputy chiefs of mission in Washington have been regular occurrences since 1975, typically being held ten to twelve times per year. More junior embassy officials have their own meetings concerned with specific sectors. Organisational responsibility rests with the embassy of the government currently holding the EC presidency, aided by the EC Commission's delegation office. The presidency's embassy is then responsible for any relevant communications to the US administration, though throughout the foreign ministries of EC governments back home instruct their ambassadors in Washington as to the appropriate action to be taken. These arrangements offer exceptionally high profile to the smaller EC states' ambassadors when their government holds the presidency. Yet this sphere of activity remains supplementary to the direct contacts between the US State Department and the EPC process.

The increasing importance of EPC in the late 1980s led the US administration to give greater recognition to the role played in this process by the EC government holding the (EPC) council presidency. The US administration typically increases the number of its staff in its embassy in the country acting as the EC president (e.g. from the US mission to the EC). This is the primary channel through which the US administration conveys its demarches and opinions. Similarly, the EC presidency government may increase the number of its staff in its Washington embassy for the duration of its term of office (this is often the case with the smaller EC governments). The US administration has also acknowledged the role of the troika of EC council presidents in the EPC process (that is, the past, present and future governments holding the council presidency).

The contacts of the US administration with the EPC mechanism grew significantly in the late 1980s. The administration is involved in meetings at different levels. In 1987 annual consultations were established between the US Secretary of State and EC Foreign Ministers. These were typically held in the US at the time of the United Nations General Assembly meeting each autumn. These supplemented the *ad-hoc* consultations between the US Secretary of State and the EC presidency (or troika) foreign minister(s). In addition, the US Assistant Secretary of State for European and Canadian affairs has, since 1984, met biennially with initially one, but later each, of the political directors of the troika foreign ministries, the meetings now alternating between the US and Western Europe. In 1989, US contact was expanded to enable *ad hoc* meetings to take place between State Department officials (e.g. the Deputy Assistant Secretary) and the troika representatives of EPC working groups. During 1991, there were approximately twenty meetings of this kind involving the Deputy Assistant Secretary. The State Department responds to the schedule of EPC meetings set by the Council presidency. The EPC process is secret, but it is understood that in recent years EPC working groups have been concerned with Eastern Europe (especially Yugoslavia), the Soviet Union, the Middle East, Africa, Latin America, Asia, human rights, international organisations (including the UN), terrorism, and drugs. The US State Department is given the opportunity to have its representatives and specialist staff meet with troika officials after such working groups have met, in order to exchange opinions and information. The frequency of such meetings depends on how often the EPC working groups meet and the relative importance of the issues to the US. The emphasis in the meetings is on 'closing the perception gap' between the two sides in a meaningful exchange, as one close observer commented.

The increasing role of the EC in international affairs has thus elicited some response from the US administration. The EC's role in the Yugoslavian crisis in 1991, for example, was recognised by a joint US–EC declaration and co-operation at the level of the US and the EC. Moreover, US recognition of the EC's role depends on the strength of the EPC process itself. The European governments have been slow to co-ordinate their foreign policies: at the European Council meeting at Maastricht in December 1991 they did agree, though, on new measures to promote common foreign and security policies in the future. US and EC foreign policy interests are distinct – the 1970s and 1980s saw a sequence of policy differences – and it is not clear whether both sides want the same thing from each other. US–EC foreign policy co-operation in the 1990s thus remains unpredictable in a world in flux.

The EC's role in international affairs has been strengthened by both the Single European Act (SEA), which took effect on 1 July 1987, and the draft Treaty on European Union agreed in principle by the European Council at Maastricht in December 1991. The SEA provided for the 'political and economic aspects' of security to be discussed within the EPC process, and it also enhanced the role of the EC Commission in the EPC domain. At Maastricht, it was agreed that the EC 'shall define and implement a common foreign and security policy, covering all areas of foreign and security policy', including 'the eventual framing of a common defence policy, which might in time lead to common defence' (Millar, 1991). Joint action will be introduced in those areas where member-governments 'have essential interests in common' (Millar, 1991). The European Council will decide on joint action and on those matters which will be decided by majority vote. The EC will act in defence matters via the Western

European Union (WEU), which is now 'an integral part of the development of European Union' (Millar, 1991). Co-ordination between the EC and the WEU Council of Ministers will be strengthened and the membership expanded. Moreover, it is envisaged that a further intergovernmental conference in 1996 will review these arrangements and consider the question of the EC itself establishing its own common defence system.

In any event, Maastricht gave the EC a defence role for the first time. EC governments have thereby prepared themselves for the continued withdrawal of US military forces from Europe. The effect of Maastricht is to significantly upgrade the EC's role (albeit on a largely intergovernmental basis) in foreign and security matters. Some observers saw this as potentially the most significant outcome of the Maastricht negotiations. The US will have to take account of these new developments in the 1990s. They are part of a momentum of change already under way in the late 1980s.

The general framework of US–EC relations became the subject of fresh attention in the late 1980s. In the US, some within the Reagan administration were responding to the implications of the Single European Act (the internal market programme and a stronger EPC process) in their last period of office. Much more significant changes occurred, however, in the first two years of the Bush presidency.

Early in 1989, the Bush administration included the EC in its examination of US foreign policy. An inter-agency review was established to co-ordinate the US response. Rather than any organisational changes within the Administration, however, it was the influence of key individuals that was most evident in the new approach being developed. The new Secretary of State, James Baker, was already familiar with the EC's economic role from his previous post as Secretary of the Treasury, as was Robert Zoelleck, a continuing member of his staff. Zoelleck, the Department's Chief Counsel and also later Under-Secretary of State for Economic Affairs, played a prominent part in the administration's inter-agency review. He pressed for a fresh approach to the EC, which would end what he saw as the traditional overemphasis on US–NATO relations at the expense of the EC. Other agencies also paid closer attention to the EC: the National Security Council, for example, created a new specialist post on the EC in 1989 (Director of European Economic Affairs). In Congress, hearings were held to investigate fears of the single market programme leading to a 'fortress Europe'. Both the administration and the Congressional Research Service undertook studies on this theme.

By the middle of 1989 the Bush Administration already appeared to have concluded that (a) a 'fortress Europe' was less likely than previously envisaged; (b) if only to maintain its own influence in Europe, it could not be seen to oppose further integration; and (c) the EC had a special role to play in Eastern Europe, on behalf of wider Western interests. The latter point had already been reflected in the administration's acceptance of an aid co-ordinating role for the EC at the July 1989 Paris Economic Summit. With the progress of events in Eastern Europe, the administration's new approach was obliged to go further.

For its part, the EC also seemed to become more favourable to closer co-operation with the US Administration. During his June 1989 visit to Washington, EC Commission President Delors stated that 'for the free world, it is a necessity to have a good understanding between the US and the EC. This is more important than soybeans and hormones . . . than the vanity of heads of states; it's the model for freedom, for liberty, for the future of the world.' Many credit Delors during this visit with helping to allay American fears of a 'fortress Europe' after 1992. Later, in September 1989, Delors issued a notable plea for harmony and understanding between both sides in a speech at Harvard.

The new approach of the Bush administration was to suggest structural changes in the US–EC relationship. In May 1989 Bush stated that he was 'ready to develop new mechanisms of consultation and co-operation with the EC' and, rather more assertively, that 'the United States is and will remain a European power'. In December of the same year, in a Berlin surrounded by political change, Secretary of State James Baker proposed that 'the United States and the European Community (should) work together to achieve, whether in treaty or some other form, a significantly strengthened set of institutional and consultative links'.[3]

At the start of the 1990s, US and EC leaders were thus debating a new European order. The future of NATO, the CSCE, the WEU and possible extensions of the Rome Treaty to include *inter alia* security matters dominated the transatlantic debates. The future shape of US–EC relations seemed less predictable than for many years.

The initial reforms to the US–EC relationship were, however, relatively modest, when set against the profound changes in the international system. The annual US–EC Commission high-level meeting in December 1989 in Brussels noted the intention of both sides 'to strengthen' their links as 'world stability is enhanced by a strong (bilateral) relationship'. During the course of 1990 the US administration and the EC Council agreed to a new set of meetings and, after a slight delay, to a new joint declaration of principles.

Two previous attempts at codifying US–EC political consultations had failed. In President Kennedy's 1962 'Grand Design', the US challenged the emerging EC to act as a political as well as an economic partner in managing the affairs of the Western world. However, the initiative was unsuccessful owing to French opposition, and to the EC's own lack of political and institutional development. In President Nixon's 1973 'Year of Europe', a similar challenge was issued to the EC. However, the condescending and hegemonic attitude of the US, reflected by Kissinger in particular, along with EC members' unease with US leadership, led to the failure of the initiative.

Unlike the previous attempts at politically upgrading US–EC consultations, the US–EC 'Transatlantic Declaration' of 1990 succeeded in reaffirming basic principles and institutionalising new forms and areas of co-operation (see Appendix 1). In both US and EC official circles, though, the declaration was described as a 'half-way' document, unable to meet more ambitious objectives owing to hesitations on both sides. With major changes occurring in the international system in the 1990s, both sides may come to re-examine their consultation procedures at a later date.

In 1990 the EC leaders and governments were not ready to go so far as the US had first suggested. The EC has always had difficulty in formulating a common policy towards the US. Hans Dietrich Genscher, the West German Foreign Minister, suggested a joint statement as an outcome in April 1990. Genscher was concerned to balance the *rapprochement* in German–Soviet relations with a positive signal to the US, and to indicate his government's gratitude for US backing for German reunification. In any event, a declaration seemed to be the most realistic outcome. Many EC governments (notably the French) were loathe to agree to anything more ambitious at a time when the Community was preoccupied with internal reforms (Economic and Monetary Union, Political Union, etc.) as well as dealing with Eastern Europe. Moreover, when some were calling for the EC to assume a defence role, it seemed premature to consider new forms of relations with Washington, which continued to emphasise the role of NATO. A declaration would, nevertheless, balance the EC's relations with the US with the agreements it had recently signed with Canada and with Japan.

For its part, the Bush administration appeared to retreat from more ambitious objectives. Despite Baker's initiative, the administration itself did not take the lead and propose a draft document; it waited for the EC to respond to Baker instead. Given the myriad of interests and the diffusion of power within the US administration, it might have proved impossible for the US to come up with a firm proposal. The best strategy seemed to be one of response. Initially, the picture had looked quite different, however. The administration had seemed concerned to reach a stronger form of agreement, in order to maintain its influence in the region. The State Department, for example, had been surprised by the willingness of the EC in January 1990 to announce unilaterally its endorsement of President Gorbachev's proposal for a CSCE summit on Europe, before consulting the US administration. There were also fears that the looming EC negotiations on Political Union might lead to a European security dimension, independent of NATO. As a result, it was important to underline the value of US–EC relations and of the NATO alliance. In addition, given the final phase of the GATT Uruguay Round negotiations, which had stalled over an agreement on agricultural subsidies, some in the US Administration had also wanted to remind the EC of the broader political context of these trade negotiations. As the matter progressed, however, complex inter-agency negotiations watered down the text the administration was comfortable with: the Treasury, for example, successfully resisted tangible commitments on monetary co-operation, as did others on the environment. In some respects, the administration might find it difficult to live with the new commitments it did agree with the EC: for example, on the frequency of high-level meetings.

The final negotiations on the declaration were conducted with the Italian presidency of the EC Council, after an initial draft had been prepared by the German government. The Declaration was 'adopted' by the relevant parties while they were in Paris for the November 1990 CSCE conference. The opportunity to have it formally signed was lost, as a result of last-minute objections by the French government.[4] The issuing of the declaration took place, however, at a time when the Gulf crisis over Kuwait dominated the attention of Western governments. The publication of the declaration on 23 November 1990 received only modest attention.

In parallel to the joint policy declaration, the new structural arrangements for US–EC dialogue were agreed upon at a meeting in Washington on 27 February 1990 between Bush and Charles Haughey, the Irish Prime Minister acting as EC Council President. They were later incorporated into the new Declaration, which outlines the following meetings:

(a) 'bi-annual consultations to be arranged in the United States and in Europe between, on the one side, the President of the European Council and the President of the Commission, and on the other side, the President of the United States';
(b) 'bi-annual consultations between the European Community Foreign Ministers, with the Commission, and the US Secretary of State, alternately on either side of the Atlantic';
(c) '*ad hoc* consultations between the Presidency Foreign Minister or the Troika and the US Secretary of State';
(d) 'bi-annual consultations between the Commission and the US Government at Cabinet level';
(e) 'briefings, as currently exist, by the Presidency to US Representatives on European Political Cooperation (EPC) meetings at the Ministerial level'.

The new arrangements revised the existing set of meetings in several respects. Firstly, the US president was now committed to regular, six-monthly meetings with the EC Commission and Council presidents. These officially began in 1991: the first meeting being in April in Washington (with Jacques Delors, President of the Commission, and Jacques Santer, Prime Minister of Luxembourg) and the second in The Hague in November (with Dutch Premier Ruud Lubbers and Delors). The second category of meetings were not new, but they were expanded. As already noted, since 1987, there had been similar meetings to those mentioned in (b) above during the annual autumn sessions of the UN General Assembly in New York. After the Declaration it was understood that there would now be a spring session held in Europe, to begin in 1991. This took place on 17 April 1991 in Luxembourg. An earlier meeting under the new arrangements was held, however, in Washington in January 1991, with Frans Andriessen representing the Commission and Jacques Poos the EC foreign ministers. The reference to the third set of meetings was simply an acknowledgement of existing arrangements, as was the reference to the fifth set. The fourth category expanded the existing arrangements, by reverting back to the biannual (rather than annual) meetings operating prior to 1983. EC Commissioners, led by Delors, met US Cabinet members, led by Baker, in April 1990 in Washington, and again in November 1990 in Brussels.

These early changes had the effect of upgrading US meetings with EC leaders, and thereby improving dialogue, but they fell well short of establishing a common institutional forum or a joint treaty. Thus, whatever the other evidence of their shared interdependence, the political relations existing between the US and the EC continue to be played out within structures that might have been created twenty years previously, rather than them being tailored directly to the new circumstances of the 1990s. The processes linking the US and the EC display a complex and confused character: a jigsaw comprising traditional bilateral intergovernmental contacts, EC institutions and international regimes which extend beyond the US–EC relationship. The policy content of each is distinct. The exclusively US–EC linkage within the Western system remains fragile and loosely organised, despite the recent changes. In reality, this is partly the result of the lack of definition of the EC's role in this regard. Moreover, historically, such ambiguity has been fostered almost as much by the approach of the US Administration to the EC as by that of the Europeans themselves.

It is not clear whether the US and the EC are looking for the same kind of dialogue. At the start of the 1990s, the US administration, in response to overtures from some quarters in the EC, took the initiative only to find the Community unwilling or unable to respond. The EC did not have its act together: internally, the disputes between EC governments over Political Union in 1990–1 gave further indication of the opposition to the Community being able to carry new responsibilities. For its part, Washington seemed afraid that the EC might shun the US role in Europe in favour of other interests in a period of increased opportunities for the Community. The US still saw its prime European link as being that of NATO, rather than any new pan-European structure based on the CSCE. NATO sustained US military hegemony in the region: it offered reassurance amid political instability. On the other side, EC opinion seemed confused or unformulated: Washington was pushing it beyond what it was ready to shoulder. The US was urging closer ties with Western Europe, when the EC was grappling with internal union and expansion on a pan-European basis. The Atlantic link seemed less pressing than matters closer to home. The US placed a high priority on security policy, whereas the EC responded to the new political and economic

agenda of a post-cold-war Europe. Although it was the US administration which had taken the original initiative, it became clear that
it would be the EC, not the US, which would set the parameters
which bilateral relations would advance in the 1990s. The EC's role
here was symptomatic of the new international conditions, post-
hegemony.

In the late 1940s the Americans and the Europeans made key
decisions that would mould their political relations for the ensuing
four decades. In the 1990s a similar historic opportunity exists to
re-fashion US–EC political relations. The 1990 'Transatlantic Declaration' was an important, though modest, step in that direction. As
the momentum of change in international relations unfolds, the Declaration may yet presage a more extensive revision of the US–EC
relationship. The Declaration would then have been only the first bite
at the cherry.

PATTERNS OF BEHAVIOUR

Patterns of behaviour offer tangible evidence of the character of
US–EC relations. Long-term trends can be assessed and patterns
distinguished. An analysis is presented here of the pattern of meetings held over the period from the 1950s to the mid-1980s involving
US and EC national government leaders. International meetings are
a matter of public record; the limitation is that the content of the
discussions is not. Yet data on the meetings held help to illustrate the
nature of US–EC interdependence. Easier communication has made
international contacts more feasible. But wider policy trends have
themselves encouraged a greater frequency of bilateral and multilateral meetings.

Data on the frequency of meetings held between US Cabinet
members and EC national government ministers are given in Table
3.1. Given the difficulties in obtaining a complete record, the data
should be regarded as providing an estimate only. The data cover
alternate years in two periods: 1956–66 and 1974–84. The two periods
have been chosen to reflect changing circumstances: the first covers
the emergence of the EC, the second the development of new
arrangements in the 1970s for multilateral co-operation (e.g. G7
annual economic summits). The data were compiled from the *New
York Times* and supplemented by official US information, as available. The coverage terminates in 1984 owing to the belief that the

TABLE 3.1 *Meetings reported between members of the US cabinet and ministers of EC nations, selected years 1956–84*[1]

	1956–66[2]	*1974–84*[3]
Economic		
Agriculture	0	6
Commerce	1	0
Energy[4]	—	1
Transport[5]	—	16
(Trade Representative)[6]	0	13
Labour	2	5
Treasury	5	30
Sub-total	8	71
Social		
Education[7]	—	4
Health/HS[8]	0	8
Housing/UD[9]	0	0
Interior	0	2
Justice (Attorney-General)	3	0
Sub-total	3	14
Politics/Security		
Defense	11	27
State	91	65
Vice-President	3	2
Sub-total	105	94
Total	116	179

1. Data compiled from the *New York Times* and supplemented by official information from departments of the US administration, as available. The US Trade Representative has been included because of the relevance of the post, despite not being a full member of the cabinet. Data for the US President are shown in separate tables. The data covers the EC12 throughout.
2. Data cover only the years 1956, 1958, 1960, 1962, 1964 and 1966. The changes are charted over alternate years to highlight general patterns only. This made the collation of the data more practicable. Specific entries have been double-checked, but ultimately they depend on the quality of the sources used.
3. Data cover only the years: 1974, 1976, 1978, 1980, 1982 and 1984.
4. The Department of Energy was only created in 1977. For more recent years, official data from the Department indicate: 1986: one foreign visit to EC government(s); 1987: 2 visits; 1988: 1 visit; 1989: 2 visits; a total of 6 visits in 4 years.

5. The Department of Transportation was established in 1966.
6. The post of US Trade Representative was created in 1963 in the Executive Office of the President.
7. The Department of Education was only established in 1979.
8. Data here cover the Department of Health, Education and Welfare from 1953 to 1979, prior to creation of the Department of Health and Human Services.

New York Times was becoming less reliable as an information source in this regard. International meetings *per se* appeared to be less 'newsworthy' by the 1980s. The data suggest, however, the important general patterns that emerged during these years. Moreover, the data should be read as highlighting general trends, rather than specific frequencies.

Following the classification of cabinet posts given in the table, it is clear that those members having economic-related responsibilities were engaged in far more meetings with their European counterparts after 1974 than in the earlier period. Indeed, although the meetings of the traditional diplomatic posts (Defense, State, Vice-President) remained relatively high and stable, those involving the cabinet's economic members had risen to approximately three-quarters of their number. This is a clear indication of the 'internationalisation' of economic policy: national ministers now regularly engage in discussions and negotiations with their foreign counterparts over economic management issues.

Moreover, the increase in meetings dealing with economic issues illustrates the erosion of the traditional monopoly on external contacts by foreign ministries. In systems of interdependence, national bureaucracies are linked internationally by multiple channels. This has manifold implications for the internal policy process of national administrations (East, 1981) and the ability to achieve effective policy co-ordination (Wallace, 1978). The overlap between domestic and external policy changes the manner in which individual government departments operate (Karvonen and Sundelius, 1990). As Wallace has noted: 'All major ministries in London, Paris and Bonn are involved in the formulation, management and implementation of foreign policy' (1978: 35). Moreover, ministries concerned with domestic policy engage in policy borrowing from other nations (see Chapter 5).

Meetings between US and EC national government representatives have increased on not only a bilateral but also a multilateral

basis. It was primarily during the 1970s that the frequency of multilateral meetings involving representatives from a number of Western
governments increased. This was particularly noticeable with respect
to economic policy issues. The 'World Economic Summits' of the
Group of Five, and then the Group of Seven, have been held on an
annual basis since 1975, with the participation of the EC Commission
President (from 1977 onwards) and the EC Council President (see
Appendix 1). The degree of co-ordination among the Group of
Seven finance ministers has also been much closer than that existing
in other areas (see Chapter 4). They now typically meet at least
four times per year to review their policy co-ordination (*Financial
Times*, 29 April 1991).

The expansion of multilateral contacts is symptomatic of an interdependence which extends beyond the US–EC relationship. As in
other spheres, the political interactions within the bilateral relationship have been obliged to respond to wider, multilateral pressures. Yet it is likely that US–EC interactions have been relatively
more frequent than those which either the US or the EC nations have
with most third parties.

Some evidence of the higher intensity of US–EC contacts is given
in Tables 3.2 and 3.3, which record the meetings involving heads of
government. Such data reflect their will to meet, rather than necessarily their world importance. US presidential contacts with Britain
and Germany during the post-war period have been notably more
frequent than those with Japan, for example, and much more so
than with the Soviet Union. US presidential contacts with Canada
(a NATO ally) have also been high.

More generally, the data in Tables 3.2 and 3.3 again show an
increase in the number of meetings, and in particular a rise in multilateral meetings, from the mid-1970s onwards. US presidents have
increasingly sought multilateral international meetings: after 1975,
they were typically involved in more than one such meeting per year
with their major European counterparts. Multilateral meetings may
be a more efficient use of time, but they also reflect the increasing
sense of interdependence and the need for collective decisions.

With regard to individual national governments, the data on the
US President illustrate the 'special relationship' existing not only
between the US and Britain, but also between the US and West
Germany. Contacts between the US and France suffered during the
presidency of de Gaulle and only began to improve under Giscard
d'Estaing. Moreover, a clear differentiation is apparent between the

TABLE 3.2 *Frequency of visits to the US by heads of selected Western governments*

	Belg.	Den.	Fr.	W. Ger.	Gr.	Ire.	It.	Lux.	Neth.	Port.	Sp.	UK	Total	Can.	Jap.
Up to 1939 inclusive	1	0	2	0	0	0	0	0	0	0	0	2	5	5	0
1940–45	0	0	0	0	1	0	0	0	0	0	0	7	8	12	0
1946–55	2	1	4	3	1	0	3	0	1	0	0	4	19	4	2
1956–65	0	4	3	11	3	2	5	0	0	0	0	11	39	11	5
1966–75	0	6	2	11	0	3	4	1	4	2	0	11	44	3	8
1976–78	2	2	4	4	1	1	4	2	1	2	1	6	30	5	3
Total	5	13	15	29	6	6	16	3	6	4	1	41	145	40	18

The lists available from the US State Department cover the period 1789–1978 inclusive. The visits included cover only those where the visitor met with the US President, or in the event of his ill-health, the Vice-President. Included here are only those visits by heads of government (and heads of state in appropriate cases, e.g. France after 1958). The authors would like to record their gratitude for the kind help extended by the staff of the State Department during this research.

SOURCE Adapted from lists produced by the US State Department.

TABLE 3.3 Selected overseas visits by US Presidents[1]

	Bel.	Den.	Fr.	W. Ger.	Gr.	Ire.	It.	Lux.	Neth.	Port.	Sp.	UK	Total	Can.[2]	Jap.	International[3]
Up to 1939 inclusive	1 (0)	0 (0)	4 (0)	0 (0)	0 (0)	0 (0)	1 (0)	0 (0)	0 (0)	0 (0)	0 (0)	1 (0)	7 (0)	3	0	3 (Paris Peace Conference)
1940–5	0 (0)	0 (0)	0 (0)	0 (0)	0 (0)	0 (0)	0 (0)	0 (0)	0 (0)	0 (0)	0 (0)	0 (11)	0 (11)	0	0	0
1946–55	0 (0)	0 (0)	0 (0)	0 (0)	0 (0)	0 (0)	0 (0)	0 (0)	0 (0)	0 (0)	0 (0)	0 (1)	0 (1)	2	0	1
1956–65	0 (0)	0 (0)	5 (0)	2 (1)	1 (0)	1 (0)	2 (1)	0 (0)	0 (0)	1 (0)	1 (0)	3 (3)	16 (5)	4	0	5
1966–75	3 (0)	0 (0)	5 (1)	3 (0)	0 (0)	1 (0)	4 (0)	0 (0)	0 (0)	2 (0)	2 (0)	3 (1)	23 (2)	3	1	7
1976–83	1 (1)	0 (0)	2 (0)	2 (0)	0 (1)	0 (0)	2 (0)	0 (1)	0 (1)	1 (1)	1 (0)	2 (0)	11 (5)	2	2	10
Total	5 (1)	0 (0)	16 (1)	7 (1)	1 (1)	2 (0)	9 (1)	0 (1)	0 (1)	4 (1)	4 (0)	9 (16)	57 (24)	14	3	26

1. In order to incorporate the wide variety of visits, they are defined as follows:
   (i) the first figure in each column records visits by US Presidents when the President has met the head of government of the host country;
   (ii) the second figure (given in brackets) records those meetings the US President has had with the head of government of the country indicated *outside the territory of either country*. In the case of the UK, this is defined as outside the UK itself.

2. Only visits to the territory of Canada and Japan are recorded here. Two visits to Canada during the Second World War to meet Churchill are excluded.

3. 'International meetings' are defined as those involving the US President and the heads of at least two other Western governments. The President's visit to the host country is also recorded under the relevant column for that nation. Of necessity, this is a varied category covering all types of international gatherings: the 1919 Paris Peace Conference, meetings of the NATO (Heads of Government) Council, international economic summits, and overseas state funerals where the US President has engaged in a series of sessions with foreign leaders (e.g. the Adenauer funeral in 1967).

bigger and smaller EC nations. The leaders of the UK, West Germany, France (and Italy) each had approximately twice the frequency of contact with the US administration as had any of their other EC counterparts.

Further data collated on ministerial contacts displays similar trends. Over the full period (1956–84), the highest frequency of meetings US secretaries had was with their UK counterparts. By comparison, those involving the US and West Germany (-16 per cent), France (-32 per cent fewer), and Italy (-64 per cent) were significantly less frequent. This was due primarily to the strength of the UK 'special relationship' in the 1950s and 1960s. From 1974 to 1984, however, US secretaries had more frequent meetings with their West German counterparts than with the British. Such data illustrate the changing status of both Britain and West Germany in the political economy of the West.

The patterns of behaviour examined here reflect an intense and wide-ranging relationship between the US and EC governments. Such rudimentary quantification helps to highlight important trends, and other contacts extend well beyond the formal meetings of political leaders. They embrace large numbers of government officials and representatives, involved in different forms of contact. Evidence of the nature and consequence of such interactions – should it be made available – could offer important insight into their complex relations. Such high levels of interaction have greatly increased the personal knowledge between the actors involved (a cognitive effect), though the impact on attitudes is less clear (the affective response).

International meetings form part of the multiple channels of interdependence, but they also stem from mutual sensitivities. Beyond the occurrence of intergovernmental meetings is the evidence of the policy effects of US–EC interdependence.

POLICY AGENDAS AND OUTCOMES

As noted in Chapter 2, inherent in the concept of interdependence is the notion that it effects and constrains the policy agendas and choices of actors such as national governments and the European Community. Indeed, Keohane and Nye regard policy costs and constraints as the central element in interdependence. 'Interdependent relationships will always involve costs, since interdependence restricts autonomy', they argue, pointing to policy considerations (1977: 9).

In reality, analysing and evaluating the policy effects of inter-dependence is highly problematic. This is especially so with respect to policies in the political and security domains. Policy effects here are less clear than in economics or trade where, for example, changes in the interest rates of one nation might quickly produce a reaction in another. Moreover, while interdependence might restrict policy options, just how some alternatives have been foreclosed is difficult to determine. Some issues or options might never reach the governmental agenda as a result of the constraints of interdependence. Yet discerning 'non-issues' here is reminiscent of the analytic problems of the (behavioural) local community power studies of the 1960s, which have been the subject of much controversy (Dahl, 1961; Parenti, 1970). A major hazard lies in obtaining appropriate evidence of the policy effects stemming from external pressures; causality is difficult to determine.

Moreover, there are further problems which arise from the particular case of US–EC relations. In the political and security domains, the EC has traditionally played much less of a role than in areas such as trade and economics. Thus, studies of US–EC interdependence must take account of this and distinguish between the respective roles of the EC Commission and the EC national governments. In the contemporary international system, the EC institutions cannot be kept out of the picture, though.

Indeed, the EC has emerged as an important foreign policy actor in its own right. Its actions are helping to change the nature of the international system. In an earlier work, Ginsberg (1989a, 1991b) analysed foreign policy actions taken by the EC. He reported that the total number of foreign policy actions taken has increased significantly: from approximately 11 such actions per year between 1958 and 1972 to 28 per annum from 1973 to 1990. Moreover, since the 1970s the EC has taken more action of a multilateral nature (dealing with international organisations, conferences and issues) and also of a bilateral kind (with the EC acting as a unit towards non-member states). Ginsberg has further categorised individual EC foreign policy actions according to which one of three possible explanations primarily accounted for them.[5] According to Ginsberg (1989a, 1991b) almost all the actions taken by the EC up to and including 1972 can be best explained by a regional integration logic. From 1973 onwards, however, new trends developed: other explanations became increasingly relevant. Most actions continued to be best explained by the logic of regional integration, but an approximately equal number were provoked by the 'logic of interdependence' and by a 'European interests' logic (varying between 14 and 22 per cent of all actions each) (Ginsberg, 1989a, 1991b).

The conclusion is that the EC itself is an increasingly important foreign policy actor. It behaves more and more in response to the global pressures of interdependence and its own perceived self-interests. The externalisation hypothesis of the regional integration logic remains an important determinant, but it has become relatively less so. For their part, traditional realist accounts are an inadequate explanation of the EC's role in world affairs. The EC is a *sui generis* actor and it must be placed in the context of an international system of increasing and widespread interdependence.

Turning to the bilateral US–EC relationship, two forms of evidence can be cited to illustrate the mutual sensitivities associated with their interdependence. These involve, firstly, the occurrence of US–EC foreign policy disputes and, secondly, cases of mutual (foreign) policy effects. The occurrence of US–EC foreign policy disputes is indicated by the entries in Table 3.4. This development must be placed in context.

Until the early 1970s, the EC lacked any organisational mechanism to handle external relations issues concerning politics and security. The launch of the 'European Political Co-operation' (EPC) process initiated modest and tentative reform to facilitate such discussions, which were later enhanced by the Single European Act. During the 1960s, therefore, there were no disputes in political or security matters between the US and the EC *per se*; only with the launch of the EPC process did the Community emerge as a significant foreign policy actor in these matters.[6] The fact that the EC took on this role in the 1970s is itself indicative of the changing nature of Western relations and the decline of US hegemony. The EC increasingly perceived its own foreign policy interests to be distinct from those of successive US administrations. Indeed, Washington has also become more conscious of its separate interests and more prepared to press them. More frequent policy clashes between the US and the EC are the consequence.

The rise in the number of such disputes can be understood as the result of increasing 'mutual sensitivities' and tensions borne out of disagreement. Mutual sensitivities in a narrow sense are not exclusive to systems of interdependence. They could also be understood within a revised realist interpretation. It is in such spheres that 'complex interdependence' and neo-realism have a tangential quality and a

TABLE 3.4   *A chronology of major US–EC Foreign policy disputes (as distinct from economic or trade disputes)*

Period	Nature of Dispute
1958–70	No disputes between US and EC *per se*; EPC not yet developed. [US disputes with individual European governments: e.g. with de Gaulle over French withdrawal from NATO and the veto of UK entry to EC; with various European governments over their lack of support for Vietnam War.]
1973–4	Middle East: EC governments refused to put their air bases at the disposal of the US in its efforts to resupply Israeli war effort. EC statement recognising 'legitimate rights' of Palestinians; France refused to join other EC governments and EC Commission in the IEA, a US policy initiative. EC and Arab League members created the 'Euro-Arab Dialogue' against US wishes. EC disunity over Arab oil embargo of Netherlands: a major upset of US expectations of the EC, which had long-term repercussions for US perceptions of the Community.
1979–80	US saw EC response to Iranian hostage crisis as weak. US saw EC response to Soviet invasion of Afghanistan as weak.
1981–2	EC slow to support US sanctions against Poland after its imposition of martial law; EC continued with food aid. EC slow to support US sanctions against Soviet Union after its backing for martial law in Poland. US opposition to the participation of EC nations in the scheme to build a Soviet gas pipeline from Siberia to Western Europe. EC opposition to the extension of the US embargo of the USSR to foreign subsidiaries of US firms and to foreign companies granted licenses to produce pipeline equipment with US technology. Reagan administration lifted ban after outcry. EC opposition to US support for repressive regime in El Salvador in its war against leftist rebels. EC opposition to US support for right-wing rebels battling to overthrow elected left-wing government in Nicaragua, after reports of 'death squads'.

	US opposition to EC support for Contradora peace process in region, and new EC co-operation accord with Central American states. US embarrassment over EC's repeated condemnations of human rights violations of (US-backed) Pinochet regime in Chile. EC opposition to US support for Israeli actions in Lebanon.
1986	Opposition among EC governments (though no EPC action) to US bombing of Libya, after Libyan-backed terrorist attacks. EC tariff preferences on imports from Gaza and the West Bank highlighted US–EC divergences.
1987	EC support for Contradora peace process, contrasted with US policy of opposition.
1990–1	Failure of some EC governments to provide armed forces for US-led military action to remove Iraqi forces from Kuwait. Limitation of EC itself to act militarily.

SOURCE   Ginsberg (1989a, 1991b).

synthesis may be appropriate (see Chapter 2, and Keohane, 1986: 191). Yet, the cases cited here extend beyond some traditional realist notions: they assume the EC to be an important foreign policy actor in its own right; they involve the EC taking action towards other regions and groups, rather than individual nations (e.g. the Arab League); and, they include the use of economic sanctions for the purposes of 'high politics' (e.g. EC punitive action against Turkey for human rights violations in 1980). Mutual sensitivities abound in a system of interdependence such as the US–EC relationship and to fully capture them within a realist perspective presents various analytical difficulties.

Finally, further interpretation of the policy consequences of interdependence is possible on the basis of a brief examination of individual US and EC foreign policy actions. This follows a tentative lead set by Keohane and Nye (1977, 1987).[7] Here, the focus is on policy sensitivity, involving effects (and, ultimately, constraints), rather than policy response (and 'vulnerability' as defined by Keohane and Nye).

Several well-known cases can be cited to illustrate aspects of US–EC interdependence in the political and security domains. The cases are varied in nature, but they each suggest certain common aspects.

They indicate mutual sensitivities: the extent to which action taken by one party affects the other. The effects have been significant. The autonomy of the actors involved has been limited, both in the policy options they have considered and in the manner they have pursued their objectives. The cases can be distinguished according to the types of action concerned and the degree of US–EC co-operation involved. The wider picture on US–EC foreign policy disputes was suggested earlier by the inventory given in Table 3.4.

The first case is that of aid to Eastern Europe in 1989–90. A common interest led to joint action with respect to another region. Both the US and the EC alone felt inadequate for the task. Yet the initiative served the interests of both as well as the recipient nations. If either the US or the EC had acted unilaterally, the policy would have had less chance of success and would inevitably have affected the interests of the other party. The joint action was thus indicative of a mutual interest, but also a mutual sensitivity.

In 1989, the US and the EC were the major actors in establishing a co-ordinated Western response to the collapse of communism in Eastern Europe. The Western Economic Summit in Paris in July agreed on a programme to aid Poland and Hungary and that the EC should act as the chief co-ordinator for this initiative. The European Bank for Reconstruction and Development began operating in 1991 in part to service the programme. The initial subscribed capital of the bank was ECU 10 billion, borne by 39 nations plus the EC institutions. Just over half the bank's capital was committed by the twelve EC nations (45 per cent) and the EC institutions (6 per cent) combined. The US contribution, the largest individual share, was 10 per cent. The programme was later extended to cover Bulgaria, Czechoslovakia, East Germany (prior to German reunification), Yugoslavia and Romania.

The magnitude of the programme was thus considerable. Economic aid was elevated to 'high politics', with an international programme developed on the basis of a multilateral, interdependent interest. Actual and potential mutual sensitivities abounded in a profoundly interdependent situation. No other explanation would seem to capture these important aspects of how and why the policy developed.

The second case is that of the Gulf crisis in 1990–1. This also involved a common interest, but incomplete joint action. It involved military action in response to common interests, including economic needs. Here, the EC as an entity was not able to act fully, as the action came to involve military means.

Sharing a common understanding of international law and the rights of sovereign nations, and also a mutual economic interest, both the EC national governments and the US supported economic sanctions against Iraq for its invasion of Kuwait. It was in the interest of neither the US nor the EC nations that Iraq should be allowed to annex Kuwait; any action taken to try to remove the Iraqi forces would have had major consequences for both the US and the EC.

While joint action only involved economic sanctions the EC institutions had a role to play and all EC governments could support it.[8] The EC imposed full-scale sanctions against Iraq and occupied Kuwait in advance of the UN sanctions. In addition, the EC participated in the Gulf Crisis Financial Co-ordination Group which offered aid to countries adversely affected by the Persian Gulf conflict. The EC also provided direct emergency aid to Egypt, Jordan and Turkey.

Once military intervention was used, however, the EC institutions were sidelined, the decision to become involved lay with the individual national governments (acting, in part, via the Western European Union), and some governments were unable or unwilling to participate in the action. Yet the interests of the EC nations and the US in freeing Kuwait overlapped very substantially. This prompted Germany, for example, as a non-combatant nation, to pay $11.4 billion to the allied nations and to Israel, as well to give economic assistance to neighbouring Arab states.

This mutual effort and support amongst the 'coalition' partners thus stemmed from shared interests, a belief that joint action was more appropriate and effective, and a recognition that they were each dependent on any action taken in the Persian Gulf. The statements made by the respective government leaders at the time support such an interpretation. When economic action was used, there was a symmetry in the US–European response; but military action produced an asymmetric outcome. The asymmetry reminded the world that the US was a military superpower, while the EC was not. This contrast was raised later in the context of the EC's debates over 'Political Union'.

The third case involves peace initiatives in the Middle East. Separate political initiatives, dating back to the 1970s, by the US and the EC affected the strategies of both parties and the policies of both came to nought.

For the US, President Carter had placed great store by his 'Camp

David' initiative, which he launched in 1979, to reconcile Israel and Egypt and thereby contribute to peace in the region. The improved relations that were established were symbolised by the understanding reached between Menachem Begin and Anwar Sadat.

Many in Europe, however, grew sceptical about whether a general peace could be secured in this fashion and they believed that fresh action was necessary to break the logjam. The EC did not throw its support behind the Camp David process, as it excluded the Palestinians. As a result, a new initiative was launched by the EC (under 'EPC') with its 1980 Venice Declaration. This called for a Palestinian homeland, Palestinian participation in peace talks, and international guarantees for mutually recognised borders. EC leaders visited capitals in the Middle East for talks with all sides. Neither the Camp David initiative nor that launched by the EC led to any noticeable improvement in relations between Israeli and Palestinian leaders, however, as peace remained elusive. Yet, the US was dismayed by what it saw as the EC's meddling and it felt that its own actions were undermined by the EC's intervention. Similarly, the EC initiative clearly stemmed from the belief that the Camp David process was going nowhere and the continuing failure to secure peace in the Middle East threatened European interests. Shared interests led to separate action and to policy failure.[9] Indeed, it could be argued that failure was in part the result of separate action. Certainly, the policy of each party was clearly affected by (sensitive to) that of the other. Subsequent actions by the US and the EC in the Middle East continue to point to divergent interests.

A fourth case of US and EC mutual policy sensitivities is that involving the US bombing of Libya. President Reagan ordered the attack in 1986 in response to terrorist actions supported by the Libyan government. This was after US attempts to have the EC adopt a strong and unified stance against terrorism had failed.

Most EC governments, and public opinion generally, disapproved of the US bombing. This was because of evidence that it had been mistargeted, and a feeling that it was an overreaction and a misuse of power. In addition, Europeans feared that it might exacerbate terrorist activity in Europe, and were concerned as to its affects on travel and tourist safety on that continent. As a consequence of the Libyan action, the tourist industry in Europe suffered greatly as Americans feared they might be high-risk targets for terrorist action.

In sum, action taken by the US towards a non-EC country was criticised, in part, for fear of its consequences inside the Community.

For the US, the Europeans appeared pacifist and disunited; for the Europeans, the US appeared trigger-happy. Yet both sides were equally affected by the threat of terrorism. There was an immediate and obvious recognition of the policy sensitivities involved.[10]

A fifth and final case to be highlighted is that involving US and EC policy towards conflict in Central America in the 1980s. To many Europeans, the US was supporting a repressive dictatorship in El Salvador, and was backing guerrillas seeking to overthrow the elected left-wing government in Nicaragua. Many saw US actions as hypocritical and in breach of international law. Consequently, EC action in America's 'backyard' seemed justified. By contrast, the Reagan administration saw both conflicts in terms of supporting pro-Western forces and stopping the spread of communism in its backyard.

In any event, in 1982 the EC launched its own dialogue with Central American states and the following year it co-operated with the Contadora Group of countries to pursue a joint peace initiative for the region. The EC then signed a co-operation accord with six Central American states to foster their development and to provide a framework for EC aid to them (Ginsberg, 1989a: 82–3).[11] To the Reagan administration, the EC's actions seemed an intervention into its own sphere of influence and threatened its own policy objectives. That is, non-military action by the EC seemed set to undermine the security policies of the US in a third region. In reality, the political embarrassment of Washington stemmed more from the EC's disagreement with US policy, rather than any serious threat to it. Nevertheless, policy sensitivities and effects were once again apparent: Washington felt the cost of separate EC action.

This brief overview indicates the existence of mutual policy sensitivities between the US and the EC in five different cases. Altogether, the cases are best understood in terms of the concept of interdependence. Again, however, they might be interpreted within a revised realist perspective. Yet the cases cited go beyond some traditional realist notions. This is reflected most strongly in economic aid being elevated to 'high politics', but also in the use of sanctions, the recognition of mutual sensitivities arising from action in third countries, and the decision to act via international fora (e.g. the Group of 24 and the UN). In sum, the cases illustrate the new conditions of the international system: the significance of reciprocal effects between the US and the EC (national governments and the EC institutions).

Of course, this mutual interdependence has not necessarily led to policy accord between the US and the EC. The cases cited range from joint action to policy disagreement. Shared interests seem best served by joint action and understanding, but this is not easily forthcoming. Indeed, lack of policy accord may be a consequence of the processes currently linking the US and the EC.

CONCLUSIONS

The political relations of the US and the EC have changed significantly since the 1950s. These changes are themselves an important element in the overall transition of the international system during this period. The significance of both EC national governments and EC institutions in US–EC bilateral relations creates a complex and varied situation, which must be incorporated into any analysis. Traditional realist notions emphasising government-to-government relations are increasingly inadequate in this regard.

US–EC relations in the political sphere do reflect interdependence, though it is of a different form from that existing in the economic or security spheres. It is an interdependence with little formal organisation, parsimony, or exclusivity. The increased contacts between the US Administration and the EC governments and institutions are symptomatic of their shared interdependence (multiple channels). There has been a growth and expansion of US–EC contacts, on both a bilateral and multilateral basis. US–EC interdependence is also reflected in policy matters. Policies in the political and security fields display sensitivities and mutual effects. The EC itself is emerging as an important international actor, and one best understood within the perspective of an interdependent world. The US Administration has been obliged to give greater recognition to the EC's enhanced role in political and economic matters, and indeed, in some security issues (multiple issues).

These developments pose new challenges for policy actors on both sides. As *The Economist* commented as far back as 1973, in the context of increased contacts between governments: 'There is going to be a lot more whizzing about by all concerned,' yet, 'The question is whether there is the necessary leadership at the top, on both sides of the Atlantic, and particularly in Europe, to pull all the various whizzings together' (3 March 1973). The management of US–EC interdependence to elaborate and achieve shared objectives remains a major item on the agenda of both parties in the 1990s. In this decade, US–EC relations could well undergo their most important transition since the start of the European integration process. Already, a momentum of change was under way in 1989–91. These themes are taken up in Chapter 6.

NOTES

1. Title III of the Single European Act incorporates 'European co-operation in the sphere of foreign policy' into the EC treaties, building upon the earlier intergovernmental agreements. It includes the EC Commission in the EPC process, recognises an EPC secretariat in Brussels, and outlines the basic working procedures of EPC. These are its main innovations; on crucial policy matters it remains limited in scope.

   EPC decisions are on the basis of unanimity. Title III contains exhortations for member governments to seek common policies and actions, but in the security sphere the EPC process is to be concerned only with its 'political and economic aspects'. Moreover, co-operation in EPC is not to 'impede' the work of NATO or the Western European Union.

2. Based on comments made by the former head of the US mission, George Vest, at the conference of the European Community Studies Association, in Washington, DC, May 1991.

3. Though Jacques Delors had himself broached the idea of closer US–EC links much earlier than Baker's own speech. (Interview in *Wall Street Journal*, cited in *European Community News*, 41/90, 27 November 1990, p. 1.)

4. The French are said to have forced the deletion of the references to consultation at EPC working group level. In reality, such consultation continues to occur.

5. The explanations which seemed most relevant were those he described as follows:

   (a) A regional integration logic, involving an 'externalization' hypothesis as developed by Schmitter (1969). This seeks to explain 'why non-members press the EC to act as a unit; what effects this outside charge has on the EC; and the outcome of EC foreign policy actions that are executed in response to outside pressure' (Ginsberg, 1989a: 25).

   (b) A global interdependence logic, following Keohane and Nye's concept of 'complex interdependence'. These are 'areas of foreign policy not connected to EC internal economic policies and their effect on outsiders' but to the EC's response to the pressures of the international system (Ginsberg, 1989a: 30).

   (c) A 'self-styled logic', or a European interests model. This recognises that 'the EC is capable of acting as a unit with its own regional interests' to promote on an international scale (Ginsberg, 1989a: 35).

These actions are not solely dependent on the need to respond to external stimuli, but instead are the products of (i) habits of working together; (ii) EC and member-state initiatives; and (iii) a sense of what the Europeans want in foreign policy questions.

6. The French departure from the integrated military command structure of NATO in 1965, of course, had implications for US–EC relations, but was not a direct aspect of those relations.

7. Keohane and Nye note that their own analysis is concerned not with 'national policy, but . . . the development and decline of international regimes' (1977: 223). To apply their systemic model at the national level, and 'analyse national policies under conditions of complex interdependence, one would need to ask two questions that are quite different from those that we have posed: (a) What range of choice is available to societies confronted with problems arising from interdependence; that is, how severe are the external constraints? (b) What determines the responses that are chosen and their success or failure?' (1977: 223).

Producing evidence to answer these two questions falls prey to the problems cited earlier on analysing policy constraints. Some progress is possible on the basis of further differentiation. 'Policy sensitivity' refers to the extent of the impact felt by one nation as a result of action taken by another: involving both the speed and cost of the effects being felt. This is a partial revision of Keohane and Nye's notion of 'sensitivity interdependence'. They note that, 'Sensitivity involves degrees of responsiveness within a policy framework – how quickly do changes in one country bring costly changes in another, and how great are the costly effects' (1977: 12). Here, we wish to separate out the speed and cost of the policy effect, from subsequent policy response and change. Analysing and differentiating policy change deserves careful consideration by itself, but it is not essential to our concerns here (Hall, 1989). We further put aside Keohane and Nye's notion of 'vulnerability interdependence', which they define as 'an actor's liability to suffer costs imposed by external events even after policies have been altered' (1977: 13). They cite the example here of oil-substitution policies by consuming nations after a supplier's price increase to illustrate vulnerability following an initial impact. 'Vulnerability dependence can be measured only by the costliness of making effective adjustments to a changed environment over a period of time' (1977: 13). In the political and security domain such assessments are very difficult to make. Moreover, evidence of policy sensitivity itself suggests the existence of interdependence (in so far as it involves significant costs): vulnerability is a different facet of the same phenomenon.

8. Like the US, the EC governments kept their embassies in Kuwait open for some time after the Iraqi invasion, despite Saddam Hussein's military threat to have them removed. The EC members agreed to protect EC nationals whose embassies were forcibly closed by the Iraqi forces. In response to the forced entry of Iraqi troops into the embassies of EC member states in Kuwait City, the EC expelled all military staff from

Iraqi embassies in EC member states and restricted the movement of Iraqi diplomats remaining in the EC.
9. An example of policy success, fuelled by mutual policy sensitivities, was the EPC's 1980 decision to endorse the participation of four EC member countries in the multilateral force which oversaw Israel's disengagement from the Sinai peninsula under the Camp David accord.
10. In this case, however, no action was taken by the EC under the auspices of EPC; see Ginsberg (1989b).
11. In 1989, however, the EC tied its aid to Central America to progress in realising political pluralism.

REFERENCES

Allen, D. Rummel, R. and Wessels, W. (1982) *European Political Cooperation: Towards a Foreign Policy for Western Europe* (London: Butterworths).

Bergsten, C. F. (1976) 'Interdependence and the Reform of International Institutions', *International Organization*, vol. 30, no. 2 (Spring).

Cerny, P. (1980) *The Politics of Grandeur: Ideological Aspects of De Gaulle's Foreign Policy* (Cambridge: Cambridge University Press).

Dahl, R. A. (1961) *Who Governs?* (New Haven: Yale University Press).

East, M. (1981) 'The Organizational Impact of Interdependence on Foreign Policy Making: The Case of Norway', in C. Kegley and P. McGowan (eds), *Sage International Yearbook of Foreign Policy Studies*, vol. 6 (Beverly Hills, CA: Sage).

Freedman, L. (1983) (ed.) *The Troubled Alliance: Atlantic Relations in the 1980s* (New York: St Martin's).

Ginsberg, R. (1989a) *Foreign Policy Actions of the European Community: The Politics of Scale* (Boulder: Lynne Rienner).

Ginsberg, R. (1989b) 'US–EC Relations', in J. Lodge (ed.), *The European Community and the Challenge of the Future* (London: Pinter).

Ginsberg, R. (1991a) 'Political and Institutional Relations Between the United States and the European Community', in L. Hurwitz and C. Lequesne, (eds), *The State of the European Community, 1990–91* (Boulder: Lynne Rienner).

Ginsberg, R. (1991b) 'European Community Foreign Policy Actions in the 1980s', paper presented to the Second Biennial International Conference of the European Community Studies Association, George Mason University, Washington, DC, May 1991.

Hall, P. (1989) 'Policy Paradigms, Social Learning and the State: The Case of Economic Policymaking in Britain' (Cambridge, Mass.: Harvard University).

Hanrieder, W. F. (1989) *Germany, America and Europe: Forty Years of German Foreign Policy* (New Haven: Yale University Press).

Harrison, M. (1981) *The Reluctant Ally* (New York: Praeger).

Hassner, P. and Roper, J. (1990) in F. de la Serre (ed.) *French and British Foreign Policies in Transition: The Challenge of Adjustment* (Oxford: Berg).

Hiden, J. and Featherstone, K. (1991) *West Meets East: Policies for a Common European Home* (London: Fabian Society).

Ifestos, P. (1987) *European Political Cooperation: Towards A Framework of Supranational Diplomacy?* (Aldershot, UK: Avebury/Gower).

Karvonen, L. and Sundelius, B. (1990) 'Interdependence and Foreign Policy Management in Sweden and Finland', *International Studies Quarterly*, vol. 34, pp. 211–27.

Keohane R. (1986) *Neorealism and Its Critics* (New York: Columbia University Press).

Keohane, R. and Nye, J. S. (1977) *Power and Interdependence: World Politics in Transition* (Boston: Little, Brown). See also second edition (1987).

Lodge, J. (ed.) (1989) *The European Community and the Challenge of the Future* (New York: St Martin's).

Louis, W. R. and Bull, H. (eds) (1986) *The Special Relationship* (Oxford: Oxford University Press).

Millar, D. (1991) 'Draft Treaty on European Union: Synopsis of Section on European Political Union' (Edinburgh: Europa Institute).

Parenti, M. (1970) 'Power and Pluralism', *Journal of Politics*, vol. 32.

Pijpers, A. (eds) (1988) *European Political Cooperation in the 1980s: A Common Foreign Policy for Western Europe?* (Dordrecht: Nijhoff).

Rummel, R. (1982) 'The Future of European Political Cooperation', in Allen (1982).

Rummel, R. (1988) 'Speaking with One Voice – and Beyond', in Pijpers (1988).

Schmitter, P. (1969) 'Three Neofunctional Hypotheses about International Integration', *International Organization*, (Winter) pp. 161–166.

Serre, F. de la (ed.) (1990) *French and British Foreign Policies in Transition: The Challenge of Adjustment* (Oxford: Berg).

Taylor, P. (1979) 'EC Political Cooperation: The Washington Connection', paper presented to International Studies Association conference, Toronto, March 1979.

Wallace, W. (1978) 'Old States and New Circumstances: The International Predicament of Britain, France and Germany', in Wallace, W. and Paterson, W. E. (eds), *Foreign Policy-Making in Western Europe* (Farnborough: Saxon House).

Waltz, K. N. (1979) *Theory of International Politics* (Reading, Mass.: Addision-Wesley).

4 The Economic Dimension

INTRODUCTION

The objective of this chapter is to apply the concept of complex interdependence (introduced in Chapter 2) to the US–EC economic relationship. The study of this relationship is organised in two parts. Part One examines the economic and monetary relationship across the three time periods introduced in Chapter 1. Historical trade, investment and employment data are provided to empirically substantiate the existence and magnitude of mutual dependence. The evidence indicates that interdependence existed throughout. However, interdependence in earlier periods was manifested in an asymmetric form, whereas the state of complex interdependence emerged fully only in the post-hegemonic period. Chapter 2 noted that complex interdependence typically entails both harmony and disharmony in bilateral relations. Part Two therefore considers disharmony by way of sector-specific trade conflict. It finds that such conflicts are part and parcel of interdependence and thus do not stand alone; rather, they are entwined by a wider swath of interdependence devoid of such conflict.

US–EC economic relations are very dense and mutually beneficial. Total two-way trade and investment, coupled with sales generated from investment, surpassed $1 trillion in 1990.[1] The US and EC have the world's largest trade and investment partnership and the value of their two-way trade and investment has grown annually. Many attribute this growth to the liberal multilateral principles and rules enshrined in the GATT which have eased the flow of goods and money across borders. NATO, too, played a key role because it provided a secure and protected environment within which the US and EC could expand bilateral and multilateral trade. What now throws into question the future of US–EC economic relations is not the mutual benefit of huge trade/investment flows, but the early post-war commitments to multilateralism and liberalism which served as rubrics for those flows.

Restrictive trade practices by both the US and EC in the 1980s–90s coupled with the end of the cold war have made economic cooperation in the GATT and elsewhere seemingly less politically

115

urgent, with very serious repercussions to the world trade and financial order. In the hegemonic period, commitments to free trade and GATT principles were enshrouded in cold war terms to bolster the Western economy as a bulwark against communism. The urgency of the security alliance tended to soothe trade and other disputes by virtue of its overriding necessity. Yet in the 1990s (as shown in Chapter 1), the policy process of US–EC relations lags far behind epic changes in Eastern and Central Europe. The cold war is over, but the economic (as well as political and military) institutions and processes of US–EC relations are rooted in the cold war.

Realistically, NATO will shrink in relative importance to the economic partnership and the EC's own emerging security identity. Just when the commercial component of US–EC and international co-operation needs to be strengthened, the GATT system (on which that co-operation had largely rested) is weak. Its members' political commitment to GATT rules is insufficient. Indeed, the broad Western consensus on a multilateral free world trade order has been challenged by the emergence of managed trade agreements, countless non-tariff barriers, and regional trade blocs (e.g, EC–EFTA and the emerging North American Free Trade Association, or NAFTA). The GATT is static and ill-equipped to provide a cogent forum for resolution of the world's trade problems in the 1990s. Part of its inadequacy has to do with the diverse interests of its 108 members and their lack of political will to update the GATT for the next century.

Even if current negotiations to complete the Uruguay Round are realised, the GATT will still not be able to cope with a changing world short of a wholesale strengthening of the organisation's rules and powers of enforcement. As of this writing, no political will is discernible among the GATT members to upgrade the 1948 agreement to the kind of full-blown international trade organisation which was proposed but not adopted forty-three years ago. Growing interdependence has led to GATT negotiations over new areas of domestic policy, encroaching more deeply into the domestic arena. This has given rise to new types of disputes not countenanced in the past. Interdependence exposes deeper sensitivities.

As pointed out in Chapter 1, the demise of the cold war is as much a historic turning point in US–EC relations as was its onset. Key policy decisions made now will shape bilateral economic relations for decades to come, much as the policy decisions made in the late 1940s shaped relations that lasted until only recently. Risks and opportunities to mould the future abound once again. Will the cold war era partnership of the United States and the EC withstand the test of a shrunken NATO and an ineffective GATT in a post-cold-war order? Chapter 6 will spell out the economic and other policy decisions that await action. This chapter serves as the empirical basis for that analysis.

PART ONE   THE US–EC ECONOMIC PARTNERSHIP

To begin, what do we mean by the 'US–EC economic partnership'? The United States and Europe traded with one another long before the Second World War. What made post-war economic relations different? The pre-war economic relationship was between the United States and individual European states. There was neither a legal nor a political framework for such relations. Indeed, a breakdown of the international economic order occurred in the 1930s with the demise of the League of Nations and functional co-operation, trade protectionism, competitive depreciation, and other forms of economic nationalism wreaking havoc upon the world trading system.

The post-war US–EC economic relationship became a 'partnership' because it took on a legal and political framework which entailed commitments (e.g., IMF, OECD, GATT, COCOM); had political, ideological, and security objectives (anticommunism, liberalism, multilateralism, collective self-defence); and dealt with exclusive bilateral links between the United States and the EC (diplomatic relations, policy consultation/co-ordination). The economic partnership helped to contain Soviet influence by strengthening the economic – and thus political – foundations of post-war Western Europe. Indeed, one of the most striking aspects of US–EC economic relations was and is its implications for the broader set of political and security links between the United States and the EC members.

The economic partnership during the hegemonic period was one in which the partners did not hold equal shares of power. The United States took on the role of hegemon with all the benefits and costs associated with that position. European security, political and economic needs were far more urgent than those of the United States. After all, the United States dominated world trade, investment and money. The United States possessed 70 per cent of global financial assets (Cafruny, 1989: 116), substituted international activism for neo-isolationism and accepted international responsibilities previously eschewed. Cities in the United States did not lie in ruins as did those in Britain and Germany. US industrial supremacy and relative insulation from the world economy maximised policymakers' freedom of action to devote substantial resources to military spending and foreign aid to reconstruct and integrate Europe into a unified Atlantic order. While US banks and multinational corporations benefited from the post-war economic system engineered by the United States, the United States still bore many of the costs of the system (Cafruny, 1989: 116).

The United States accepted (a) the trade discrimination that would follow the establishment of a European customs union and (b) the inconvertibility of currencies at least until reconstruction was achieved and supplied the Europeans and Japanese with liquidity through foreign investment, defence spending and high aid levels (Cafruny, 1989: 116). In the first few years after the establishment of the EEC and EFTA, US exports to Europe dropped by $200 million annually. Although this amount was a small dip in export trade, it came at a time when the United States was already carrying a substantial payments deficit (Krause, 1968: 223). The US mobilised other developed countries for management of the international economic order, and in some cases managed the system alone. It acted as the world's central banker, provided the major initiatives on international trade negotiations and dominated international production.

For their part, many European countries suffered a high human toll as a result of the war and this left a deep mark on European political culture. The European countries were economically exhausted and actively sought US leadership. They needed US assistance to rebuild their domestic production and to finance their international trade. The political implications of US leadership were viewed in positive terms because it was felt that US economic assistance would alleviate domestic economic and political problems and encourage international stability. Europeans feared not US domination but isolation, given the late entry of the United States into the two world wars (Spero, 1990: 24).

Yet the US–EC relationship was still a partnership in the hegemonic period in the sense that, while unequal, the EC states accepted the costs and benefits of American leadership of the international monetary/trade order and of NATO. 'The Europeans did more than merely follow the Americans; confounding sceptics, they created the EEC, moving farther along the road to unification than most Americans thought possible' (Ball: 8). An early, though isolated, precursor of a shift in the relative balance of power within the US–EC partnership came in 1962 when the United States withdrew its GATT concession on carpets and glass. The EC refused the US offer of compensation and instead retaliated against American goods (Krause, 1968: 225).

Both partners benefited from two decades of historically unprecedented economic growth. Both perceived a common threat to their security and, while Western Europe was more geographically vulnerable to Soviet power, the United States felt its security too was in danger. As a result, there was a mutual dependence in terms of their respective security needs. Before the outbreak of the cold war, the realities of economic interdependence were apparent because both sides agreed to turn away from the economic nationalism of the 1930s and to create a new international economic order in the 1940s designed to institutionally manage economic interdependence. The partners' common interest in economic co-operation was enhanced – not solely precipitated – by the cold war (Spero, 1990: 22).

The US and EC governments developed rules, institutions and procedures to regulate key aspects of international economic integration: management was made easier 'by a high level of agreement among the powerful on the goals and means of the international economic system. The foundation of that agreement was a shared belief in capitalism and liberalism' (Spero, 1990: 22). Although they could not have known it then, the early post-war institutions of international co-operation moulded and accepted by the United States and the future EC states would in just a decade provide the multilateral structure of today's US–EC relationship. The coincidence of three favourable political conditions – the concentration of power, shared interests and leadership of the US – provided the political capacity equal to the task of managing the international economy. It enabled the Europeans to recover from the devastation of the war, and to establish a stable monetary system and a more open trade and financial system that led to a period of unparalleled economic growth (Spero, 1990: 24).

Asymmetry existed in the monetary field. The weight of the dollar in international trade and capital markets made the European economy dependent on the vicissitudes of US economic performance, and US monetary policy and interest rates set by the US Federal Reserve Board. That said, the United States did entail costs by guaranteeing dollar convertibility (into gold) and thus fixed exchange rates. Since the US dollar is still a major, although no longer dominant, currency of international commodity trade a strong European sensitivity to its fluctuations remains.

It was not possible for the EC to be an equal partner of the United States during the hegemonic period. First, it had yet to develop a level of political integration sufficient for it to speak with one voice in foreign affairs. Second, the heavy hand of French nationalism robbed the EC of its influence as a single actor in Europe and abroad until after 1969. With European reconstruction completed by the 1960s, the EC developed its own economic and political power base in the 1970s. The development of European Political Co-operation (EPC) and the growth of EC foreign policy actions in the 1970s occurred in partial response to the preoccupation by the United States with non-European matters, e.g. the Vietnam War and the payments and trade/payments deficits of the 1970s. The partnership was destined to become more equal as the Europeans began to catch up with US economic performance during the period of hegemonic decline. In this period, the EC became the 'most important member of the GATT' and was able to determine in large measure 'the success or failure of any attempt to liberalise [international] trade' (Krause, 1968: 225). In partial response to the Nixon Administration's decision in 1973 to break with fixed exchange rates, the EC created the European Monetary System in 1979 to stabilise intra-EC exchange rate fluctuations. This action spoke to the EC's attempt to reverse its dependence on the vicissitudes of US monetary policy.

As the United States grappled with its own economic problems in the period of hegemonic decline, its political support for the notion of European integration was made increasingly contingent on US market access to the EC. Trade disputes increased in number. The EC itself as early as 1972 concluded that

> the points of friction and strain continue to be very numerous, and they are even increasing with the growth of the EC, the more so as the future intention of the United States to dissociate the political principle of its support for the objective of European union and the unbending defence of its economic interests whenever it considers that the integration of Europe calls these into question. Never before has the US . . . scrutinised and evaluated so systematically down to the last detail the scope and possible effects of European policies.[2]

The economic partnership of the post-hegemonic period is much more equal in terms of major indicators of economic power (GDP, GDP per capita, industrial output and performance) and independence (food, energy and industrial self-sufficiency). The EC now has a larger population than the US and a roughly equal GDP. Indeed the EC has 'the largest concentration of wealth and human resources in the world' (Jannuzzi, 1991: 3). It is the world's largest trader and boasts the world's largest single market. It has stood up to American pressures for market access or reforms of farm and industrial policies on numerous occasions, particularly during the current post-hegemonic period. Furthermore, as the EC moves from the success of the EMS to EMU, the dollar will be sensitive to the European Currency Unit (ECU) and EC monetary policies set by the new European Central Bank. These developments will pave the way for a more symmetric US–EC monetary interdependence at the turn of the century. Thus, the monetary as well as commercial side of the economic partnership has grown more symmetric as the two adjust to their relations in the post-hegemonic period.[3]

Finally, no introduction to US–EC economic relations would be complete without a word about the significance of these relations in both bilateral and multilateral terms. Bilaterally, the two sides have huge stakes in world trade, accounting for nearly half of all world imports and exports and the lion's share of total world investment. Trade-related and investment-related employment account for approximately 6 million jobs in the United States and the EC. Multilaterally, the two have favoured a liberal world trade order (to varying degrees) by concluding GATT rounds of multilateral trade negotiations (MTNs). These rounds have reduced international tariffs from about 50 per cent before the Dillon Round to roughly 5 per cent by the Tokyo Round. Although the future of multilateralism and the GATT in their current form are increasingly questioned, without the United States and the EC there would be neither a GATT nor a liberal world trade order to save. In addition, the economic security of the OECD states hinges on amicable US–EC relations. A prosperous, growing and amicable US–EC bilateral trade and investment partnership positively affects the broader Western international economy because of the dependence of other OECD states on the US and EC markets. To the developing states, the US and EC – with their markets and foreign investment – are indispensable assets in the quest for economic development (Ginsberg, 1989a: 262–3).

COMPLEX INTERDEPENDENCE

This chapter applies the Keohane–Nye concept of complex interdependence (defined in Chapter 2) to the US–EC economic relationship and finds that it generally meets the conditions set out
by Keohane and Nye. Neo-mercantilist notions help to explain the
background for some of the more vociferous sectoral disputes that
intermittently plague bilateral relations. Yet sectoral disputes are as
old as the US–EC relationship itself, form part of the pattern of
complex interdependent relations that has developed, and are
accepted by both sides as necessary evils in a peacetime, and highly
competitive, international system.

Data collated in this chapter point to dense bilateral economic ties
which intimately connect the US and Europeans economies to a
non-hierarchical, multivaried bilateral agenda. The US–EC agenda is
noted for:

- its absence of the use of military force to realise national interests
  in bilateral relations;
- the widespread external effects of internal economic decision-
  making; and
- a substantial reduction in international economic decision-making
  autonomy.

Although Keohane and Nye introduced the concept of complex
interdependence in the late 1970s, they – nor subsequent writers on
the subject of international political economy – did not seek to test its
validity as an explanation of US–EC economic relations.

Whereas complex interdependence provides an overarching explanation of US–EC economic relations, Gilpin (1987), Haus (1991)
and others have questioned its validity as an explanatory concept.
Gilpin surmises that interdependence 'is a phenomenon to be studied, not a ready-made set of conclusions regarding the nature and
dynamics of international relations' (Gilpin, 1987: 18). For Gilpin, an
economic nationalist perspective does this. Economic nationalists
stress the conflictual nature of international economic relations; they
argue that 'economic interdependence must have a political foundation and that it creates yet another arena for interstate conflict,
increased national vulnerability, and constitutes a mechanism that
one society can employ to dominate another' (Gilpin, 1987: 18). For
Haus, a neo-mercantilist perspective best explains US–EC trade dis-

putes that result from complex interdependence and end up in trade war and other forms of coercion barring peaceful settlement (Haus, 1991). Blake and Walters describe mercantilists as those who see politics as determining economics. 'Economics are to be understood in terms of competition for the distribution of wealth and power among states, as distinct from the individual and global welfare maximisation stressed by liberal economists or the class competition emphasised by radical economists' (Blake and Walters, 1987: 9). 'Mercantilists explain contemporary conflicts over trade and industrial policies between the US and its leading economic partners as a struggle by governments to secure a favourable position in an evolving international division of labour' (Blake and Walters, 1987: 9).

Neo-mercantilist thought offers some insight into some of the methods used by the US and, indeed, the EC in settling disputes, e.g. threats of or actual punitive action restricting access to a market. After all, the EC, like the US, represents state and producer interests with strong motives to expand export trade and protect domestic markets. However, this body of thought has its limitations. While neo-mercantilism enables us to focus on the causes, effects and outcomes of certain kinds of disputes, it does not explain how US–EC commercial disputes are functions of complex interdependence accepted by both the US and EC. Within the interdependent relationship, conflict may exist on one among many levels. Hallmarks of US–EC economic relations are that

- disputes are either settled by compromise or by unilateral action, in which case the parties agree to disagree and return to normalcy;
- commercial competition is understood to be sharp and unremitting, given what are essentially capitalist or mixed–capitalist societies; and
- when disputes are put into the broader context of the relationship between the world's largest bilateral traders and investors, they are not very significant in terms of value and volume of trade.

As a result, though a neo-mercantilist explanation of conflict may provide some insight into trade conflict, it is – at most – a partial explanation limited to one segment of US–EC relations. Neo-mercantilist, indeed realist, concepts may be more applicable to other sets of international relationships than they are to US–EC relations.

In short, if neo-mercantilism is at work in US–EC relations then broadly speaking there would not be co-operation; investment/trade flows would drop as trade disputes, one after another, whittle away at broad consensus. Neo-mercantilists account for only the conflictual aspects of bilateral relations rather than the full picture. US–EC relations frame, contain, and minimise disputes. Few disputes hit hard. Some disputes evade resolution, but the overall relationship is not permanently set back. Complex interdependence, with conflict built into its assumptions of how states manage the stresses of inter-dependent life, better captures the dynamics of US–EC economic relations. Yet current theoretical understanding remains inadequate: further refinement is necessary to fully encompass the complexities of US–EC relations.

MULTILATERAL INSTITUTIONS AND BILATERAL PROCESSES OF US–EC ECONOMIC RELATIONS

By way of introduction, official day-to-day US–EC economic rela-tions are conducted in two spheres. In the multilateral sphere, the US and EC members (and/or the EC itself), as members of international organisations (UN) and regimes (GATT, G7) abide by certain rules, engage in consultations and negotiations, and make common poli-cies. In the bilateral sphere, the US and the EC are engaged in economic summitry, diplomacy, negotiations, consultations, conflict resolution (or, conversely, when resolution fails, trade war) and policy co-ordination. At first glance, it would appear that the bilateral sphere is most directly relevant to trade relations because the US and EC (not the individual EC member-states) are the exclusive partici-pants. However, upon closer analysis, US–EC relations are much more regulated by the multilateral agreements to which both parties belong than to a structure of bilateral institutional arrangements that frame, for examples, US–Canadian, US–Israeli, EC–Lomé Conven-tion or EC–EFTA relations. The regimes governing US–EC trade relations are found in the multilateral rather than bilateral sphere (COCOM, GATT, OECD, IMF, G7). The formal bilateral sphere is characterised by a process of conducting relations, (e.g., negotiations to end trade disputes), not an institution. The multilateral sphere consists of both processes (consultations at Western Economic Sum-mits) and institutional structures (IEA, UNCTAD, EBRD).

MULTILATERAL FORA

Appendix 1 identifies the various fora of US–EC economic (and political) relations. Even before the beginning of the establishment of the US–EC relationship in 1951 with the founding of the ECSC, the United States and the future EC members were engaged in multi-lateral organisations dealing with international codes for labour (ILO, 1919), currency stabilisation (IMF, 1944), international economic development (IBRD, 1944), international peace and security (UN, 1945), atomic energy (1945), agricultural development (FAO, 1945), economic reconstruction (OEEC, 1948), international trade liberalisation (GATT, 1948) and collective self-defence (NATO, 1949). Appendix 1 shows that of the 25 fora in which the US and EC interact, 18 are multilateral. As a result, the management of US–EC relations is tied heavily to the future of multilateral co-operation.

The most relevant multilateral fora are the GATT, NATO, COCOM, OECD, Western Economic Summits (G7) and CSCE. At multilateral organisations and meetings, the US and EC members are part of a group that is not specifically related to the US, EC or US–EC relationship. Of all the multilateral fora established during the hegemonic period, the GATT was (and remains) the most central to US–EC relations. US–EC trade relations are dependent on the GATT as a framework of rules, dispute settlement procedures and trade liberalisation. Despite the many challenges worldwide that put the future of the GATT system in some doubt, it has to date provided the US and EC with what they do not have at present on a bilateral basis, i.e. a framework to avoid commercial chaos.

It is at the GATT that the US and EC submit trade disputes to bilateral consultations for resolution, and, if that fails, then to panels which investigate and make nonbinding opinions. It is also at the GATT that the two partners engage (with the other members) in periodic rounds of negotiations to reduce trade barriers. GATT rules affect international trade on which the US and EC so heavily depend. The GATT has been criticised for ineffective dispute settlement mechanisms and GATT members (including the US and EC) have been criticised for either blocking or ignoring dispute settlement procedures. GATT decisions are determined by consensus – polite language for the veto each member has over initiation and adoption of GATT reports on trade disputes.

The GATT sets up a panel of independent experts to examine disputes, reach conclusions, and, in some cases, make recommendations for a solution. The dispute settlement process has five stages: consultations and conciliation enabling the parties to settle their dispute through bilateral consultations, and, if that fails, GATT-sponsored conciliation; establishment of a formal panel, if bilateral conciliation fails, to consider findings and make recommendations; and follow-up and implementation (US International Trade Commission, 1985: vi–vii). Panel findings are adopted by consensus, which offers disputants the opportunity to block adoption of the findings. If bilateral settlement cannot be reached after the panel findings are made then the findings are circulated at the next meeting of the GATT Council (body of representatives of the members) for decision to adopt the report. As a last resort, the complainant may request GATT authorisation to suspend concessions or other obligations with respect to the defendant at an amount of trade equivalent to the traded item in dispute. Part 2 of this chapter on trade disputes and their resolution addresses US–EC relations in the GATT.

In addition to the GATT dispute settlement procedures, there are codes covering non-tariff measures. Dispute settlement procedures under these codes are similar to the regular GATT procedures. GATT codes include subsidies and countervailing duties, government procurement, standards, import-licensing procedures, customs valuation and antidumping measures. There are also sectoral agreements over trade in civil aircraft, bovine meat and dairy products. The GATT Standards Code of 1980, for example, obliges the US, the EC and other signatories to ensure that standards and certification systems are not used as trade barriers. Signatories must use open procedures when developing new standards or certification systems or revising old ones before being finalised. The Code includes dispute settlement provisions to deal with violators.

The US and EC are heavily involved in GATT proceedings. They are the two largest and most powerful parties to the MTNs, and are the two most involved parties in dispute settlement procedures. The majority of US–EC trade disputes make their way to the GATT for possible settlement. The United States has participated in more GATT dispute settlement cases than any other single GATT member, most often as the complainant (ITC: 1985). From 1948 to 1985 it was a party to more than one-half of all cases. The US filed complaints in 33 cases and was named in 13 complaints. The most frequent target of US complaints was the EC, against which about two-thirds of US complaints were filed. In 14 cases, US complaints concerned farm products and 10 of these were against EC measures (US International Trade Commission, 1985: 49). The second ranking target of US complaints was Japan, which was the subject of five US complaints.

Despite the many trade problems the US faces with Japan, particularly with regard to barriers to Japan's import trade, and given the two-way value of trade and investment between the US and EC, the vast majority of US complaints at the GATT are levelled against the EC. That the EC is the largest target of US complaints is not a sign of grave crisis in US–EC relations. It instead testifies to the magnitude and intensity of their relations. Either side can issue a complaint against the other and does not expect other aspects of bilateral relations to be adversely affected. A sign of complex interdependence, then, is tolerance of discord and an agreement to disagree. The above suggests the high sensitivity of the US market to EC actions and testifies to the existence of complex interdependence between the United States and the EC. Complex interdependence triggers trade disputes because of the high degree of mutual sensitivity.

Complaints against US measures have also become more common. Over the period 1975–85, 8 panel cases were filed against US trade measures. In the 27 years prior to 1975, only 5 of the cases reviewed names US measures. The EC filed 5 of these cases on US measures, 3 of them since 1975. The EC or its members have been heavily engaged in formal dispute settlement procedures as well. The EC was involved in 62 cases, accounting for 74 per cent of all GATT and Code panels, most often as the target of complaints (US International Trade Commission, 1985). While EC countries filed 20 panel requests, they were the subject of complaints in 42 of the panel cases. Since 1975, the EC has been a party to 24 of 42 panel cases filed. Over 40 per cent of all panel complaints against the EC have been filed since 1975. Complaints against the EC have concerned subsidies more frequently than any other type of measure. Subsidies were the topic of 13, or one-third, of the cases.

Whereas the GATT has provided a multilateral framework for trade liberalisation and dispute settlement for the US and EC, NATO has provided the security umbrella. At NATO, 11 of the 12 EC members form the majority of the 16-member organisation and work with the United States on many issues that have an impact on bilateral and multilateral economic relations: government procurement, product standardisation, restrictions on exports of strategic products and economic sanctions against aggressor states. In the integrated common structure, 9 EC members (not France, Spain and Ireland) and the United States are committed to collective self-defence. At COCOM, 11 EC members and the US are involved in controls of exports with military applications to selected countries, such as North Korea, Iraq, Vietnam and Cuba.

At the OECD, the US and EC have another opportunity to interact. The OECD is a forum for industrialised democracies to consult on and co-ordinate a broad range of economic issues. The objectives of this organisation are to: promote the members' financial stability and economic growth; promote economic development of LDCs; and expand multilateral, non-discriminatory world trade. Heir to the old 1948 OEEC, the OECD produces economic studies, prescribes economic policy, and makes economic forecasts. It also promotes an open, non-discriminatory, multilateral world trade order. The OECD has legal agreements in which the EC members and the US are signatories, e.g. the Civil Aircraft Code and the Export Credits Agreement Accord. Since 1990 the OECD has been committed to promoting economic reforms in Central and Eastern Europe, and OECD observers point to the organisation's potential role as a productive force in the transformation of the economies of the former Soviet bloc states. The organisation provides an important forum for the US and EC to meet and consult on matters of multilateral significance (GATT round, aid to Eastern Europe) and on bilateral significance (farm subsidies).

At the CSCE, where the EC (through the EPC and the EC Commission) has played a central and dynamic role since the negotiations began that produced the 1975 Helsinki Accords, the EC works with the United States and the other members in promoting trade and economic, scientific, industrial and environmental co-operation between East and West Europe. The CSCE is the only forum in which the West (NATO, EC and the EFTA states) can meet alone with the East. The United States has had to learn to adjust to the leading and proactive role of its former client at CSCE deliberations.

On 21 November 1990 the CSCE states signed the 'Charter of Paris for a New Europe', which reassigned the content of the three previous Helsinki baskets (trade, security and human rights) to seven new sectors (human dimension, security, economic co-operation, environment, culture, migrant workers and the Mediterranean). CSCE was institutionalised by establishing (a) a permanent secretariat in Prague, a conflict prevention centre in Vienna and an office for free elections in Warsaw; and (b) the practice of regular high-level political consultations (head of government, foreign minister).

As a consequence of the adverse effects of economic interdependence on the ability of national governments to independently make economic policies, leaders of the western industrialised states have convened annual summits since 1975. At these Western Economic Summits (of the G7), the EC Commission President and the EC Council President (who are actually the eighth and ninth members of the Group) join the United States President and the leaders of Canada, Japan, France, Germany, Italy and the UK in seeking consultation and co-operation concerning macroeconomic trade, monetary policies and international political events. It was at the 1989 Western Economic Summit in Houston that the EC Commission was asked to co-ordinate Western aid to the reforming economies of Central and Eastern Europe. The EC Commission now co-ordinates multilateral aid from the Group-24 (OECD members) to the countries of the former Soviet bloc. The G7 finance ministers and central bankers also meet at the summit and during the year to discuss, monitor, and co-ordinate exchange rate fluctuations and interest rate policy. The G7 has been actively involved in questions pertaining to the reconstruction of the economies of the former Soviet Union. The EC Commission is represented at and participates in these meetings as well.

Multilateral fora in which the US and the EC and/or EC states are members, but whose work is not directly and immediately relevant to the US–EC relationship include the IMF and the World Bank, the IEA, UNCTAD, the European Bank for Reconstruction and Development (EBRD) and the IAEA. At the World Bank, founded in 1944 to pave the way for post-war reconstruction, the US and EC states, among the other 150 members, finance Third World economic development projects. The US and EC member states together have the lion's share of voting power: 15.1 per cent for the US and 29.7 per cent for the EC states (8.7 per cent for Japan). At the IMF, also founded in 1944 to help the Europeans meet their debt obligations, the US and EC states join 150 other members in providing loans to countries with payments problems. Here too the US and EC again grab the lion's share of voting power: 19.6 per cent for the US and 28.9 per cent for the EC states (6.1 per cent for Japan). At the IEA, founded in 1974 in the wake of the OPEC oil cartel embargo and price hikes, the EC Commission, EC members (minus France) and the United States, among other major oil-consuming states, devise plans to deal with any future oil embargo. At UNCTAD, founded in

1974 as a UN body to promote international trade as a means of supporting Third World economic development, the US and EC states are among other UN members who exchange views on development issues and are involved in various areas under the auspices of UNCTAD, e.g. the Generalised System of Preferences and international commodity agreements (rubber, sugar, wheat, coffee, timber and so forth). Lastly, and most recently, at the EBRD, established in 1990 to provide Western loans to the reforming economies of the former Soviet bloc, the EC Commission and the United States are the two principal shareholders. At the IAEA, the US, EC and other UN members work together on setting up agreements to enable IAEA authorities to undertake inspections of the nuclear facilities of member countries.

These and other fora listed in Appendix 2 comprise the broader basis for US–EC relations. Because the US and EC are so intimately and comprehensively involved in multilateral flows of trade, services, investment, capital and labour, it is not surprising that the number of international organisations in which they are involved in is so large. These bodies give the US and EC multiple opportunities to discuss and work on not only multilateral questions but also bilateral ones. Chapter Six investigates the benefits and costs of the US and EC operating at so many and such diverse levels of international activities.

BILATERAL FORA

Formal bilateral relations began with the exchange of diplomatic recognition between the United States and the ECSC in 1951 and the setting up of an ECSC mission to Washington and a US mission to the ECSC High Authority in Luxembourg – which later became the US mission to the EC Commission in Brussels. Since then the US and EC have raised and expanded the level of their diplomatic interactions (see Chapter 3). For example, in 1990 the new EC Head of Delegation to the United States, Andreas van Agt, was accredited to the White House, whereas before EC Delegation Heads were accredited to the State Department. Thus, in one fell swoop, the Bush administration upgraded the diplomatic status of the EC Commission in the United States and of the broader US–EC relationship (although the move had been under consideration for several years).

Appendix 2 shows that of the 25 fora in which the US and EC interact, eight are bilateral. For the purposes of studying economic relations, the most relevant bilateral fora are (a) the biannual US–EC high-level meetings of the EC Commission President and relevant Commissioners and the US Secretary of State and relevant Cabinet members; (b) the US–EC biannual summits of the EC Council President, the EC Commission President, and relevant EC Commissioners and the US President, Secretary of State, and relevant Cabinet members; and (c) biannual meetings of the US Secretary of State and the EC foreign ministers with the EC Commission President. There are also *ad-hoc* consultations between the Presidency Foreign Minister or the Troika (including the Political Directors) and the US Secretary of State.

The November 1990 Transatlantic Declaration (see Appendix 1 and Chapter 3 for more information) pulled under one rubric the bilateral principles and objectives of US–EC economic (and other) relations and the levels, frequency, and content of bilateral consultations. Although some in the US Administration had hoped for a treaty institutionalising US–EC relations, the Declaration was all that could be reached by negotiation. In the realm of economics, the Declaration commits the US and EC to:

– promote market principles, reject protectionism, and expand, strengthen, and further open the multilateral trading system;
– inform and consult each other on important matters of common economic interest with a view to bringing their positions as close as possible and to co-operate in appropriate international bodies;
– expand their dialogue to include discussion of matters such as technical and non-tariff barriers to industrial and agricultural trade, services, competition policy, transportation policy, standards, telecommunications, high technology and other relevant areas; and
– strengthen mutual co-operation in exchanges and joint projects in science and technology, including research in medicine, environment protection, pollution prevention, energy, space, high energy physics and the safety of nuclear and other installations.

On 23 April 1990, the EC Commission President and the US Secretary of State led their respective delegations to the first of the new biannual ministerial meetings provided for in the Transatlantic Declaration. The EC side was also represented by the EC Commissioners responsible for external relations and trade, science, research and development, agriculture and rural development, environment, nuclear safety and civil protection, and employment,

industrial relations, and social affairs. The US side was also represented by the Secretaries of Commerce and Agriculture and the US
Trade Representative. They discussed the Uruguay Round, US–EC
trade relations from agriculture to aircraft to science and technology,
and developments in Europe.

There is no EC–US co-operation accord; trade and other relations
are regulated and conducted within the multilateral fora previously
discussed. The 1990 US–EC Declaration provides a framework for
bilateral relations, but it is neither a binding treaty nor an institutional arrangement. As a result, the US and EC must rely on
multilateral institutions to provide a legal context for economic relations. While there is no bilateral institutional framework, there are
bilateral agreements. They include steel exports to the US (1982,
1988); fishing in US coastal waters (1977), the supply of nuclear fuels
(1958) and co-operation in the field of peaceful use of atomic energy
(1959). There has also been an exchange of letters on environmental
protection.

Ad-hoc consultations occur frequently between US and EC officials
on economic issues and are too numerous to quantify. For example,
in the two-year period between 1989–91, US Secretary of Commerce
Moshbacher met three times with EC Commissioner and Vice-
President Bangemann to discuss controversial trade issues (specifically, standards, testing and certification) concerning both the GATT
and the EC 1992 project. One cannot discount the significance of
these meetings for US–EC relations in terms of crisis management
and policy co-ordination. In addition, the US Department of the
Treasury and the EC Commission have a formal programme of
exchange of professionals, as do other agencies of the Federal Government and the Commission.

A curiosity of US–EC economic relations, in a sense, is that
important as these relations are for Americans and Europeans, there
is no fixed bilateral economic organisation, whereas there are fixed
organisations at the multilateral level. Depending on one's view, the
absence of a fixed organisation of bilateral relations points to (a) a
lack of commitment and an institutional vacuum leading to anarchic
conditions or, conversely, (b) the strength of ties because they are so
firmly rooted, mutually advantageous and pacific that they need not
be organisationally structured. Beyond fixed institutions and processes, the informal axis of US–EC economic relations – the vast flow of
trade, investment, capital, people and ideas across the North Atlantic
– is a self-propelling process requiring little management. This points

to the level of trust and the degree of peace that exists between the US and the EC as well as among the OECD states. The complex economic interdependence that exists between the US and the EC to date has not required a complex organisational structure such as NATO.

INDICATORS OF US–EC ECONOMIC RELATIONS: MACROECONOMIC COMPARISONS

At the core of their economic relations is the dependence of the US and the EC on each other for trade and investment and on a fluid international economic environment that remains conducive to the flow of goods, services, and capital. US–EC trade and investment continue to expand greatly so that, for example, in 1990, total two-way trade and investment was over $570 billion (a 100 per cent increase over 1985 levels in real terms). Total two-way trade coupled with sales generated from two-way investment surpassed the historic $1 trillion mark in 1990. US–EC trade and investment represent such large components of the GDP of the US and EC that they cannot be duplicated by any other set of external economic relationships in existence.

The EC stopped being the passive junior partner of the United States in the international economy back in the period of hegemonic decline in the 1970s. Not only is the EC now, in some respects, a larger economic entity than the United States but the international economic weight of the EC is so heavy that it, together with the US, dominate international economic policy. The EC's 1991 population of 345 million is a third bigger than the US population of 251 million (while Japan's population is just 124 million). With the expected expansion of the EC in the 1990s to include new members, its population and internal market will continue to grow. The EC's 1990 GDP of $4.7 trillion has nearly caught up with the United States's 1990 GDP of $5.4 trillion (compared with Japan's $2.9 trillion). As discussed below, the EC is the world's largest importer and exporter. However, in terms of the number of companies in Fortune 500, a list of the world's largest corporations, the US has 164 corporations compared with the EC's 129 and Japan's 111.

Large markets like the EC and the US must function in a wider international trade system. The EC is more heavily dependent on exports and imports as a percentage of GDP than the United States or Japan. EC exports of goods and services account for about 28 per cent of the EC's GDP compared with Japan's 14 per cent and the United States's 8 per cent. EC imports of goods and services account for about 25 per cent of GDP compared with Japan's 12 per cent, and the United States's 9 per cent. Thus, over half the EC's GDP is accounted for by imports and exports compared with 26 per cent for Japan and 17 per cent for the United States.[4] The heavy dependence on trade as a very high (EC) or high (US) percentage of GDP speaks to both partners' dependence on a fluid and peaceful world trade order. In practice, however, the logic of that argument must compete with powerful protectionist sentiments.

MULTILATERAL TRADE

The extensive and balanced flow of US–EC trade is an indicator of complex interdependence. What follows is an analysis of US–EC commercial interdependence, first from the perspective of their dependence on, and dominance of, the world market and second from the perspective of the dependence on each other's markets. Mutual dependence on multilateral and bilateral trade is a hallmark of US–EC relations.

Multilateral trade is one of the two pivots around which the international economy revolves (the other one being investment, which is handled in the subsequent section). Both the US and EC shares of world trade have increased in the post-war period. In 1989, world imports and exports totalled almost $6 trillion. Table 4.1 shows that in 1989 total imports and exports of the US and EC accounted for one-half of world trade (up from one-third in 1950). Japan's share of world trade rose from just 1 per cent in 1950 to 8 per cent in 1989. Table 4.2 shows that the US and the EC account for 55 per cent of total world imports, a percentage that has held steady since the 1950s. Over a forty-year period, the EC has taken nearly 40 per cent of world imports and the US has taken between 13 and 19 per cent. Conversely, Japan has taken only 6 to 7 per cent of world imports in the 1970s and 1980s (up from 3 to 4 per cent in the 1950s and 1960s). The US and EC together account for about one-half of world export trade. Table 4.3 shows that between 1950 and 1989 the EC share of world exports rose from 29 to 38 per cent, the US share dropped from 17 to 13 per cent and Japan's share rose from 1 to 9 per cent. As a percentage of total world exports, the EC's share is three times

TABLE 4.1 Total trade of the EC, the US and Japan as percentages of total world trade, 1950–89

	1950	1955	1960	1965	1970	1975	1980	1985	1989
EC	16	34	36	40	40	38	38	35	38
US	16	15	15	14	14	13	12	15	15
Japan	1	2	3	5	6	7	7	8	8

SOURCE Based on *International Financial Statistics Yearbooks* (Washington: International Monetary Fund, 1988, 1989, 1990).

TABLE 4.2 Imports of the EC, the US and Japan and as percentages of total world imports, 1950–89 (*$US billion*)

	1950	%	1955	%	1960	%	1965	%	1970	%	1975	%	1980	%	1985	%	1989	%
EC*	21	(34)	22	(24)	47	(37)	74	(41)	125	(41)	326	(39)	773	(40)	661	(35)	1,150	(39)
US	10	(16)	12	(13)	16	(13)	23	(13)	43	(14)	106	(13)	257	(13)	362	(19)	493	(16)
Japan	1	(1)	2	(2)	4	(3)	8	(4)	19	(6)	58	(7)	141	(7)	130	(7)	210	(7)
WORLD	61		93		126		182		304		837		1,946		1,890		2,975	

*Includes intra-EC imports.

SOURCE Based on statistics from the International Monetary Fund, the US Department of Commerce and the US International Trade Commission in current prices.

TABLE 4.3 Exports of the EC, the US and Japan and as percentages of total world exports, 1950–89 ($US billion)

	1950	%	1955	%	1960	%	1965	%	1970	%	1975	%	1980	%	1985	%	1989	%
EC*	17	(29)	29	(33)	43	(36)	67	(39)	116	(40)	309	(38)	691	(37)	647	(36)	1,108	(38)
US	10	(17)	15	(17)	21	(17)	27	(16)	43	(15)	108	(13)	221	(12)	213	(12)	364	(13)
Japan	0.8	(1)	2	(2)	4	(3)	8	(5)	19	(7)	56	(7)	130	(7)	177	(10)	274	(9)
World	59		88		120		173		291		822		1,892		1,799		2,891	

*Includes intra-EC exports.

SOURCE Based on statistics from the International Monetary Fund, the US Department of Commerce and the US International Trade Commission in current prices.

higher than that of the US and four times higher than Japan's.

The dominance by the US and EC of world trade speaks to their dependence on foreign markets as a source of their power (exports) and vulnerability (strategic imports). If the world market contracts for any reason then the damage to US and EC business and employment interests is felt widely. The US and the EC are dependent on working with one another and with the wider international trade community to keep trade open. As the United States grapples with a massive merchandise trade deficit, exports are vital in the quest to achieve a more even balance of trade. For the EC, with its mercantilist heritage, exports are a way of life and are vital to economic growth and employment. Japan also is dependent on export trade but its commitment to multilateral import trade is captive to domestic social and cultural customs that stymie imports.

BILATERAL TRADE

The framework for bilateral trade between the US and EC is the multilateral rules of the GATT and the OECD. The two partners are governed by GATT (and some OECD) rules and regulations and often submit bilateral trade disputes to the GATT for conciliation when their bilateral consultations fail to resolve them. On the whole, more GATT rules are honoured than are violated, although there are instances when either one tries to evade GATT rules and findings. The OECD has established several multilateral rules pertaining to export credits and aircraft trade. There are a few bilateral agreements governing fishing, atomic energy and trade in steel. Despite disputes in some sectors of US–EC trade, the vast flow of two-way trade goes undisturbed by controversy.

Table 4.4 depicts two-way trade between the United States and the EC, Canada and Japan as a percentage of total US trade with the world from 1981 to 1990. The EC is the largest trading partner of the United States, although Canada has been close on the EC's trail. Indeed, US–Canadian trade exceeded US–EC trade in value from 1983 to 1985. In 1990, two-way trade between the US and EC amounted to $183.9 billion compared with Canada's $170.2 billion and Japan's $134.9 billion. The EC took 21 per cent of the total two-way trade between the US and world (up from 19 per cent in 1981), compared with Canada's 20 per cent (up from 17 per cent) and Japan's 16 per cent (up from 12 per cent). The high and growing

TABLE 4.4   *Two-way trade between the US and the EC, Canada and Japan as percentages of total US trade with the world, 1981–90 ($US billion)*

	EC	(%)	Canada	(%)	Japan	(%)	World
1981	92.9	(19)	83.9	(17)	58.8	(12)	487.9
1982	88.0	(19)	80.0	(18)	58.4	(13)	449.4
1983	86.2	(19)	88.5	(19)	62.1	(14)	452.6
1984	107.9	(20)	110.8	(21)	79.4	(15)	535.0
1985	114.2	(20)	120.0	(21)	89.8	(16)	556.5
1986	125.6	(21)	121.3	(21)	104.9	(18)	585.2
1987	137.3	(21)	127.8	(20)	110.9	(17)	646.0
1988	155.3	(21)	148.9	(20)	125.1	(17)	747.4
1989	166.5	(20)	163.0	(20)	134.6	(16)	817.4
1990	183.9	(21)	170.2	(20)	134.9	(16)	865.0

SOURCE   Based on data from the US International Trade Commission and the US Department of Commerce in current prices.

proportion of trade between the US and the EC, Canada and Japan is a function of the complex interdependence that exists between the United States and these trade partners.

Table 4.5 depicts US imports from the EC, Canada and Japan as a percentage of total US imports from 1981 to 1990. Canada accounted for $92.0 billion (19 per cent) of total US imports from the rest of the world, followed by the EC which accounted for $90.8 billion (18 per cent) and Japan which accounted for $88.8 billion (18 per cent). Although the US and the EC maintain the world's largest bilateral trade relationship, the EC is not the largest source of US imports. For example, in 1986, 1987 and 1988 this position was held by Japan. In 1989 Japan was the largest source of US imports followed by Canada and then the EC. In 1990 Canada was the largest source of US imports followed by the EC and Japan. The adjacency of Canada and the appeal and price of imports from Japan have much to do with the prominence of these countries in the US market.

What these figures mean for US–EC interdependence is that the United States market is represented nearly evenly by its three main suppliers – the EC, Canada and Japan. The fact that the EC is not the dominant supplier to the US market has worried some Atlanticists and gives grist to the mill of those who point to the emerging pre-eminence of transpacific trade to US interests. It is not as if the US market was turning its back on imports from the EC or that the EC is turning its back on exports to the US. The EC's market share has

TABLE 4.5 *US imports from the EC, Canada and Japan and as*
percentages of total US imports, 1981–90 ($US billion)

Year	EC	%	Canada	%	Japan	%
1981	41.4	(17)	45.8	(17)	37.5	(14)
1982	42.3	(18)	46.3	(19)	37.4	(15)
1983	43.8	(17)	52.0	(20)	40.9	(16)
1984	56.9	(18)	66.3	(20)	56.7	(17)
1985	67.5	(20)	68.9	(20)	68.2	(20)
1986	75.4	(20)	68.1	(18)	82.0	(22)
1987	80.1	(20)	70.8	(18)	84.0	(21)
1988	84.0	(19)	80.7	(18)	89.1	(20)
1989	84.0	(18)	88.0	(19)	91.8	(20)
1990	90.8	(18)	92.0	(19)	88.8	(18)

SOURCE Based on data from the US International Trade Commission, the
US Department of Commerce and the International Monetary Fund in
current prices.

TABLE 4.6 *US exports to the EC, Canada and Japan and as percentages*
of total US exports, 1981–90 ($US billion)

Year	EC	%	Canada	%	Japan	%
1981	50.6	(24)	38.1	(18)	21.3	(9)
1982	45.7	(24)	33.7	(17)	21.0	(10)
1983	42.4	(23)	36.5	(21)	21.2	(10)
1984	44.8	(22)	44.5	(23)	22.7	(10)
1985	46.7	(22)	51.1	(24)	21.6	(10)
1986	50.2	(23)	53.2	(24)	22.9	(11)
1987	57.2	(23)	57.0	(23)	26.9	(11)
1988	71.3	(23)	68.2	(22)	36.0	(12)
1989	82.5	(24)	75.0	(21)	42.8	(12)
1990	93.1	(25)	78.2	(21)	46.1	(12)

SOURCE Based on data from the US International Trade Commission, the
US Department of Commerce and the International Monetary Fund in
current prices.

remained steady throughout the 1980s. It rather suggests that as the
US has increased its total imports, the Japanese have expanded their
trade and the Canadians have maintained theirs.

Table 4.6 depicts US exports to the EC, Canada and Japan as a
percentage of total US world exports from 1981 to 1989. Whereas in
US imports the EC is not the dominant source of supply, in exports
the EC is the dominant market for the United States. The EC absorbs

TABLE 4.7   *US trade balances with the EC, Canada, Japan and the world*
and as percentages of the total US trade balance with the world,
1986–90 ($US billion)

	1986	%	1987	%	1988	%	1989	%	1990	%
EC	−25.3	(16)	−22.9	(14)	−12.7	(10)	−1.5	(1)	+2.3	(–)
Canada	−14.9	(10)	−13.8	(9)	−12.5	(10)	−13.0	(11)	−10.6	(9)
Japan	−59.1	(38)	−57.1	(36)	−53.1	(42)	−49.0	(41)	−42.7	(37)
World	−155.2		−158.2		−126.8		−118.6		−116.0	

SOURCE   Based on data of the US International Trade Commission and the
US Department of Commerce in current prices.

a quarter of US exports to the world, compared with Canada which
takes a fifth and Japan which takes just 12 per cent. In 1990, US
exports to the EC reached $93.1 billion compared with exports to
Canada of $78.2 billion and to Japan of $46.1 billion. US dependence
on the EC market points to a complex interdependent relationship
which, despite sectoral disputes outlined in Part 2, is most lucrative in
terms of US production, revenues, employment, and contribution to
balance of trade.

The US merchandise trade balance with the EC went into deficit in
1983 after a decade-long US trade surplus with the EC. The US
merchandise trade deficit with the EC amounted to $1.35 billion in
1983, rising to $12.1 billion in 1984 and $20.9 billion in 1985. The
level of the US dollar remained high, which made imports cheaper
for the US consumer and exports more expensive abroad. The economic recovery in the United States also had something to do with the
imbalance between imports and exports. Table 4.7 shows that the US
had a trade deficit with the EC from 1986 to 1989 which turned into a
small surplus in 1990. At its zenith, the US trade deficit with the EC
accounted for 16 per cent of its total deficit with the world. Over the
years in which the United States experienced a trade deficit with the
EC, a more tense US attitude toward the EC developed. It comes as
no surprise that the number of trade disputes initiated by the United
States with the EC was greater in the 1980s than in the 1970s. With a
small deficit and then small surplus in trade with the EC in 1989 and
1990, the US and EC ended the 1980s with a rough symmetry in the
balance of their trade flows. This was not the case for the US trade
balance with Canada and Japan. Although the US merchandise trade
deficit fell each year since 1985, the deficit with Canada and Japan
remained high.

TABLE 4.8 *Composition of US merchandise trade with the EC and as percentages of total US trade by SITC numbers,* * *1980, 1985 and 1990* *($US billion)*

SITC item	Description	1980	%	1985	%	1990	%
Exports							
0	Food/Live animals	5.0	(9)	3.1	(7)	3.7	(4)
1	Beverages/Tobacco	.9	(2)	1.1	(2)	2.7	(3)
2	Crude materials†	7.5	(14)	4.8	(10)	6.3	(7)
3	Mineral fuels	2.2	(4)	2.9	(6)	3.7	(4)
4	Oils/Fats‡	.2	(—)	0.2	(—)	0.1	(—)
5	Chemicals	5.2	(10)	5.7	(12)	10.5	(11)
6	Manufactures	11.3	(21)	2.6	(6)	5.6	(6)
7	Machinery/transport	18.7	(35)	20.4	(44)	44.9	(48)
8/9	Other	2.0	(4)	5.4	(12)	15.5	(17)
Total exports		53.0		46.2		93.0	
Imports							
0	Food/Live animals	.9	(2)	2.1	(3)	2.1	(2)
1	Beverages/Tobacco	1.6	(4)	2.3	(3)	2.5	(3)
2	Crude materials†	.5	(1)	.8	(1)	1.0	(1)
3	Mineral fuels	2.4	(7)	5.5	(8)	4.5	(5)
4	Oils/Fats‡	§	(—)	§	(—)	0.2	(—)
5	Chemicals	3.3	(9)	6.1	(9)	9.5	(11)
6	Manufactures	10.7	(30)	10.8	(16)	13.3	(15)
7	Machinery/transport	15.5	(43)	27.2	(40)	39.3	(45)
8/9	Other	1.3	(3)	12.6	(19)	14.0	(16)
Total imports		36.2		67.4		86.4	

* Standard International Trade Classification.
† Inedible, includes soybeans but not fuels.
‡ Includes animal and vegetable products.
§ Less than $100 million.

SOURCE Compiled from official statistics of the US Department of Commerce and the US International Trade Commission in current prices.

Table 4.8 depicts the composition of US merchandise trade with the EC in the 1980s. Machinery and transport equipment comprised the largest share of total US exports to the EC in 1990 (48 per cent), followed by chemicals, agriculture and manufactures. Machinery and transport equipment comprised the largest share of total US imports from the EC in 1990 (45 per cent), followed by manufactures and chemicals. Trade in the same sectors is a function of a sophisticated, complex, interdependent relationship. The US and EC produce many of the same industrial products yet their consumers recognise, are comfortable with, and purchase products from 'the other side' despite those products being available at home. In some cases, for example, a US purchaser of an EC-made product is actually purchasing something manufactured in the EC by a US subsidiary. The main items in US exports to and imports from the EC are listed below.

Main Items in US Exports to EC
Transportation equipment and parts – railway and tramway vehicles, aeroplanes, helicopters, ships.
Office machines and automatic data-processing equipment and parts – computers and ADP equipment and electrical components.
Coal.
Electrical machinery, apparatus, and appliances, power generating machinery and equipment.
Professional, scientific and controlling instruments and apparatus.
Soybeans, vegetable oilcake and oilcake meal, corn.
Cigarettes.
Non-grain feed ingredients (corn gluten feed).

Main Items in US Imports from EC
Passenger motor vehicles and parts.
Crude petroleum (shipped through the Netherlands), motor fuel.
Aeroplane and aeroplane parts – jets, engines.
Machinery for particular industries – agricultural machinery, lawn-mowers, construction vehicles, washing machines.
Power-generating machinery and equipment.
Miscellaneous manufactured articles – printed materials, office supplies, jewelry, musical instruments.
Wine.

Tables 4.9 and 4.10 depict the share of total US farm and manufactures exports to and imports from the EC, Canada and Japan from 1980–88. The statistics are revealing because they help to explain why agricultural trade is such a volatile issue in US–EC relations. In 1988, 20 per cent of total US farm exports went to the EC, down from a high of 28 per cent in 1982 (20 per cent also went to Japan, up from 15 per cent in 1980 and 6 per cent went to Canada). In 1988, 20 per cent of total US farm imports came from the EC, up from 14 per cent in

TABLE 4.9   *Share of US agricultural exports to/imports from EC, Canada and Japan, 1980–8*

	1980	1981	1982	1983	1984	1985	1986	1987	1988
Exports									
EC	27	26	28	25	21	22	25	24	20
Canada	5	5	6	6	6	6	7	7	6
Japan	15	15	15	17	17	18	19	20	20
Imports									
EC	14	15	18	18	18	20	20	20	20
Canada	6	7	9	9	9	9	9	11	11
Japan	0.6	0.7	0.8	1	1	1	1	1	1

SOURCE   US Department of Commerce.

TABLE 4.10   *Share of US manufactures exports to/imports from EC, Canada and Japan, 1980–8*

	1980	1981	1982	1983	1984	1985	1986	1987	1988
Exports									
EC	25	22	22	23	22	22	23	24	24
Canada	21	23	21	26	28	29	28	27	25
Japan	6	6	6	7	7	7	9	8	9
Imports									
EC	24	22	22	21	21	22	22	22	21
Canada	20	21	21	21	21	20	18	17	17
Japan	23	25	25	24	24	26	27	26	25

SOURCE   US Department of Commerce.

1980 (11 per cent came from Canada, up from 6 per cent in 1980 and just one per cent came from Japan).

The drop in the EC share of total US farm exports, at the same time the EC share of total US farm imports has risen, has coincided with (and has played a role in) the rise in the number of US-lodged agricultural disputes with the EC in the 1980s. That the US and EC now supply one another with equal shares of agricultural commodities is a sign of complex interdependence, but the reduced share of the EC in the export of US farm products has been politically explosive in the US farm belt, which blames the CAP for the reduced share in that historical market. The increase in Japan's share of total US farm exports, despite the general restrictiveness of the Japanese food import market, is noteworthy.

Table 4.10 shows that the EC takes nearly one-quarter of all US wine manufactures exports, as does Canada (whereas Japan's share is just 9 per cent). Of total US manufactures imports, the EC supplies about one-fifth and Canada 17 per cent. Japan is the largest supplier with its share of 25 per cent. Japan has been the largest supplier of manufactures to the United States for most of the decade. The huge asymmetry in US–Japan trade in manufactures is the main cause of the serious political frictions between the two countries. Conversely, a rough symmetry in US–EC trade exists because the two have roughly equal shares of each other's markets for agriculture and manufactures. US–EC trade conditions meet the conditions for a complex interdependent relationship, despite the agricultural trade disputes which have multiplied in the 1980s over the 1970s (see Part Two of this chapter for further analysis).

Tables 4.11 and 4.12 show that the US is the largest single supplier to, and market for, the EC. EC imports from the US in 1989 amounted to $69.5 billion or 19 per cent of total EC imports of $361.9 billion from the world in 1989. This compared to EC imports from EFTA – a trade bloc – which amounted to $74.5 billion or 20 per cent of total EC imports. Imports from Japan and the former Soviet bloc amounted to 10 per cent and 6 per cent, respectively, of the world total. EC exports to the US in 1989 amounted to $59.7 billion or 20 per cent of total EC exports of $299.2 billion to the world in 1989. This compared to EC exports to EFTA, which amounted to $60.0 billion or 20 per cent of total EC exports. Exports to Japan and the former Soviet bloc amounted to just 5 per cent of total exports.

BILATERAL INVESTMENT

Bilateral trade has been shown to be very important to the US and EC, but this section reveals that two-way investment, rather than trade, constitutes the lion's share of US–EC economic interactions. For example, in 1987, total US exports to the EC (of $59.7) amounted to only 12 per cent of $503 billion in sales of affiliates of US companies in the EC. US multinational corporations (MNCs) produce abroad many times the value of US exports in any one given

TABLE 4.11   *EC imports* from selective trading partners and as percentages of total EC imports from the world, 1984–89 ($US billions)*

Source	1984	%	1985	%	1986	%	1987	%	1988	%	1989	%
EFTA	58.2	(19)	60.7	(19)	75.1	(23)	92.9	(23)	80.4	(22)	74.5	(20)
US	52.3	(17)	53.0	(17)	56.8	(18)	66.3	(17)	59.4	(16)	69.5	(19)
Japan	21.0	(7)	22.6	(7)	34.0	(10)	42.0	(10)	38.6	(10)	35.5	(10)
East Europe/ USSR	28.3	(9)	25.8	(8)	25.0	(8)	28.0	(7)	25.3	(7)	21.4	(6)
World	307.9		311.0		322.0		398.8		365.4		361.9	

*Extra-EC imports.

SOURCE   Compiled from statistics of the United Nations OECD External Trade Database and the US International Trade Commission; 1988 statistics from OECD Monthly Statistics of Foreign Trade; 1989 data compiled from preliminary statistics of the UN OECD External Trade Database.

TABLE 4.12   *EC exports* to major trading partners and as percentages of total EC exports to the world, 1984–9 ($US billion)*

Source	1984	%	1985	%	1986	%	1987	%	1988	%	1989	%
EFTA	58.9	(21)	63.9	(22)	84.3	(25)	102.9	(26)	99.4	(28)	60.0	(20)
US	57.6	(21)	65.0	(22)	73.4	(22)	82.7	(21)	64.5	(18)	59.7	(20)
East Europe/ USSR	17.3	(6)	17.8	(6)	19.8	(6)	22.1	(6)	21.8	(6)	14.4	(5)
Japan	7.4	(3)	7.9	(3)	11.2	(3)	15.7	(4)	16.6	(5)	14.8	(5)
World	277.8		291.6		338.3		394.1		355.6		299.2	

*Extra-EC exports.

SOURCE   Compiled from official statistics of the United Nations OECD External Trade Database and the US International Trade Commission; 1988 statistics from OECD Monthly Statistics of Foreign Trade; 1989 Data compiled from preliminary statistics of the UN OECD External Trade Database.

year.[5] US–EC foreign direct investment and the sales generated by that investment are the largest of their kind in the world.[6] Although the US continues to be the world's largest overseas direct investor, its position has declined in relative importance to that of the EC, Japan and other investors. By 1987, US direct investment abroad accounted for less than one-third of worldwide foreign direct investment, down from one-half in 1960 (Jackson, 1991: 2).[7]

Foreign investment in the United States in the 1980s, when the trade and payments deficits soared, became a divisive domestic political issue. The huge flow of capital into the US from abroad during the 1980s meant that the amount of foreign-owned assets in the United States surpassed the amount of assets Americans owned abroad. The net international investment position (the differences between assets Americans own abroad and the assets foreigners hold in the US) declined from a surplus of $141 billion in 1981 to a deficit of $664 billion in 1989. According to Jackson, this position is not as adverse as it seems. The negative direct international investment position is undervalued in current dollars by up to $400 billion because the data available are carried at book value or the value at the time the investment occurred (Jackson, 1991: 3). While public opinion polls show that Americans generally hold negative views of foreign investors and are more inclined to limit or restrict foreign investment than they were a few years ago (Jackson, 1991: 1), the negativism is directed more against Japanese investment than European.

With few exceptions, investment as a source of friction in US–EC relations is minimal. Whereas European takeovers of US companies are not controversial in the United States, Japanese takeovers are. Many Americans think Japanese companies have invested too much in the United States. Congressional concerns about foreign investment of certain firms in the US were reflected in the 1988 passage of the Exon-Florio provision. The law enhances the President's authority to suspend, delay, or prohibit acquisitions, mergers or takeovers of US businesses which threaten to impair national security. The law also widens the scope of industries which fall under the national security rubric and has the potential to substantially alter the foreign direct investment process in the United States. It is not intended to inhibit foreign direct investment, but the EC has registered its protest over the law. The EC, while not an intended target, is concerned about the law and it remains a potential source of friction in US–EC relations.

Following the end of the Second World War, US businesses rapidly expanded abroad and US direct investment abroad propelled the United States into being the world's largest net investor. Europeans generally view US subsidiaries in their country as European firms, even though some Europeans have been concerned over the apparent high level of US investment:

the Europeans held almost exactly the same amount of private investment in the United States as the Americans held in Europe. . . . The difference [was] that in Europe the investors were US MNCs whereas in the United States two-thirds of the investors were individual Europeans . . . who invested in US securities without obtaining control over US MNCs. (Goodman, 1974: 250)

As early as 1974, Goodman observed accurately that the whole structure of industry was being reformed on a worldwide basis and predicted that US firms in the EC would meet tough competition from EC companies

whose horizons have been widened beyond the tightness of the national border. . . . European investment is flowing into the US at a rate unheard of a few years ago. Some EC firms are beginning to view the US market not as the intimidating biggest market in the world but as one that offers opportunities to investors. . . . The picture that emerges is both a movement of European MNCs toward a position of parity with their American counterparts and an increasing interdependence between European and Americans on the part of each other. (Goodman, 1974: 252)

EC INVESTMENT IN THE UNITED STATES

Table 4.13 shows that the EC is the largest investor in the United States, accounting for $235 billion or 59 per cent of the $400.8 billion in total foreign direct investment in the United States in 1989 (up from 51 per cent in 1980). In 1989 the EC direct investment position in the United States was over three times the position held by Japan and over seven times that of Canada. The largest areas of EC investment in the United States are found in Table 4.14. Of total foreign investment in the United States in 1989, the EC accounted for 86 per cent in the petroleum industry, 66 per cent in manufacturing, 65 per cent in the insurance industry, 53 per cent in the banking sector and 51 per cent in wholesale trade. Sales generated by EC investment in the United States amounted to $325 billion in 1987 according to data in Table 4.15. The leading items in these sales were manufacturing ($116 billion or 36 per cent of the EC total), followed by wholesale trade ($89 billion or 27 per cent), petroleum ($49 billion or 15 per cent) and retail trade ($26 billion or 8 per cent).

TABLE 4.13   *Foreign direct investment in the United States by the EC,
Canada and Japan and as a percentage of total, 1980, 1985–89
($US billion)*

	1980	%	1985	%	1986	%	1987	%	1988	%	1989	%
EC	42.5	(51)	104.3	(56)	123.9	(56)	162.1	(60)	194.0	(59)	235.0	(59)
Canada	12.2	(15)	17.1	(9)	20.3	(9)	24.0	(9)	27.4	(8)	31.5	(8)
Japan	4.7	(6)	19.3	(10)	26.8	(12)	35.2	(13)	53.4	(16)	69.7	(17)
World	83.0		184.6		220.4		271.8		328.9		400.8	

SOURCE   Based on data from the US Department of Commerce, Bureau of Economic
Analysis, *Survey of Current Business*, various issues, in current prices, and Jackson
(1991: 8).

TABLE 4.14   *Composition of foreign direct investment position* in the
United States by the EC, Canada and Japan and as percentages of
total investment in the US, 1988–9 ($US billion)*

	EC	%	Canada	%	Japan	%	All countries
1988							
All industries	194	(59)	27	(8)	53	(16)	329
Petroleum	31	(88)	2	(6)	0	(0)	35
Manufacturing	79	(65)	9	(7)	12	(10)	121
Wholesale trade	33	(51)	3	(5)	19	(29)	65
Banking	9	(53)	1	(6)	4	(23)	17
Finance	2	(25)	1	(12)	3	(37)	8
Insurance	13	(65)	3	(15)	†	†	20
Real estate	10	(31)	4	(13)	10	(31)	32
Other services	16	(44)	4	(11)	†	†	36
1989							
All industries	235	(59)	31	(8)	70	(17)	401
Petroleum	30	(86)	2	(6)	0	(0)	35
Manufacturing	106	(66)	11	(7)	17	(11)	160
Wholesale trade	36	(51)	3	(4)	21	(30)	71
Banking	10	(53)	1	(5)	4	(21)	19
Finance	5	(45)	1	(9)	6	(54)	12
Insurance	15	(65)	3	(13)	†	†	23
Real estate	10	(28)	4	(11)	14	(39)	36
Other services	21	(47)	5	(11)	†	†	45

* Direct investment as measured by valuation adjustments plus capital outflows. Capital outlfows are defined as the net equity capital plus reinvested
earnings plus net intercompany debt. The overall position is also generally
regarded as the book value of US direct investors' equity in, and net outstanding loans to, their foreign affiliates. A foreign affiliate is a foreign

business enterprise in which a single US investor owns at least 10 per cent of the voting securities, or the equivalent.

† Suppressed to avoid disclosure of data of individual companies.

SOURCE   Data compiled from the US Department of Commerce and the US International Trade Commission in current prices.

TABLE 4.15   *Sales generated by direct investment by EC firms in the US by industry, 1987*

	Sales		Employment	
	$ Billion	*%*	*Thousands*	*%*
All industries	325	100	1,593	100
Petroleum	49	15	94	6
Manufacturing	116	36	823	52
Food	10	3	70	4
Chemicals	38	12	208	13
Metals	8	2	70	4
Machinery	22	7	194	12
Other machinery	37	11	307	19
Wholesale trade	89	27	141	9
Retail trade	26	8	308	19
Finance (except banking)	7	2	141	9
Insurance	15	4	42	3
Real estate	3	1	6	0.4
Services	9	3	88	5
Other industries	9	3	66	4

* US employees of EC firms in the United States

SOURCE   *Foreign Direct Investment in the United States* (Washington: US Department of Commerce, Bureau of Economic Analysis, July 1989) and Harrison (1990: 9).

US INVESTMENT IN THE EC

The EC is the largest market for US investment. Table 4.16 shows that the EC took 40 per cent (or $150 billion) of total US foreign direct investment of $373 billion in 1989. The EC was followed by Canada's 18 per cent ($67 billion) and Japan's 5 per cent ($19 billion). The EC is the largest market for US investment and a much larger market for US than Japanese foreign direct investment.[8] The EC 1992 plan has proven to be a stimulus to US foreign direct investment

TABLE 4.16   *US direct investment position* in the EC, Canada and Japan as percentages of total US investment in the world, 1980–9 ($US billion)*

	EC	%	Canada	%	Japan	%	All countries
1980	77	(36)	45	(21)	6	(3)	215
1981	80	(35)	45	(20)	7	(3)	226
1982	78	(35)	46	(21)	7	(3)	221
1983	79	(35)	47	(21)	8	(4)	227
1984	70	(33)	47	(22)	8	(4)	213
1985	81	(35)	47	(20)	9	(4)	230
1986	98	(38)	50	(19)	11	(4)	260
1987	122	(39)	57	(18)	14	(4)	309
1988	131	(39)	63	(19)	18	(5)	333
1989	150	(40)	67	(18)	19	(5)	373

* The position is the book value of US direct investors' equity in, and net outstanding loans to, their foreign affiliates at year's end includes reinvested earnings

SOURCE   Data compiled from Statistics of the Organisation for Economic Cooperation and Development and the US Department of Commerce in current prices.

in the EC. Some US producers have been attracted by the expectations that after 1992 the EC's growth rate and productivity will expand more rapidly. Others have sought to establish production facilities or joint ventures in the EC before 1993 out of fear that the EC will clamp down on certain imports by using antidumping measures and rules of origins, and local-content requirements. The EC has created a 'positive investment climate by using the 1992 programme as both a carrot (benefits of market integration) and as a stick (not so subtle hints that firms lacking an EC presence may be shut out of the market)' (Harrison, 1990: 5).

The composition of US direct investment in the EC, Canada, Japan and the LDCs is found in Table 4.17. In nearly all sectors, the EC was the largest recipient of US investment. For example, US direct investment in the EC in 1989 was the largest in the general manufactures sector ($75 billion or 48 per cent of total US direct

TABLE 4.17 Composition of US direct investment position* in major partners and as a percentage of total investment, 1987–9 ($US billion)

	EC	%	Canada	%	Japan	%	LDC	%	All countries
1987									
All industries	120.1	(39)	58.4	(19)	14.7	(5)	70.7	(23)	308.0
Petroleum	15.4	(25)	12.1	(19)	2.7	(4)	18.1	(29)	61.8
Manufacturing	64.7	(51)	26.8	(21)	7.1	(5)	21.5	(17)	127.1
Wholesale trade	11.3	(36)	3.1	(10)	2.9	(9)	5.6	(18)	31.4
Banking	5.8	(38)	0.6	(4)	0.3	(2)	6.0	(39)	15.2
Finance/Insurance	17.9	(34)	9.6	(18)	1.1	(2)	14.4	(28)	52.0
Real estate	2.9	(45)	1.0	(16)	0.1	(1)	1.4	(22)	6.4
Other services	2.0	(14)	5.2	(37)	0.3	(2)	3.7	(26)	14.1
1988									
All industries	131.1	(39)	62.6	(19)	17.9	(5)	76.8	(23)	333.5
Petroleum	15.5	(27)	11.7	(20)	3.3	(6)	16.0	(28)	57.7
Manufacturing	68.2	(49)	28.8	(21)	8.9	(6)	25.0	(18)	139.5
Wholesale trade	12.6	(36)	3.5	(10)	3.4	(10)	6.0	(18)	33.8
Banking	6.4	(34)	0.8	(4)	0.3	(2)	6.8	(36)	19.0
Finance/Insurance	22.8	(38)	10.9	(18)	1.3	(2)	17.3	(28)	60.5
Real estate	3.3	(42)	1.3	(17)	0.2	(3)	1.5	(19)	7.8
Other services	2.5	(17)	5.6	(37)	0.3	(2)	4.2	(28)	15.0

continued on page 152

TABLE 4.17 *continued*

	EC	%	Canada	%	Japan	%	LDC	%	All countries
1989									
All industries	150.0	(40)	66.9	(18)	19.3	(5)	n.a.	—	373.4
Petroleum	17.0	(29)	10.9	(19)	3.2	(5)	n.a.	—	57.9
Manufacturing	74.9	(48)	32.3	(21)	10.0	(6)	n.a.	—	155.7
Wholesale trade	13.7	(36)	3.9	(10)	3.4	(9)	n.a.	—	37.7
Banking	6.5	(33)	1.0	(5)	.2	(1)	n.a.	—	19.9
Finance/Insurance	31.2	(40)	11.6	(15)	2.0	(3)	n.a.	—	77.1
Real estate	3.9	(44)	1.3	(15)	.2	(2)	n.a.	—	8.8
Other services	2.7	(17)	5.7	(35)	0.4	(2)	n.a.	—	16.2

* Direct investment as measured by valuation adjustments plus capital outflows. Capital outflows are defined as the net equity capital plus reinvested earnings plus net intercompany debt. The overall position is also generally regarded as the book value of US direct investors' equity in, and net outstanding loans to, their foreign affiliates. A foreign affiliate is a foreign business enterprise in which a single US investor owns at least 10 per cent of the voting securities, or the equivalent.

SOURCE Official economic data compiled from US Department of Commerce BEA Statistics and the US International Trade Commission in current prices.

TABLE 4.18   *Sales generated by US foreign direct investment in the EC by industry in 1987**

	Sales		Employment[†]	
	$ Billion	*%*	*Thousands*	*%*
All industries	503	100	2,569	100
Petroleum	83	16	70	3
Manufacturing	268	53	1,741	68
Food	28	6	138	5
Chemicals	48	10	215	8
Metals	12	2	111	4
Machinery	57	11	315	12
Electrical equipment	25	5	260	10
Transportation equipment	46	9	316	12
Other manufacturing	51	10	387	15
Wholesale trade	91	18	230	9
Finance[‡]	16	3	72	3
Services	18	4	156	6
Other industries	26	5	145	6

* Sales by non-bank affiliates of non-bank US parents (private sector only).
[†] European employees of US subsidiaries.
[‡] Except banking, insurance, real estate.

SOURCE   *United States Foreign Direct Investment Abroad* (Washington: US Department of Commerce Bureau of Economic Analysis, July 1989) and Harrison (1990: 9).

investment position in all countries), followed by finance and insurance ($31 billion or 40 per cent), petroleum ($17 billion or 29 per cent) and wholesale trade ($13.7 billion or 36 per cent). Table 4.18 shows that sales generated by US direct investment in the EC amounted to $503 billion in 1987. Manufacturing sales amounted to $268 billion (or 53 per cent of total sales generated by US foreign direct investment in the EC), wholesale trade sales amounted to $91 billion (or 18 per cent) and petroleum sales amounted to $83 billion (16 per cent).

Investment interdependence between the US and EC more tightly enmeshes their economies than does bilateral trade. There is no larger investment partnership in the world between two separate economic entities. What this section has attempted to show is that, with the exception of Exon–Florio, investment relations are largely peaceful and roughly balanced.[9] Indeed, the EC has been a creditor to the United States since the early 1970s. This has never become a source of strain in bilateral relations, because capital has come from 'so many diverse national autonomous sources and went to such varied destinations'.[10] Contrary to the explanations of the neo-mercantilists, the two sides, given all they have at stake, cannot afford to wage trade wars beyond the occasional skirmish. Investment interdependence produces many more benefits than costs in the overall contours of US–EC relations. In addition, the trade wars that have occurred have not interrupted the increase in two-way investment flows. The major strains the US and EC experience with investment interdependence come instead from the Japanese. Just as Japanese investment in the US and EC has expanded, the US, and particularly the EC, have encountered many cultural and other obstacles to the expansion of investment in Japan. The danger in the heavy dependence of the United States on imported capital is that the same capital can be withdrawn. In 1987, up to 62 per cent of the US current account deficit was financed by the inflow of private capital (Kashiwage, 1990: 8). There would be adverse repercussions to the United States economy should foreign capital inflows substantially decrease.

EMPLOYMENT EFFECTS OF BILATERAL
TRADE AND INVESTMENT

In a report of the US International Trade Commission (ITC), the number of full-time jobs in the United States associated with exports to the EC was estimated at 1.3 million on average during the period 1978–84.[11] The number of full–time jobs in the EC associated with US imports from the EC was 1.2 million on average during the same period. The largest employment sector of US–EC trade is manufacturing. The number of full–time US jobs associated with US manufactures exported to the EC was 658,000 on average during 1978–84, while in the EC the number of full-time jobs associated with exports to the US was 757,000.[12] Table 4.15 shows that, in 1987, the sales generated by direct investment by EC firms in the United States of $325 billion accounted for 1.6 million jobs in the United States. Table 4.18 shows that, in 1987, the sales generated by direct US investment in the EC of $503 billion accounted for 2.6 million jobs in the EC.

Altogether, over 6 million jobs in the United States and the EC are estimated to have been generated by trade and sales from foreign investment. Revenues from export sales and sales generated by investment are crucial indicators of US–EC complex interdependence, but among all indicators perhaps the one which cuts most deeply into the body politic of the US and EC states is employment. More jobs are associated with US trade with the EC and EC trade with the United States than with any other single trading partner. Thus, for better or worse, the US and EC depend on each other for trade–investment-related employment: drops in employment levels due to restrictive trade practices fuel bilateral tensions because of the immense political value attached to the rate of employment in all democratic and capitalist–oriented countries.

MONETARY RELATIONS

It is an understatement to characterise US–EC monetary relations as interdependent. Bilateral trade and payments balances have always been heavily affected by exchange rate fluctuations and fiscal policies.[13] This section shows how monetary interdependence has mirrored other spheres of US–EC relations and has grown from an asymmetric to a more symmetric form between the Bretton Woods conference of 1944 and the establishment of EMU in the 1990s. It also shows how the two sides have dealt with friction over monetary interdependence and concludes with a brief analysis of the impact of EMU on US–EC relations.

Of the many dimensions of the US–EC economic relationship, the monetary one is among the most difficult. There is neither a bilateral nor a satisfactory multilateral framework for the management of international exchange rate fluctuations, so co-ordination that does exist is *ad hoc*. The IMF has some influence, but most of its clout is limited to governments who seek loans. Secretive and *ad-hoc* policy co-ordination is done through the G7 finance ministers. The US–EC economic relationship is affected by G7 monetary decisions, and indeed the US and EC are heavily involved, but it has not been the central component in the making of those decisions.

The US and EC are not independent actors in monetary affairs; policies pursued by one side carry enormous implications for the interests of the other. Scholars refer to the 'myth of national monetary authority'.[14] National control of international capital movements is impractical. An example of the myth of independent US and EC monetary authority is the case of the overvalued US dollar in the 1980s, its implications for the EC, and the corrective action taken with the G7.

A brief historical examination of the impact of monetary issues in US–EC relations shows that, during the hegemonic period, the dollar, like the political and economic power of the United States, was supreme. At Bretton Woods in 1944, forty-four states committed themselves to fixed exchange rates pegged to the value of the US dollar, which was convertible into gold at $35 an ounce. The US acted as the benevolent hegemon, offering incentives and leadership to keep the system in place. This entailed costs such as exposing the US dollar to risks as the world's reserve currency and meeting other economic obligations and expectations; yet it also entailed benefits with most of world trade invoiced in dollars – a convenience to US traders and a saving to US consumers – and the influence the US Government derived from weighted voting in the IMF. Yet despite the preponderance of US power, the US and EC needed one another to make the international monetary–trade system work. An asymmetric interdependent relationship best describes US–EC monetary ties during this time. The US was at the helm but without the EC members as shipmates there would be no crew. That asymmetry in relations would begin to be replaced by a more mixed interdependent relationship as changes both within the United States and the international system ushered in the period of hegemonic decline.

The supremacy of the US dollar helped to stabilise international trade and finance during the first twenty-five years after the Second World War. However, the Nixon administration, in response to internal and external pressures enumerated below, broke with the gold standard in 1971 and abandoned fixed exchange rates in 1973. That shift from an internationalist to a nationalist approach to US foreign monetary relations marked the formal dissolution of the Bretton Woods system and the retreat of the United States from a hegemonic role. Explanations of the US action are rooted in US domestic politics as well as in changes in the international system.

What prompted the action from the view of US internal politics was: the weakening effect of the US budget and trade deficits on the US international economic position; the apparent breakdown of the early post-war domestic consensus underpinning US international economic leadership and the emerging perception that costs associated with leadership outweighed gains; the relative decline of US industry which reduced foreign confidence in the dollar; and the benign neglect of the dollar at home and abroad by a US leadership preoccupied with domestic opposition to the Vietnam War.

The factors that prompted action from the view of international politics were (a) the high European accumulation of dollar holdings in amounts which posed a potential threat to US gold stocks; (b) the opposition in the EC to the US wish to devalue the overpriced dollar, which in the late 1960s was helping to cause a massive payments deficit; (c) the economic reconstruction and strength of the EC and Japanese economies, which caused some in the US to question the need for, and the advantage of, its currency being subjected to external pressures without the expected benefits; (d) the reduced Soviet threat to the EC, which made dependence on the US less palatable; and (e) the Vietnam War, as well as other US foreign commitments, whose costs drained the US treasury and contributed to the rapidly expanding payments deficit.

The break with Bretton Woods testified to the power of the EC states who held dollars and resisted change necessary to forestall the US action, as well as to the power of the United States to engineer change unilaterally. The split with Bretton Woods was a turning point in US–EC relations because the US was not willing to shoulder former responsibilities, yet the EC was not willing or ready to replace the United States. Thus there were elements of symmetry and asymmetry in US–EC monetary relations during the period of hegemonic decline. A mixed monetary interdependent relationship was in evidence. New formulas would be devised that would emphasise plural over hegemonic approaches to dealing with the effects of exchange rate fluctuations. Yet the transition from hegemony to hegemonic decline left scars. According to a former US Ambassador to the EC, the Nixon administration in 1973 treated the EC as it would a hostile state (Schaetzel, 1975: 95).

The US and EC currencies were not destined to float completely freely after the 1973 break: the actions of the G7 and the European Monetary System (EMS) were attempts to substitute fixed exchange rates with some semblance of currency stability in the otherwise volatile international monetary order of the 1970s–80s. The G7, an informal regime of finance ministers and central bank governors, began exchanging views and information with one another in 1975. When group decisions are reached, they are not binding on the members. By the 1980s, the G7 was co-ordinating the actions of national authorities in foreign exchange markets. It has helped to limit extreme fluctuations in exchange rates, contributed to financial market stability and facilitated current account adjustment (Henning, 1990: 19). The EMS, established in 1979 after previous attempts to stabilise exchange rate fluctuations (the so-called snakes), showed that the EC was able to adopt its own system of controlling the adverse effects of internal exchange rates on trade. The EC's quest for a zone of monetary and exchange rate stability through the EMS was a response to the 'bad experience of the independent floating exchange rates of the major currencies and to the undisputed recognition that such a monetary situation negatively affected European integration and economic recovery'.[15] It was also a response to the adverse effects of US monetary policy on the EC. Despite the subsequent (fluctuating) success of the EMS, it will be shown below that the EC was neither willing nor able to replace the United States during the period of hegemonic decline as the western monetary leader after the demise of the Bretton Woods system.

The G7 and EMS testified to the decline of US hegemony and the arrival of a more pluralist and symmetric international monetary order requiring co-operation among the major currency countries. Although the establishment of the G7 and EMS helped to usher in a new era in international monetary relations, elements of US hegemony persisted. The dollar still reigned supreme as the premier world reserve currency well after the collapse of Bretton Woods, yet the German mark, in conjunction with the EC currencies, and the Japanese yen were gaining more weight and influence in international monetary affairs. The asymmetry in US–EC monetary relations that existed previously was being replaced by a mixture of symmetric and asymmetric interdependent elements. The US retained significant power but not enough to force others into submission. The EC gained significant power, but it was not in any position to present a viable alternative to the US role in the international monetary system. Cafruny best sums up the contradictions of US monetary relations after 1973:

> The US Government's benign neglect of the dollar expressed the contradictory nature of US power. On the one hand, it indicated that the US was no longer powerful enough to enforce or manage a return to unchallenged dollar supremacy; on the other hand, it laid bare the extraordinary power of the US, given its structural position in the world economy, to act unilaterally and, within very wide bounds, with impunity. . . . The US removed the dollar from gold, but the dollar world remained unchallenged and the rest of the world had to bear much of the cost of adjustment.[16]

As fixed exchange rates were replaced by floating exchange rates, it was expected that the uncoupling of national economies from international controls and trends would be beneficial. Floating exchange rates were expected to permit swift and nearly autonomous balance-of-payments adjustments, so that governments would be relieved from concerns over external equilibrium to concentrate on pursuing full employment and stable prices, and would have more discretionary power over their economic and monetary policies – as disruptive outside influences were barred by exchange rate changes (Kashiwagi, 1990: 5). The opposite occurred and the US and the EC became more interdependent in terms of the relationship between monetary and fiscal policies on the one hand, and import–export trade on the other. Floating failed to offset competitive disadvantages owing to different rates of inflation and thus to ease trade conflicts by means of natural realignment (Thiel, 1983: 345). Devaluation and revaluation of individual currencies occurred as exchange rates overshot the German mark, leading to competitive distortions that tended to heighten the trend toward protective countermeasures. Individual governments often resorted to trade restrictions as a measure to partially avert the impact of monetary disturbances (Thiel, 1983: 374). The correction of current account imbalances proved to be a very long process. Under conditions of close interdependence of national economies and liberalised capital flows, the economic policies of the major currency countries have had considerable influence on one another. The misalignment of exchange rates which emerged after the collapse of Bretton Woods has resulted in wasteful resource allocation at the domestic and international levels (Kashiwagi, 1990: 9).

The overvalued dollar in the first half of the 1980s, its impact on the EC and on US–EC relations and the concerted international action taken to avert further imbalance is a study of complex interdependence. The overvalued US dollar (*vis-à-vis* the yen and mark), a policy of the Reagan administration, caused a flood of imports and capital into the US and widened the US payments imbalance. This then fuelled domestic protectionist pressures and contributed to a rise in the number of US–EC trade complaints against the EC. The massive inflow of capital helped the US government to finance its huge budget deficit which, while expedient in the short term, was costly in the long term and disruptive to the international monetary and trade order. The US took actions to maximise national independence in fiscal and monetary policy, but the influx of capital to finance the budget deficit had the effect of expanding the dependence on, and vulnerability to, external control. This was the case until the US government entered into international co-operation to make belated adjustments. In the 1985 Plaza Accord, the G7 (minus Italy and Canada) agreed to co-ordinate action to bring down the value of the dollar and to raise the value of the yen and mark. The result, with some delay, had the effect of increasing US exports to Japan and Germany. The EC was forced to adjust as well. Dollar appreciation had repercussions for EC capital movements, interest rates, investment, inflation and trade flows.[17] The Plaza Accord symbolised not just the decline of American hegemony but its replacement with a post–hegemonic order of major currency and political powers on which the United States must depend.

In the post-hegemonic period, a complex interdependent monetary relationship between the US and EC has begun to replace the vestiges of asymmetry that lingered on during the period of hegemonic decline. The dollar declined in the late 1970s and early 1980s as an anchor of stability in the international monetary system.[18] The decline of the dollar's pre-eminent position as the world's key currency was accelerated in the 1980s when other economies grew faster and as investors, worried over growing US inflation and budget deficits, sought security in other currencies (Stokes, 1991: 3013). According to the IMF, the dollar share of total official foreign exchange reserves held by the world's central banks fell from 71.4 to 56.4 per cent between 1981 and 1990. The share of trade invoiced in dollars by the major trading countries fell from 32.8 to 25.7 per cent between 1980 and 1987 (Stokes, 1991: 3014). In the early 1980s, banks denominated 83 per cent of their external loans in dollars but by 1989 that percentage dropped to 71 per cent (Stokes, 1991: 3014). The dollar accounted for 63 per cent of external bonds issued in the first half of the 1980s but was used for only 44 per cent of such securities in the second half of the decade (Stokes, 1991: 3014).

The decrease in the role of the dollar in trade invoicing, bond issues and asset holdings[19] occurred at the same time as the EMS enjoyed unexpected success in stabilising European exchange rate fluctuations. Indeed the EC, through the success of the EMS, grew considerably more independent of the US dollar (Kashiwagi, 1990: 9), helping it become symmetrically interdependent with the United States according to the myth of independent monetary authority in a post-hegemonic world. The EC's decision at Maastricht in December 1991 to move ahead with the establishment of European Monetary Union (EMU) at a time when the dollar continues to decline as the premier reserve currency heralded a potentially new era of emerging symmetry in US–EC relations.

Both G7 and EMS continued to perform important functions during the 1980s, although co-ordinated action in the G7 by the end of the decade was hamstrung by the apparent lack of success on the part of the Bush Administration to make further inroads into the US budget deficit.[20] The decline in the value of the US dollar pursuant to the Plaza Accord of 1985 expanded US exports and helped put a cap on the increase in the US trade deficit. In the Louvre Accord of 1987 the leading currency countries agreed that the dollar, which had fallen to about 40 per cent of its 1985 peak, had declined enough and took steps to stabilise the dollar within a set (though undisclosed) range. The EMS in general was the success story of the 1980s – defying initial (Germany) and lingering (UK, US) sceptics. Both nominal and real exchange rates among the EMS members have become more stable and economic policies have become more convergent (Ifri, 1990: 60).

At Maastricht, the EC leaders agreed to set up EMU by 1999 with a single currency, the ECU, and a European Central Bank. To gain admission, each EC member must meet stringent economic criteria. Although it is not likely that all EC members will meet the criteria before 1999, some will, and they may accede to EMU before the others. In 1990 the EC had entered the first stage of EMU, so the process had already begun before Maastricht. While EMU, in its final stage, is still a few years off, and some argue that much can happen before then to change plans, the impact of the emerging ECU and the unity of EC monetary policy have broad implications for US–EC monetary relations. Deadlines are less critical as the emerging reality of a unified EC monetary order, if not by 1999, then sometime in the early part of the next century.

IMPACT OF EMU ON US–EC MONETARY RELATIONS

Although the implications of EMU for US–EC monetary relations are little understood, and the response from the US government thus far muted, some expected effects may be surmised. In general, EMU will confirm recent trends toward more symmetry in US–EC monetary interdependence as the EC develops the ECU as a possible rival reserve currency to the US dollar.[21] The following briefly suggests ways in which EMU will affect (a) the EC and its role in the international monetary system and (b) US–EC monetary interdependence. Since EMU is still in its early stages, only tentative observations can be made at this point.

EMU is likely to improve the EC's economic performance; for

example, the removal of currency transaction costs will result in large savings for EC businesses. The flow of intra-EC trade will be substantially enhanced because the disappearance of risks due to currency fluctuations (small but real under EMS) and the deduction of time and paperwork spent on currency conversions will add to the cost savings mentioned above.

The EC's international political and monetary profile will be enhanced by EMU. EMU will strengthen the EC's identity in the international economy and in policy-making circles. EMU will make the relationship among the major international currencies more balanced and equal. Whereas in the past, the US had to bear the brunt of responsibility as the key reserve currency country, that burden in the future will be more spread out and alleviated. The extent to which a potential dollar crisis would affect world trade and finance would be greatly reduced and the world monetary system would be much more stable (Kashiwagi, 1990: 10). At the same time, the rise of the ECU as an international reserve currency, along with the dollar and the yen, could cause more frequent capital flows that may prove unstable. The G7 may be reconstituted into a G3 (US, EC and Japan) and thus negotiations among fewer associates could steamline decision-making and make the EC a more formidable partner.

In the past, the Bretton Woods system, the IMF and the G7 have provided fora in which the US and EC conducted their monetary relations. This was always unsatisfactory because (a) the US was a dominant force in these fora up to recently, (b) the EC lacked the unity to speak with one voice on monetary issues and (c) the vast flow of goods and services between the US and EC was heavily affected by exchange rate fluctuations but the bilateral relationship did not have the authority or structure to address monetary issues. EMU will unify the monetary relationships of the EC states with the United States into a single US–EC monetary relationship. With EMU, dollar fluctuations will not drive wedges between EC currencies. Therefore, 'the effect on interest rate changes on the US and EC economies will be far more symmetrical and . . . the circumstances under which the US could benefit from the use of the dollar weapon correspondingly more rare' (Henning, 1990: 22). In the past, the US had neglected the rapid movement in the exchange rate of the dollar (usually downward) to extract concessions from the EC and Japan in trade or macroeconomic policy. The US used the 'dollar weapon' in 1973 to dissolve the Bretton Woods system (Henning, 1990: 21).

The EMS, while successfully in control of European exchange rate fluctuations, did not catch the attention of the United States. This was due, perhaps, to a mixture of US ambivalence toward, and skepticism of, EC monetary integration (some would say a characteristic of the US Treasury Department) and the fact that the EMS itself was not a major factor in the international monetary system. The proximity of US policy interests to those of the British, who did not join the EMS until 1990, may also be another explanation of the passive US policy towards the EMS. To the German mark, however, the United States paid much attention, because of its role in helping to manage the exchange rate of the dollar (Thiel, 1990: 90). Now that the German mark may be replaced by the ECU, the United States will most likely take a much less sceptical view of EC monetary policy.

EMU is expected to reduce the autonomy of US monetary policy by limiting its policy options. Symmetry in monetary interdependence will bring about more equality in US–EC relations. Co-operation and tensions – always part and parcel of complex interdependent relationships – will emerge from the new relationship. Equality in monetary relations could prompt the US and EC to co-operate more broadly to establish more international monetary stability (Thiel, 1990: 10). Neither side will be able to neglect its own accounts, balances and exchange rates. At the same time, tensions could develop as, for example, the EC determines its own monetary policies with adverse effects on the United States.

The ECU could become a rival reserve currency to the US dollar. With a multi-currency monetary system (dollars, yen and ECU), the US fiscal and monetary policies will be tested daily by currency traders who may choose from dollars, yen or ECUs. Thus the dollar (and yen and ECU) will be subject to a daily referendum and traders will be able to drive down the value of the currency when they disagree with a government action (Stokes, 1991: 3013). In the past, US exporters benefited from most of world trade being denominated in dollars. This reduced the threat of sudden shifts in exchange rates that could turn into losses (Stokes, 1991: 3015). More than one-half of German import trade is already denominated in marks. As world trade becomes increasingly denominated in ECU and yen, US traders and consumers will suffer from the loss of stability they enjoyed when the dollar reigned supreme over world trade. Finally, US businesses in Europe will enjoy the same cost savings as EC firms when the ECU replaces national currencies and eliminates currency transaction costs.

CONCLUSIONS TO PART ONE

Part One established that degrees of economic interdependence existed throughout the history of US–EC relations. Economic interdependence first took an asymmetric form with the EC as the junior member of the US–EC partnership. As the period of hegemony was replaced by one of hegemonic decline, economic interdependence developed concomitantly into symmetric and asymmetric elements. The power of the US declined relative to that of the EC, but the EC has been unable to establish parity because of its own divisions and embryonic political development. Economic interdependence during the post-hegemonic period of bilateral relations took its current complex form. A new era of symmetry in US–EC interdependence has arrived, given the EC's economic renaissance and movement toward a completed single internal market and EMU, with their implications for the EC's international role, and the acceptance by the United States of its reduced weight in international economic and monetary affairs. Thus US–EC economic relations have been a trek from inequality to equality of partnership over the past four decades.

Part 1 has also shown that complex interdependence has been managed – not very well – by multilateral institutions that date back to the late 1940s and by the G7 which is the heir to the old Bretton Woods system. As important as these relations are for Americans and Europeans, there is no fixed bilateral economic organisation, whereas they are fixed organisations at the multilateral level. The absence of a fixed organisation of bilateral relations may point either to (a) a lack of commitment and an institutional vacuum leading to anarchic conditions, or, conversely, (b) the strength of ties because they are so firmly rooted, mutually advantageous, and pacific that they need not be organisationally structured. Beyond fixed institutions and processes, the informal axis of US–EC economic relations – the vast flow of trade, investment, capital, people and ideas across the North Atlantic – is a self-propelling process requiring little management. This points to the level of trust and the degree of peace that exists between the US and EC as well as among the OECD states. The complex economic interdependence that exists between the US and EC to date has not required an organisational structure such as NATO.

Bilaterally, the two have good, long-standing diplomatic relations but the economic management side of those relations is not as far advanced as the military co-operation represented by NATO. The

Transatlantic Declaration was an attempt to upgrade bilateral economic and political ties but it is too soon to analyse its place in history. As it now is, the Declaration was a recommitment to existing principles that guide relations. It provided an umbrella under which bilateral contacts were made more frequent and at higher levels over a wide range of issues. Only time will tell if the Declaration will serve as a foundation for a major overhaul of US–EC relations, e.g. through a bilateral treaty, or remain a blueprint without a legal basis.

The Uruguay Round was not concluded when this book went to press. Many of the trouble spots in US–EC relations outlined in this chapter – how to reconcile disputes over steel, oilseeds and wheat flour subsidies – have been referred to the Uruguay Round where they are supposed to be negotiated away. If the Uruguay Round does not succeed in sufficiently addressing these problem areas, the US and EC are going to have to either work out these problems on a bilateral basis or continue to cope with them in the future. Continuation of the subsidy war will not break the US–EC partnership, but what may erode the EC proclivity toward export subsidies is the unremitting international pressures to scale back these expenditures. Even if the GATT includes new rules about subsidy usage, the recent history of both the US and the EC blocking adoption of GATT working panel reports – because they did not like the conclusions – does not speak well for the future acceptance of GATT rules.

The indicators of US–EC economic relations show two roughly equal economic giants who depend heavily on international trade as they do on bilateral trade; they are as interdependent with one another as they are dependent on a world trade order that remains open, despite the rise of managed trade in some sectors. At the core of their economic relations is the dependence of the US and EC on each other for trade and investment and on a fluid international economic environment that remains conducive to the flow of goods, services, and capital. Total two-way trade coupled with sales generated from two-way investment surpassed the historic $1 trillion mark in 1990. US–EC trade and investment represent such large components of the GDP of the US and EC that they cannot be substituted for any other set of external economic relationships in existence.

A key observation of Section One has been that bilateral investment, not trade, represents the core of the economic partnership because more sales and jobs are generated by investment than by trade. US–EC foreign direct investment, and the sales generated by that investment, is the largest of its kind in the world. Over 6 million jobs in the

United States and the EC are estimated to have been generated by trade and sales from foreign investment. More jobs are associated with US trade with the EC and with EC trade with the United States than with any other single trading partnership.

Finally, Part One has found that, of the many dimensions of the US–EC economic relationship, the monetary one is among the most difficult. There is neither a bilateral nor a satisfactory multilateral framework for the management of international exchange rate fluctuations. The break with Bretton Woods testified to the power of the EC states who held dollars and resisted change necessary to forestall the US action as well as to the power of the United States to engineer change unilaterally. It was a turning point in bilateral relations because the US was not willing to shoulder former responsibilities, yet the EC was not willing or ready to replace the United States. A mixed interdependent relationship with both symmetric and asymmetric elements was evident during the period of hegemonic decline. New formulas would be devised that would emphasise plural over hegemonic approaches to dealing with the effects of exchange rate fluctuations. The US retained significant power, but not enough to force others into submission. The EC gained significant power, but it was not in any position to present a viable alternative to the US role in the international monetary system. The Plaza Accord symbolised not just the decline of American hegemony but its replacement with a post-hegemonic order of major currency and political powers on which the United States must depend. In the post-hegemonic period, a complex interdependent monetary relationship between the US and EC has begun to replace the vestiges of asymmetry that lingered on during the period of hegemonic decline. Part One identified some of the expected implications of the EMU for the role of the EC in the world economy and for US–EC relations. EMU will confirm recent trends toward more symmetry in US–EC monetary interdependence as the EC develops the ECU as a possible rival reserve currency to the US dollar.

In sum, the foregoing has shown that complex economic interdependence can be verified empirically and that the economic welfare of the United States is inextricably linked to that of the EC. Part Two analyses the other side of the coin, i.e. sectoral trade disputes, which underscore how interdependence may adversely affect specific producer and consumer groups. Commercial disputes notwithstanding, the overarching environment of complex interdependence places those conflicts in due context. The premium is on understanding the tit-for-tat exchange of the punitive actions which governments have taken when pressed by producer groups demanding support. Thus it is here that the neo-mercantilist approach provides a partial insight into the behaviour of governments under certain conditions. What may appear to be the neo-mercantilist behaviour of governments may in fact be the consequence of different domestic policy approaches rooted in divergent political cultures (Chapter 5). The following analysis shows that, however painful some of the trade disputes have been, they appear to form no set pattern to challenge the totality of complex interdependence.

PART TWO   TRADE DISPUTES AND DISPUTE SETTLEMENT: OVERVIEW

This part is centred on Table 4.19, which lists all major US–EC trade disputes since 1962 by year, period (in bilateral relations), complainant and status of dispute settlement. However, before analysing the historical data, Part Two introduces readers to the major US–EC trade disputes as currently identified by the US government and the EC Commission and briefly describes the most serious, and potentially damaging, bilateral trade dispute, agriculture. Whereas Part One showed that disputes are minimal in the investment area, where the lion's share of US–EC commercial transactions take place, Part Two shows that bilateral trade disputes have been settled without long-term damage to overall relations and constitute a fraction of total commerce. Although there is no 'crisis' in US–EC trade, there are three areas worthy of concern which could throw bilateral relations into a serious crisis if they are not handled carefully: (a) sector-specific trade disputes (steel, aircraft), (b) disputes over agricultural export subsidies (wheat flour) and (c) possible EC moves to increase tariffs bound (set by agreement) in previous rounds of MTNs (soybeans). Containment of these real and potential disputes from spilling over into other areas of trade peace in US–EC relations cannot be taken for granted, given the strong internal constituent political interests that line up behind them. The management of bilateral trade relations to avoid any one side from tipping the balance of interests is an issue that will be dealt with in the policy section of Chapter 6.

The chief cause of trade friction is the external effects of domestic politics and policies (see Chapter 5). Much of the disputed trade is rooted not in aggressive nationalist behaviour or hostility by one

TABLE 4.19 *Typology of US–EC disputes and dispute settlements, 1962–present*

Dispute	Year(s)	Period	Complainant	With no threats or punitive action	With threat/ warning	With punitive action	Not yet settled
					Dispute settlement		
1. US carpet and glass	1962	Hegemonic	EC			●	
2. EC poultry subsidies	1963–4	Hegemonic	US			●	
3. US imports of EC steel	1969–74	Hegemonic decline	US	●			
4. Soviet natural gas pipeline	1981–2	Hegemonic decline	US			●	
5. EC canned fruit subsidies	1981–5	Hegemonic decline	US	●			
6. EC wheat flour export subsidy	1981–	Hegemonic decline	US				●
7. EC pasta subsidies	1982–6	Hegemonic decline	US			●	
8. EC tariff cuts on citrus imports	1982–6	Hegemonic decline	US			●	

9.	US cut imports of EC steel	1982–9	Hegemonic decline	EC			•	
10.	US Wine Equity Act	1985–6	Hegemonic decline	EC	•			
11.	EC Airbus subsidies	1986–	Post-hegemonic	US				•
12.	Portugal's EC accession	1986–7	Post-hegemonic	US			•	
13.	Spain's EC accession	1986–7	Post-hegemonic	US			•	
14.	EC meat ban	1987–	Post-hegemonic	US			•	
15.	EC canned fruit subsidies	1988–9	Post-hegemonic	US		•		
16.	EC oilseeds subsidies	1988–	Post-hegemonic	US				•
17.	EC restriction of apple imports	1988–	Post-hegemonic	US				•
Totals					3	1	9	4

partner towards the other – in the neo-mercantilist vein – but in different approaches to economic, industrial, agricultural, social and trade policies that are as old as the US–EC relationship itself. For example, during the 1980s the jump in US formal disputes against EC trade policies may be explained in part by (a) the litigious nature of US society in which Washington law firms have drummed up business for potential clients, i.e. US producer groups have complaints against foreign unfair trade practices; (b) the 'Rambo style' of the Reagan administration in which the United States aggressively pressed any major trading partner who did not grant to US exports the same treatment the US granted to imports; and (c) the United States in its quest for even more liberal economic practices expected its major trading partners to respond in kind. The settlement of disputes by government punitive action is where neo-mercantilism provides more depth of insight than the liberal approach. This section shows that the majority of US–EC trade disputes were not settled before punitive action (or punitive action followed by counterretaliatory action) was taken. The most acute differences revolve around government subsidies to aid sectors targeted to achieve more competitiveness.

The US and EC have been publishing respective annual reports since the mid-1980s detailing obstacles to trade they claim to encounter in each other's market. These reports, while politically charged because of the negotiations at the Uruguay Round, domestic considerations, and the battle between the US and the EC over allegations of which side is more restrictive, still offer the reader insight into the official thinking of Washington and Brussels towards one another. The USTR's *National Trade Estimate Report on Foreign Trade Barriers* documents significant foreign (including EC) barriers to US exports. In its 1989 report, the USTR listed, among others, the following EC barriers to US trade:

– variable levies on farm products that are set sufficiently high to raise imported product prices above EC price levels;
– 'buy national' public procurement policies (and the lack of transparency on pending procurements and contract awards) on EC government-owned utilities and agencies not covered by the GATT Government Procurement Code;
– export subsidies on farm products that are based on the difference between internal EC price and the world price (or at levels below world prices);

- insufficient protection of copyrighted products;
- oilseed production subsidies for producing oilseeds, protein crops and dairy products used in feed, thus impairing trade concessions previously granted to the US;
- the ban on use of all hormones in livestock production and meat and meat products imported into the EC; and
- French, German, British, and Spanish government financial support for the Airbus aircraft producer consortium.[22]

For its part, the EC, in an attempt to show that the United States itself is not free of restrictive trade and investment practices, publishes its annual *Report on United States Trade Barriers and Unfair Practices: Problems of Doing Business with the US*. As the title shows, the report does not document foreign trade barriers to EC exports worldwide, but limits its purview to the US market. In its report, the EC documents such US barriers as

- restricted government procurement practices at the state and federal levels;
- the Buy American Act of 1988 placing certain restrictions on the purchase of foreign-produced goods by federal agencies;[23]
- Department of Defense research and development contracts to US manufacturers who enjoy the benefits of commercial application of those contracts, resulting in indirect subsidisation of commercial production;
- subsidised farm exports through the Export Enhancement Programme under the 1985 Farm Bill (requires the USDA to use food stocks to subdsidise exports);
- the extraterritorial reach of US law to foreign subsidiaries of US firms;
- export controls which are too frequent and inclusive in terms of product coverage;
- Section 301 of the Trade Act of 1974 as amended in the 1988 Omnibus Trade and Competitiveness Act which enables the US Government to take unilateral action outside the GATT to redress allegedly unfair foreign trade practices;
- restrictions on foreign ownership of certain manufacturing plants considered by the US President to adverely affect US national security and interstate commerce – barriers to investment, e.g. the Exon-Florio Amendment.[24]

Of all the disputes listed above, those involving farming have bedeviled US–EC relations since the establishment of the CAP. Both sides support farm income spending with comparably huge sums of money, but they do so in different ways, for different reasons, and with different effects. For the EC, the CAP forms the bedrock of the EC, since it was part of the original package of compromises between French agricultural and German industrial interests (see Chapter 5). Despite the logic of swifter and more comprehensive reform to bring down costs, the CAP represents very strong political, rural, social and agricultural interests, which are committed to it come what may. The EC Commission has been attempting since the mid-1980s to lower price support levels to discourage overproduction of butter, milk, beef, veal and cereals. Some limited progress has been made, but a wholesale commitment to overhaul the agricultural programs of the EC and bring farm spending within more reasonable limits continues to elude EC reformers.

The US view is that the CAP distorts European and world agricultural markets because excessively high price supports encourage overproduction. The US claims that during the thirty-year history of the CAP, the EC has gained self-sufficiency in many farm product areas through a highly protected internal market with artificially high internal support prices. Of all the EC's practices, export subsidies most upset the United States and the Cairns Group; these are restitutions the EC pays farm exporters to bridge the gap between the high internal (and thus externally uncompetitive) price and the world market price.

The EC maintains high internal price supports as the chief means of enhancing farm income and retaining rural employment. As a result of high price supports, the EC is left with unwanted surpluses too costly to be competitive on world markets, so export subsidies are used to make farm products more competitive abroad. Unlike the US, the EC does not have extensive storage facility and land-set-aside practices that are alternatives ways of supporting farm income without encouraging overproduction and depressing world prices. The EC also claims that despite its exports it is still the world's largest food importer.

Besides differences over price support policies, the US and EC are at loggerheads over agricultural export subsidies. Throughout the post-hegemonic period, a US–EC subsidy war has been waged as each side seeks to out-spend the other in enhancing sales in rival third-country markets. The EC's quest is to dislodge high-priced unwanted surpluses. The US quest is to avoid losing shares of foreign markets to EC subsidised exports. The export subsidy war is now so old that it rarely captures the headlines, yet some would argue that it robs taxpayers from Peoria to Padua of billions of dollars annually in wasteful productive resources much needed elsewhere. The US has been pressing the EC to support farm income through means other than export subsidies. The United States maintains (a) that its exporters are put at a comparative disadvantage in third-country markets where EC export subsidies have been used and (b) that EC export subsidies violate GATT rules. GATT rules permit the use of export subsidies on certain primary products so long as the measures are not used to obtain more than an 'equitable share' and so long as the subsidised exports are not priced substantially below those of other suppliers to the same market. The US and EC have been unable to agree as to what precisely constitutes an equitable market share. As a result, they have sought to outspend one another in the quest to maintain or expand third-country market shares through subsidisation.

During the 1970s, a period of hegemonic decline, the United States protested vociferously over EC export subsidies and sought bilateral as well as multilateral negotiations to end them, but to no avail. The United States did not take any action to meet the EC exports subsidies with its own subsidies, because this was not the normal practice of the United States. In addition, although its hegemony was in decline, the US's policy of support for EC integration – as a cornerstone of its cold war foreign policy – precluded openly hostile action *vis-à-vis* the EC. In the 1980s, a time of transition from hegemonic decline to post-hegemony, the United States responded to the EC policy of export subsidisation in kind by Congress passing legislation enabling the US government to retake or maintain farm export markets lost to EC export subsidies. The EC has forced the hand of the United States to act in its own defence. The result has been a war of money to determine ownership of foreign agricultural market shares. In post-hegemonic US–EC relations, shorn of cold war objectives, there are fewer restraints on US policy towards the EC. This section shows that the EC had begun to challenge the supremacy of US foreign commercial leadership and policies as long ago as the 1960s, but more actively since the mid-1980s.

In response to EC subsidy actions adversely affecting US shares of foreign markets and pressure from US farm interests, Congress enacted the Bonus Incentive Commodity Programme in 1983 and the Export Enhancement Act in 1985. These programmes were designed to subsidise sales of selected US farm exports to markets in which the EC had used export subsidies to undercut prices of US products to increase market shares. The Export Enhancement Act was particularly designed in response to losses of US shares of the Algerian and Egyptian wheat–wheat flour markets to EC sales. Funds are allocated to sell surpluses stockpiled by the US Department of Agriculture at reduced prices to precisely those third–country markets where EC subsidised sales have eroded historical US market shares. The EC's response to US legislation has been to file formal complaints through GATT procedures and to maintain, indeed increase, its export subsidies to meet the new US challenge.

One other hardy perennial in US–EC relations is the EC's on-and-off-again threat to replace the zero-duty rate on imports of corn gluten feed.[25] The EC's zero duty on corn gluten feed was bound (i.e. a concluded agreement) at the Dillon Round of MTNs in 1962 and any move to replace it with a higher duty or quota would require compensation. The US supplies the lion's share of the EC's market for non-grain feed ingredients (NGFIs), which was valued at $665 million in 1990. The import levy on corn gluten feed was bound in the GATT as a trade-off for US and others' acceptance of the EC's variable levy system for cereals. At the time of the Dillon Round, EC imports of corn gluten feed were negligible. However, EC imports of the product rose in the 1980s as an important and low-cost source of high-protein animal feed, much to the chagrin of the EC's domestic cereals producers (whose home-grown grains for animal consumption are much more costly). Since the EC would like to favour domestic production over imports, and given the power of the cereals lobby in Europe, the possible elimination of the zero-duty rate remains a perennial thorn in the side of EC relations with the United States.

For the United States, such an action would be considered a frontal assault on the sanctity of all US farm exports to the EC, not only because of the loss of trade for the corn gluten industry but because the US fears that, should it happen, it would only be a matter of time before the EC then moved to replace the GATT-bound zero-duty rate on imports of soybeans with a tariff. In the case of soybean exports, the fourth largest item of US exports to the EC, should the EC take such a hostile action, again a full-scale trade war would occur. In 1984, the EC notified the GATT of its intent to substitute the zero duty on NGFI with tariff quotas to increase the use of home-grown grains in animal feed. The threats of massive retaliation from the United States were so vociferous that the EC backed down. This matter still has the potential to seriously affect US–EC relations in the future.

A TYPOLOGY OF US–EC TRADE DISPUTES AND DISPUTE SETTLEMENT

As shown in Table 4.19 the story of US–EC trade acrimony reveals a discernible trend. Of the 17 conflicts, 2 (12 per cent) occurred during the hegemonic period, 8 (47 per cent) during the hegemonic decline period and 7 (41 per cent) during the post-hegemonic period. A clear acceleration of disputes is discernible as US–EC trade has grown and the two economies have become more interdependent. The majority of US–EC commercial conflicts have occurred in the latter hegemonic decline and the post-hegemonic periods when conditions of complex interdependence have largely replaced previous hegemonic behaviour. Hegemony, the cold war, and the EC's own embryonic development were the key explanations behind the lower number of trade disputes in the earlier history of US–EC relations.

Table 4.19 also shows that the US was the complainant in 14 (82 per cent) of the disputes, whereas the EC was the complainant in 3 (18 per cent). Part One showed how much more active the US has been as a complainant in the GATT than the EC. Part of the explanation of why the US initiated 82 per cent of all bilateral trade disputes is rooted in the misperceived expectations of the United States in its early support for the creation of the EC. The expectation was that a reconstructed Western Europe would be a trade partner of the United States. The United States would tolerate some adverse effects on its export trade as a result of the creation of the customs union and the CAP but that would be compensated for by other benefits.

Agricultural products were involved in 12 (70 per cent) of the 17 disputes. The shock of the CAP, with its high price supports, variable import levies and export subsidies, and the implications of those policies for US agricultural interests, had much to do with the rise in the number of US-initiated farm trade disputes with the EC. The cold war, and earlier rhetorical and policy support for the EC, put a lid on bilateral confrontation. However, as the EC expanded agricultural market shares in Europe, the United States, and third countries, dominated by the United States, and given the decline and later eclipse of hegemony, the seal was broken and the confrontations began.

Table 4.19 depicts the settlement status of each dispute. Of the 17 disputes, 3 (18 per cent) were settled with neither threats of punitive action nor punitive action itself. All 3 were settled peacefully during the period of hegemonic decline. One (5 per cent) was settled with a threat or warning of punitive action. Nine (53 per cent) were settled after punitive action by the US or the EC was taken. Of the 9, 2 (22 per cent) were taken during the hegemonic period, 4 (44 per cent) during hegemonic decline, and 3 (33 per cent) during post-hegemony. The majority of bilateral disputes were settled only after confrontation had occurred and, of those, most occurred in the 1980s during the transition from hegemonic decline to post-hegemony. This suggests that the number of disputes is in part a function of the shifts that were taking place between the United States and the EC and in the world around them, and the rise of complex interdependence. Four (23 per cent) of the 17 disputes have not yet been settled. Of the unsettled disputes, one dates back to the hegemonic decline period and the remainder are from the post-hegemonic period.

In the following pages, an analysis is made of each case of trade dispute, categorised according to the type of action taken. This will allow further conclusions to be drawn at the end of the chapter.

TRADE DISPUTES SETTLED WITH NO PUNITIVE ACTION

Steel (1969–74)

The first US–EC steel trade crisis resulted in the conclusion of a voluntary restraint agreement (VRA) between the United States and the EC, which was in effect between 1969–74. However, because of the worldwide boom in steel demand, the EC was not held to the VRA's provisions during 1973–4 (Tarr, 1988: 184).

Canned Fruit (1981–5)

In 1981 the United States complained that EC subsidies to processors of certain fruits discriminated against US fruit producers. The EC maintained that its subsidies compensated processors for high costs resulting from the very high minimum prices paid to the fruit growers. In March 1982 the United States requested that the matter be investigated by a GATT panel to determine if the EC's subsidies impaired US rights under Article 16 of the Subsidies Code. The panel report of November 1984 found that the production aids granted to processors of canned peaches, pears and fruit cocktail nullified and impaired tariff concessions granted by the EC on those products and suggested that the EC restore the competitive relationship between imported and domestic canned fruit. The panel report was never adopted. Instead the two sides, after protracted negotiations, signed the US–EC Canned Fruit Agreement in 1985, placing limits on EC processing aids for canned fruits. The EC agreed to cut its processing aids to peach canners by 25 per cent in the 1986–7 farm year, and to phase out processing aids for canned peaches in subsequent years. The United States agreed to accept previous reductions in the processing subsidies for canned pears.

Wine (1985–6)

In this brief tiff, the EC requested that the GATT Subsidies Code set up a panel to investigate provisions of the US Wine Equity Act which it maintained were inconsistent with the Subsidies Code. That wish was granted in February 1985. The Wine Equity Act temporarily amended the definition of the wine industry to include the grape growers as well as wine producers in order to give grape growers a chance to lodge antidumping and countervailing duty complaints against unfairly trade imports. The panel report concluded that inclusion of the grape growers in the definition of the wine industry was contrary to GATT rules, which define industry as the producer of the product concerned, i.e. only wine production in this instance. The US blocked adoption of the panel's conclusions. First, the law widening the definition of the industry was due to expire in 1986 anyway. Second, the United States stated that it would not move in this instance unless the EC agreed to resolve longstanding cases involving US complaints against EC wheat flour and pasta subsidies – two disputes that had been under examination under the Subsidies Code since 1982.

TRADE DISPUTES SETTLED AFTER THREAT OF PUNITIVE ACTION

Canned Fruit (1988–9)

In August 1988 the United States charged that the EC had violated the 1985 US–EC Canned Fruit Agreement and in March 1989 US trade officials warned the EC that domestic pressure could force the United States to retaliate against EC exports if the EC did not reduce its subsidies per the earlier agreement. The United States maintained that EC subsidies to processors of canned fruit were eliminating US sales of canned fruit to the EC altogether and threatening to reduce US industry shares of the home, Canadian and Japanese markets. The US industry claimed that up to $10 million in annual sales were being lost to the EC. The EC argued that the subsidies were in compliance with the 1985 accord. On 8 May 1989 the USTR began to undertake a preliminary investigation into the EC subsidy action and drew up a list of EC products targeted for potential punitive action. However, by June the EC agreed to lower its subsidies to processors of canned peaches and pears, which caused the USTR to terminate its investigation.

TRADE DISPUTES INVOLVING PUNITIVE ACTION

Carpet and Glass (1962)

In 1962 the United States withdrew a previous GATT concession on carpet and glass. Not satisfied with the offer of compensation from the United States, due to the EC under GATT rules, the EC retaliated against US goods.

Poultry (1963–4)

The first full-fledged agricultural trade conflict between the US and EC broke out in 1963 over a conflict between the EC's quest to promote poultry production and historical US shares of the European poultry market. The so-called Chicken War was a precursor of what was to come in the 1980s. The United Sates had reservations about the potential effects of the CAP on its agricultural producers but they were put aside in order not to delay completion of the Dillon Round of MTNs and ratification of the Rome Treaty in 1957. The Chicken

War confirmed the earlier reservations of the United States about the future impact of the EC on US commercial interests.

By 1962 the EC had incorporated poultry into the CAP and raised import levies to protect the nascent industry. However, the EC had previously bound the import levy on poultry at the Dillon Round of MTNs by unbinding the rate at which the United States was owed compensation under GATT rules. The new and higher variable levy had the effect of substantially reducing US poultry sales in the EC market. Upon failure of the US and EC to negotiate an agreed amount of compensation, the two parties submitted the matter to the GATT under Article 28. A November 1963 GATT panel report fixed the value of compensation owed at a point which did not satisfy US claims. As a consequence, the United States increased tariffs on imports of high-priced brandy, Volkswagen pick-up trucks, dextrine and potato starch from the EC. The value of the increased punitive tariffs was roughly equal to the value of trade lost to US poultry producers in the EC.

The US was no longer willing to pay a heavy price for the course of European economic integration and the EC, just five years after its formation, was prepared to assert its interests even at the expense of its patron. The irony of the Chicken War (and subsequent trade squabbles) is that the complainant (i.e. US poultry) did not receive direct compensation and innocent producers in the defendent (i.e. cognac) were punished since their export goods were targeted for punishment by the complainant.

The Chicken War was a watershed in US–EC relations because it indicated the limits of how much the patron would be willing to sacrifice to the client, how much the client was willing to pursue its own interests despite the adverse effects on its patron, and finally how both could not remain in an unequal partnership. There had to be give and take, and there was. President de Gaulle made the Chicken War into an issue of European unification and French membership in the EC. He stated that if the EC gave in to the US and reversed policy, the CAP would collapse and France would leave the EC. In retrospect, the EC action was taken, the United States responded, the GATT served a useful function, and the two trade partners survived their first major farm trade conflict.

Gas Pipeline Embargo (1981–2)

The US embargo of supplies for the construction of the Siberian gas pipeline precipitated a major crisis of confidence in US–EC economic, political and legal relations and exposed the position of the United States *vis-à-vis* the EC in the period of hegemonic decline. In response to the December 1979 Soviet invasion of Afghanistan, the US imposed economic sanctions on the Soviets and expected the EC to follow suit. The United States imposed a partial grain embargo on the Soviet Union and a boycott of the Moscow Olympics. The EC responded less speedily and with milder sanctions that essentially prevented exports to the Soviet Union from replacing suspended US supplies. The EC's reticence infuriated the United States. It was against this strain in bilateral relations that the pipeline embargo fiasco must be placed.

EC member governments and firms were involved in manufacturing parts for construction of the pipeline that would carry natural gas from Western Siberia to Western Europe and in arranging long-term contracts for the sale of Soviet natural gas. Ostensibly as a response to the Soviet role in the Polish government's crackdown on the Solidarity movement and its imposition of martial law, but also in the context of a deterioration in US–Soviet relations, the Reagan administration imposed an embargo on all components used in the construction of the pipeline, effective from 30 December 1980. The United States government warned that the pipeline, once in operation, would make the EC dependent on – and hostage to – Soviet natural gas supplies. It maintained that once the pipeline was operative then, the hard-currency revenues earned by the Soviet Union from the sale of natural gas to Western Europe would be used to further beef up Soviet military capabilities. The United States claimed that denying the Soviet Union the needed bank credits, equipment and technology would force it to divert its own huge resources away from defence.

The embargo was extended on 18 June 1982 to retroactively ban sales by subsidiaries of US firms abroad and by foreign companies manufacturing under patents licensed by US firms, including European firms. The United States threatened firms that did not abide by the embargo with punishment.

That the US government thought it could decide for the Europeans what was and was not in their security interests was more a throwback to the hegemonic behaviour of the 1950s. Of course, as a defender of Western Europe in the event of war, the United States had legitimate concerns about the security implications of the pipeline, but the methods used to impose US views on the Europeans symbolised less the hegemonic power of the United States than the decline of that power by 1981.

The effect of the embargo actions infuriated the EC and the EC Commission sought to challenge the legality of the action in the GATT in July 1982. The EC claimed that the US offered insufficient consultation on the matter, that EC firms stood to lose sales on contracts to which they were previously bound and that the US action was an illegal extraterritorial interference into the domestic legal systems of the EC. The EC argued that US subsidiaries in Europe were European firms that came under EC and member-state laws. Four EC members – Germany, Britain, Italy, and France – were involved in the pipeline construction.

Bowing to extreme pressure from the EC, the Reagan administration backed down and ended the embargo on 12 November 1982, having achieved nothing but the distrust and embitterment of the EC and its member-states. The Europeans underestimated US resolve in foiling the pipeline project as much as the United States misjudged European resolve in going ahead with it in spite of the Soviet-instigated clampdown in Poland. The US Government also failed to understand how much the Europeans considered US subsidiaries in Europe to be European firms, not American ones. The EC's concerns about the extraterritorial reach of US law to foreign subsidiaries of US firms have yet to be satisifed and the issue remains open as a source of friction in EC relations with the United States.

Pasta (1982–6)

In April 1982 the United States filed a complaint under the GATT Subsidies Code against the EC for subsidising pasta exports. The US charged that the EC action was a violation of Article 9 of the Subsidies Code. The US industry and government argued that EC subsidies were set as high as 70 per cent of the wholesale cost of pasta. According to the EC, these payments were designed to bridge the gap between the world price and the much higher price of the durum wheat component of pasta on the EC market. The US pasta industry claimed that the EC subsidies cost it up to $40 million annually in lost sales and allowed EC pasta producers to undersell their US competitors in the US market. The US argued that these subsidies were applied to a processed food, which is prohibited under the GATT Subsidies Code. The EC responded that the EC's export subsidies relate only to the durum wheat component of pasta and were thus legal under GATT rules.

In May 1983 the GATT Subsidies Code panel found that EC export subsidies on the durum wheat component of pasta violated the code. The ruling was never formally adopted because the EC chose not to acknowledge it. It was the first time the EC chose not to accept a GATT panel's conclusions and was thus another signal of its assertion and self-confidence in relations with the United States. At the time the United States took no immediate retaliatory action in response. The pasta issue, however, was not laid to rest after all.

The pasta case was resurrected when the United States raised import duties on pasta in retaliation for the adverse effects of EC Mediterranean tariff preferences on the sale of US citrus products in the EC market (see the next section). When on 10 August 1986 the US and EC signed an agreement ending the citrus dispute, they included a provision requiring the amount of subsidy on pasta to be negotiated by July 1987. Intense negotiations occurred during the summer of 1987 over the amount of EC subsidisation of pasta exports to be permitted. At stake was only $35 million in EC pasta exports, accounting for 10 per cent of the US market. An agreement was reached after much acrimony.

On 1 October 1987 an agreement ending the dispute over EC pasta exports to the United States went into effect. The United States had threatened to take retaliatory actions against EC pasta exports if no solution were reached by 2 August. Negotiations to end the 'pasta war' ended on 5 August – three days after a US-imposed deadline – avoiding retaliatory and counterretaliatory measures. The EC threatened it would respond in turn with equivalent measures. Fortunately for both, the deadline was ignored when a breakthrough seemed forthcoming.

According to the terms of the agreement, the legality of the EC subsidy would be decided within the context of the Uruguay Round of MTNs. In the meantime the 5 August settlement set up a complicated and temporary arrangement whereby the EC agreed to eliminate export subsidies on about one-half of the durum wheat component of pasta exports and to substantially decrease production subsidies to pasta producers. However, the negotiated settlement, according to one observer, left intact the EC's defence of the principle that it may use export subsidies for processed foods (Yannoupoulos, 1988: 116). Furthermore, by referring the legal question of subsidisation to the Uruguay Round, the US and EC put off reckoning to a later date and to an uncertain future, given the status of MTNs by the end of 1991.

The level of acrimony and the potential emergence of another trade war over such a small amount of disputed trade pointed to the sensitivity of the US industry over the EC action. EC officials could not understand why the US took offence over such a small amount of trade. The US Government was also concerned about using the pasta case to signal the EC to back off taking future actions that would adversely affect US farm interests. The EC's response to the US action on pasta was a watershed in bilateral relations because it alerted the United States to the rise of the EC's political power and helped bring the US–EC partnership to a new plateau of rough equality. It helped to usher in the post–hegemonic period in US–EC relations under conditions of complex interdependence.

Mediterranean Tariff Preferences for Citrus (1982–6)

In the 1970s the US citrus growers claimed that the EC's tariff cuts on imports of citrus from the non-member Mediterranean states discriminated against US citrus, which was subject to the full MFN duty rate. US citrus growers wanted equal treatment on the EC market. Even before the 1970s the US protested against earlier EC agreements with Mediterranean countries which entailed reciprocal tariff concessions. The latter were ended by the EC in the 1970s but tariff preferences not only remained but were widened.

The US initiated bilateral consultations with the EC under GATT rules in an attempt to find a solution to the conflict back in 1976 and again in 1982. The EC argued that its tariff preferences were designed to promote economic development in the Mediterranean countries. As the two were unable to agree on a mutually acceptable position, the dispute was submitted to a GATT panel in June 1982 to determine if the EC's preferential tariff treatment on imports of citrus products from certain Mediterranean countries impaired MFN treatment of the United States. The GATT panel report of 1985 found that the EC tariff preferences on fresh oranges and fresh lemons had indeed impaired concessions made to the US and recommended that the EC restore the competitive balance.

The EC blocked acceptance of the GATT panel report in the GATT Council because it claimed that the panel ignored the broader objectives of the EC's tariff preferences as a form of economic assistance. In response, the Reagan administration threatened to impose punitive duty increases on imports of EC pasta, a product (discussed above) over which the US and EC have previously disputed, to an amount equivalent to the US loss of trade due to the EC's Mediterranean tariff preferences. The EC threatened to counterretaliate by increasing duties on imports of US walnuts and lemons. The EC's threat of counterretaliation was the first of its kind, another signal that it would not be 'bullied' by its closest political–military ally! US–EC relations were again adjusting from an unequal to a more equal trade partnership, with commercial interests taking greater precedence than alliance ones.

The two agreed to a temporary truce in the summer of 1985. Both agreed to drop their threats of retaliation and counterretaliation and to work toward a settlement of the issue of US citrus access to the EC market. The US government imposed a 31 December 1985 deadline by which agreement must be reached, or else the US would raise pasta duties. Negotiations failed to settle the dispute by that deadline and the United States raised duties on imports of EC pasta. The expected loss of EC trade in the US market would be about $30 million – an amount roughly equivalent to the loss of US trade as a result of the Mediterranean tariff preferences. The EC counterretaliated by raising duties on imports of US walnuts and lemons designed in turn to rob the US of about $30 million in sales on the EC market. The EC also punished the United States by actually raising pasta subsidies. This exchange of hostile actions ushered in a more mercantilist phase in bilateral dispute settlement.

On 10 August 1986 the United States and the EC finally signed an agreement ending the citrus conflict but not the pasta dispute. They agreed to eliminate all punitive actions taken in 1985: the EC agreed to lifts its punitive duties on US lemons and walnuts and the US agreed to lift its punitive duties on pasta. The US and EC agreed to lower tariffs or raise quota levels on a variety of other products as well. The EC granted tariff quota concessions on imports of US grapefruits, lemons, certain sweet oranges, almonds, roasted groundnuts and frozen orange juice. The US agreed to lower tariffs or raise quotas on imports of EC anchovies, certain cheeses, sweet oranges, olives, capers, cider, paprika and olive oil. The US also agreed not to challenge present or future EC preferential trade accords with the Mediterranean states. Legal settlement of the pasta subsidy question was postponed until 1987, although the EC did agree to temporarily reduce export subsidies for pasta sold to the US market.

Two observations on this conflict are worth making. First, domestic politics in the United States prevailed over US foreign policy interests in the Mediterranean Basin. Second, the EC stood up to US retaliatory action and counterretaliated, pointing to a new found self-confidence in a period of American hegemonic decline. It was the second time that the EC took counterretaliatory action against the US (the first time was in regard to the steel conflict which is covered in the following section).

That the EC counterretaliated after the US imposed punitive duties against the EC in response to the citrus conflict heralded a new era in EC relations with the United States. Just as the United States had decided it could no longer idly sustain the negative implications of EC actions on its industry, the EC decided it would no longer subject itself to adverse US actions without a response. Indeed EC counterretaliation was probably responsible for hastening the resolution of the conflict. In the end, EC tariff preferences for Mediterranean citrus producers remained.

This round of trade disputes was not settled by hegemonic bullying, nor did it cause irreparable damage to US–EC relations. What it did do was put US–EC commercial relations into its logical post-cold-war–international-peace-time framework, i.e. intense commercial rivalry shorn of the political contraints of the cold war. Trade rivalry among allies is a normal function of a peace-time international system. Mercantilists are on the mark for their explanation of the intensity of the dispute and the process through which the conflict was finally settled.

Steel (1982–9)

Under the EC's 1980 steel crisis plan, capacity was slated to be cut to streamline the industry and to raise prices despite the huge losses in employment. Under ECSC rules, the EC Commission permitted certain state subsidies to steel firms for restructuring. They were suppose to be lifted in 1985, but some subsidisation has continued to this day. The US steel industry claimed the subsidies biased world steel trade and in 1982 US steel producers filed petitions with the US Department of Commerce seeking initiation of antidumping and countervailing duty actions against EC producers. To avoid US action, US–EC bilateral consultations (under GATT rules) produced a VRA in which the EC agreed to curtail shipments to the US. US steel producers refused to accept the negotiated agreement and the ITC voted affirmatively in most of the countervailing duty cases against EC steel imports into the US. Adding further to the drama, the EC agreed to develop a procedure for consultations regarding exports of steel pipes and tubes to the US just before the ITC announcement of its determination which, had it occurred, would have triggered the

US Department of Commerce to assess countervailing duties on products having caused injury. For its part, the US producers agreed to avoid diversions of trade from other steel products to pipes and tubes and to withdraw their petitions. For its part, the EC agreed to limit certain steel products to the US market, covering 64 per cent of total US imports of steel products from the EC. The accord, known as the 1982 US–EC Carbon Steel Arrangement, in effect between 1 November 1982 and 31 December 1985, was designed for the US industry to have the time necessary to restructure and create more stable conditions in US–EC trade relations, yet guarantee some share of the US market for EC suppliers.

Specialty steel products (e.g. pipes and tubes) flooded the US market in 1982. Imports of pipes and tubes from the EC, while not included in the 1982 Arrangement, were to be held at 5.9 per cent of apparent US consumption under terms of a separate letter of understanding. Consultations were to be held should EC shipments exceed this amount. As negotiations initiated by the US side in late 1984 failed to limit the surge in imports, the US invoked Section 201 of the Trade Act of 1974 and took safeguard action to restrict imports of certain EC specialty steel products from the EC and other foreign suppliers. The EC claimed that the US steel problem was the result of decreased consumption and the strength of the dollar, not imports from the EC, and that the measure did not conform with GATT rules. The EC filed a grievance under GATT procedures seeking $570 million in compensation.

When negotiations to settle the dispute broke down early in 1984 the EC on 1 March, imposed retaliatory quotas on imports of US styrene, polyethylene, guns, hunting rifles, athletic and gymnastic equipment, and snow skis and imposed new tariffs on methanol and vinyl acetate and antitheft and firm alarms valued at $119 million – roughly equivalent to the loss that the EC claimed was created by the US action. It was the first time in the history of bilateral relations that the EC took a counterretaliatory action against the United States, pointing to an assertation and self-confidence not previously exercised in this way. Claiming that the increase of imports of EC steel pipes and tubes contravened the US–EC letter of understanding attached to the 1982 Carbon Steel Arrangement, the US placed an embargo on imports of EC steel pipes and tubes which took effect on 29 November 1984.

In another attempt to diffuse the crisis the US and EC agreed in January 1985 to lower the EC share of the US market for steel pipe and tube and by June 1985 the two sides had negotiated a new steel agreement. The US allowed the EC to ship certain amounts of pipe and tube in excess of the quotas agreed to under the January agreement and the EC agreed to conclude negotiations for renewal of the Carbon Steel Arrangement and to open and conclude negotiations on limiting exports of steel products to the US not directly subject to quotas under the 1982 arrangement but to consultation if a jump in the volume of imports were to occur.

Late in 1985 the 1982 US–EC Carbon Steel Arrangement was renewed limiting EC shipments to 5.5 per cent of the US market until 30 September 1989, although the scope was broadened to cover new steel products (semifinished steel continued to be treated as a consultation product in the 1985 pact). The agreement subjected semifinished steel products to discussion if EC shipments to the US market increased significantly. On 30 December 1985 the US unilaterally imposed quotas on imports of EC semifinished steel products. EC shipments were limited to 400,000 short tons annually over the period 1 January 1986 to 30 September 1989 with an additional 200,000 short tons per year alloted to cover contracted shipments from the British Steel Corporation to a steel company in Alabama. The EC retaliated by imposing punitive tariffs against imports of US fertilisers, coated paper and animal fats from 15 February 1987 to 15 November 1989.

In June 1986 the US and EC agreed to abandon the measures and broaden the 1985 arrangement to cover semifinished steel. New limitations on EC semifinished steel exports to the US were set. The EC agreed to rescind retaliatory measures when the agreement went into effect. The 1986 US–EC voluntary restraint agreement was due to expire on 30 September 1989.

On 20 November 1989 the United States and the EC concluded a new VRA covering EC exports of steel to the US that ran from 1 October 1989 to 31 March 1992 and replaced the VRA that expired on 30 September 1989. The new accord raised the EC share of the US steel market from 6.8 per cent to 7 per cent. In January 1990 the US and EC reached an agreement to eliminate market-distorting practices in the steel sector. Under the agreement the US and EC would liberalise tariffs and NTBs in steel both bilaterally and multilaterally at the Uruguay Round. The accord prohibited export subsidies but permitted other subsidies under certain circumstances, e.g. for R & D, environmental protection, plant closures, and certain social purposes.

Given that the EC wished to continue to sell steel to the US market, and that a quota is always preferable to a punitive tariff – with its higher monetary cost and permanancy – the US appeared to use its weight to force the EC into signing a VRA when the EC would have preferred not to. The VRA has kept the peace in US–EC steel trade and indeed the agreement to work harder to combat trade-distorting practices is a model for the Uruguay Round negotiators. It has also shown the capability of both sides to work through difficult trade disputes. However, the VRA was but one step away from the desired objectives of the GATT and of a liberal world trade order that the US and EC had sought to uphold over the previous four decades. Suffice it to say that in a complex interdependent relationship, a sector so sensitive to domestic economies must be handled carefully to avoid accelerating conflict. Despite the exchange of punitive actions in the mid-1980s, the US and EC seemed to have worked out their steel trade problems so that all has remained quiet on this front since 1991. The main concern here is that too many US–EC trade problems have been referred to the Uruguay Round given the uncertainties of those deliberations.

Spanish and Portuguese Accession to the EC (1986–7)

In response to the negative implications of the Spanish and Portuguese accession to the EC on 1 January 1986, the US government threatened to place punitive duties on imports of certain EC products.

When it joined the EC, Spanish import levies on corn and sorghum rose from 20 to 120 per cent in order to meet the much higher common external tariff (CET) of the EC. The United States stood to lose sales in the Spanish market for these products to internal EC suppliers. The US and EC entered into negotiations on compensation and the United States set a 1 July 1986 deadline for a negotiated settlement to be reached should negotiations fail to produce a settlement. Beyond that date, the United States threatened to increase levies on imports of EC white wine, brandy, cognac, mineral water, cheeses, whiskey, gin, hops, meats, sausages, leather, potato starch, endives, carrots, olives, and coffee extracts, amounting to an EC loss in trade of $1 billion. This amount was designed to be roughly equivalent to the value of trade lost to the United States as a result of the Spanish accession action.

With regard to Portugal, the United States opposed an article in the country's accession treaty that (a) set aside 15.5 per cent of the

Portuguese grain market solely for EC suppliers and (b) imposed restrictions on Portugal's imports of oilseeds. The United States viewed this as an assault on its interests, not so much because such a small segment of the Portuguese grain market was in itself any great loss but because it wanted to signal the EC that it would challenge actions that set a precedent for future restrictions on sales of US agricultural products. In response to the EC action, the United States threatened to increase import levies for such EC products as beer, chocolates, confections, and pear and apple juices. In response to an EC quota established on Portuguese oilseed imports, the United States stated that it would raise import tariffs on wine as from 1 May unless action was taken.

The EC would not be pushed around either. In response, on 9 April the EC threatened to counterretaliate if the US took action. The EC Commission stated that if the US took hostile action with regard to the Portugal question then the EC would increase tariffs on imports of US corn, beer, wine, meat, honey, dried fruit, foliage for bouquets, sunflower seed, animal fats and fruit juices. With regard to Spain, the EC would impose punitive duties on imports of US corn gluten feed, wheat and rice.

In response, on 15 May the Reagan administration ordered quotas (instead of tariffs) on imports of the EC items targeted for punishment (as mentioned above) but set levels above the quantities exported in the previous year to avoid any immediate loss in EC sales. The US planned to impose restrictions on imports from the EC on 1 July 1986, when last minute negotiations produced a six-month temporary truce. In the interregnum, the EC agreed to increase its offer to 234,000 tons of feedgrains imported into Spain until year's end. The US delayed planned retaliation.

When negotiations did not yield the desired results, the United States imposed retaliatory duties of 200 per cent on $400 million worth of European brandy, white wine, gin, cheeses, canned ham, olives and other goods effective until the end of January 1987. However, on 29 January a peace accord was reached. The EC was required to ensure that Spain import 2 million metric tons of corn and 300,000 metric tons of sorghum from non-EC suppliers over each of the following four years. The EC agreed to eliminate the 15.5 per cent share of the Portuguese grain market reserved to EC suppliers.

The US–EC trade dispute over enlargement could have been avoided. It was provocative of the EC to retain 15.5 per cent of the Portuguese grain market for EC suppliers. The EC underestimated the

US response. For the US, the small amount of the Portuguese grain market so restricted was not what was at stake. What the EC failed to recognise when it included that provision in the accession treaty was that it would raise the ire of the US farm community already jittery about the impact of enlargement on its farm exports to the EC. In hindsight, the EC was sensitised to US interests and the US was reminded how important it is to clearly inform the EC of US positions and interests before policy actions are taken that could have adverse external effects. With regard to Spain's new and higher import levies, the EC had a right under the GATT to expand its customs union and to expect Spain to accede to the higher CET and the United States did not contest either. What was contested was the level at which compensation owed to the US under GATT rules would be set. A round of punitive actions and counteractions were taken before the two sides could hammer out an agreement. The US–EC dispute over the compensation issue reflected the complex interdependence conditions of the post-hegemonic period in US–EC relations.

Meat (1987–Present)

Two issues pertaining to restrictions of meat entering the EC precipitated this new round of trade disputes in 1987: a ban on imports of hormone-treated beef and the setting of new health and safety standards for third-country slaughterhouses and packing plants exporting meat to the EC (known as the EC's Third Country Meat Directive).

For health purposes, the EC banned all sales (domestic as well as imported) of meat treated with growth hormones, as from 1 January 1988. The United States Government insisted that there was no evidence indicating that growth hormones posed health risks and concluded that the EC action was an unfair trade practice. The EC's response to that charge was that the ban applied to domestic as well as imported products; thus it is was in this way not restrictive. Most US meat exports to the EC come from animals that have been treated with hormones. The value of US meat sales in the EC subject to the new ban amounted to about $100 million in 1988.

The US Government responded by threatening to impose punitive duties against EC products if the ban went through. As a result, on 18 November 1987 the EC agreed to postpone implementation of the ban for one year to 1 January 1989. The ban on the use of hormones in EC meat production went ahead on 1 January 1988 as planned. Although the US welcomed the reprieve, it listed, on 25 November

1987, thirty European food categories worth $100 million (equal to the loss of the US meat market in the EC) it would consider for retaliation should the US meat exports to the EC be banned.

By the end of 1988 negotiations failed to resolve the dispute and the EC was set to implement the ban on 1 January 1989. The EC gave a grace period for officials to have time to work out a solution. US attempts to request the establishment of a technical experts group under the GATT Standards Code to evaluate the effects of the growth hormone on consumers were rejected by the EC. In December 1988 the EC charged that the threatened unilateral retaliatory measures proposed by the United States violated the GATT and proposed that the US be judged within the GATT Council. In response, the US blocked the EC's request for a GATT Council ruling, noting that the dispute had been before a GATT Standards Code committee for the previous 18 months and that the EC had blocked any action in that committee. The EC drafted its own counterretaliatory list, raising tariffs by 120 per cent on $361 million's worth of imports from the United States should the United States proceed with its sanctions.

On 1 January 1989 the EC enacted its ban against US hormoned-treated meats and the US immediately implemented its planned retaliation. US officials estimated that the ban would cost US exporters $100 million annually. The US retaliated by imposing 200 per cent tariffs on an assortment of imports from the EC worth $100 million. EC goods targeted by the retaliatory measures included boneless beef, processed pork ham and shoulder, prepared or preserved tomatoes, soluble or instant coffee extract, certain fermented beverages with less than seven per cent alcohol content and fruit juices. The USTR has modified the value of retaliation from $100 to $92.4 million. Efforts to resolve the issue in the GATT continued to be unsuccessful. On 23 November 1990 the European Court of Justice upheld the legality of the hormone ban.

In response to the US retaliation, the EC finalised its list of US products (valued at $96 million) slated for counterretaliation. However, the EC held off on implementing the measures and in February the US and EC agreed to establish a task force to work out the technical problems with US exports of hormone-free beef to the EC. On 3 May 1989 the task force signed an interim agreement whereby EC officials agreed to take responsibility of inspecting the feedlots of US beef exporters (to the EC) to certify that the animals have not been treated with growth hormones. The task force did not resolve the issue of US exports of meats, such as tongue and liver, which are treated with hormones, and account for 70 per cent of total US beef exports for human consumption in the EC market.

In December 1989 the US Congress passed legislation requiring US military bases in Europe to purchase US beef. The US military market for beef in the EC is valued at about $55 million and will require the US to offer subsidies to cover transportation costs and the difference in price between the EC and US stock. Although the EC requested that the US modify its retaliatory measures, US officials responded that the military beef matter was unrelated to the hormone conflict.

At the end of 1989 the US still helped to resolve the issue under the GATT Standards Code but the EC repeatedly blocked the US request for a technical expert group to evaluate the effects of hormones on human consumption. The EC requested that a GATT dispute settlement panel rule on the legality of the US retaliatory measures, but the US blocked that move.

In October 1990 EC inspectors decided to remove all US meat producers from their list of approved certified plants as from 1 January 1991, alleging that poor hygiene in US meat plants posed a hazard to EC consumers. The United States rejected the EC claims, stating that there was no scientific basis for prohibiting exports. The US urged the EC to postpone implementation of the ban until further talks were held, but the EC implemented the ban on schedule.

On 28 November 1990 the US pork and meat producers lodged complaints with the USTR, demanding retaliation against the EC under Section 301 of the Trade Act of 1974. Their petition alleged that the EC actions violated GATT rules and discriminated against US exports. On 1 January 1991 the USTR initiated an investigation into the pork and meat producers' allegations. The meat dispute promises to be one of the most difficult trade conflicts between the US and EC in the 1990s.

TRADE DISPUTES NOT YET SETTLED

Wheat Flour (1981–Present)

EC export subsidies to enhance sales of wheat flour in foreign markets is the longest-running bilateral trade dispute. In December 1981 the United States alleged that the EC was subsidising wheat flour exports which gave the EC more than an equitable share of world export trade in this product and that this action was a violation of Articles 8 and 10 of the GATT Subsidies Code. A Subsidies Code panel was formed in 1982 and issued a report in March 1983 which was never formally adopted. The EC continues to challenge the US interpretation of GATT rules on what constitutes a legal export subsidy and an equitable share of foreign markets. As mentioned earlier, this unsolved dispute has resulted in a virtual subsidy war between the United States and the EC to determine which side can outspend the other in enhancing exports to retain or increase foreign market shares. As a consequence of US dismay with EC wheat flour export subsidies, Congress enacted legislation in 1985 to provide US wheat flour exporters to sell their product at subsidised rates in markets, such as Algeria and Egypt, where EC subsidies have eroded traditional US market shares. The EC has since challenged the legality of the US legislation in the GATT.

Aircraft (1986–Present)

The dispute began in 1986 when the US claimed that Airbus Industrie, a European aircraft manufacturing consortium, was being unfairly subsidised with state launch aid (subsidies granted to launch new series of aircraft) and state-backed financial incentives to potential customers of Airbus, and that this action was a violation of the GATT Civil Aircraft Code. Articles 4 and 6 of the Code prohibit trade-distorting subsidies, such as launch aid, unless there is a reasonable expectation of recovering all costs, and unfair inducement of potential purchasers. The US side claimed that Airbus has never shown a profit.

Airbus is a public–private corporation co-owned by Aerospatiale of France, Deutsche Airbus of Germany, British Aerospace of the UK and Construcciones Aeronauticas of Spain. Airbus competes with Boeing and McDonnell Douglas of the United States. The EC denied the American claims and counter-claimed that their loan system does not constitute an illegal subsidy. The Europeans maintain that the subsidies for Airbus are loans that will be repaid, although no timetable for repayment is specified. The Airbus partners charge that the US government subsidises its aircraft industry as much as the Europeans through generous defence contracts as well as tax benefits and that Airbus provided healthy competition for the US industry which itself holds three-quarters of the world aircraft market. Airbus maintained that Boeing and McDonnell Douglas have received $23 billion between 1979 and 1987 in indirect subsidies in the form of military research and development. According to the US industry, US producers – unlike their European counterparts – must bear the full market risks for new aircraft development and production, and thus limit their profit margins and ability to invest in new technologies for future competition.

After US-initiated bilateral consultations with the EC did not yield a mutually acceptable agreement, the US Government requested a special meeting of the GATT Aircraft Code Committee to begin talks within the GATT framework. Then in the summer of 1988 Airbus governments launched a new series of aircraft by providing $3.3 billion in aid. In response, the US industry threatened to file a section 301 case and antidumping and countervailing duty cases if the programme was not stopped.

US–EC meetings in 1988 failed to resolve the key issue of subsidies – the terms under which government support would be permitted; the definitions of acceptable commercial business practices; and transparency arrangements to enable third parties to gauge the actual level of subsidisation. Airbus subsidies are not transparent because it is not a public limited company; if it were, Airbus would be required to publish financial information for the first time. The EC stated that any future agreement with the US on aircraft subsidies would have to take into account exchange rate fluctuations because the world aircraft market is valued in dollars. EC official indicated that a weakened dollar had increased production costs for Airbus relative to its US rivals. The US rejected the EC request to address the exchange rate question because it would not only negate the advantage of the dollar depreciation but would also set a dangerous precedent for other industries.

In a matter related to the Airbus dispute, the US government expressed concern over an exchange rate guarantee scheme devised by the German government in the context of privatising Messerschmitt-Bolkow-Blohm (MBB) and its wholly-owned subsidiary, Deutsche Airbus. Efforts to privatise MBB through a Daimler-Benz–MBB merger was made conditional on the German Government's ability to cover the financial risk of current and future Airbus projects. One element of the support plan was for the government to finance exchange rate guarantees which cover Airbus sales to the year 2000. The German government used this mechanism to offset adverse exchange rate fluctuations between the mark, in which production costs incurred, and the US dollar.

US officials claimed that the German government distributed $390 million under this scheme which undermines the international balance of payments adjustment process. In December 1989 the United States requested conciliation under the GATT Subsidies Code to determine the legality of the German exchange rate subsidy plan. Throughout 1990 the US and EC met to seek settlement to no avail. In April 1991 the US asked that a dispute settlement panel examine the German exchange rate scheme for Airbus.

US–EC bilateral negotiations over Airbus subsidies were suspended in February 1991 on differences over how far subsidy cuts should go. The United States informed the EC in May 1991 that it would request initiation of GATT consultations on the dispute with the EC over Airbus. For its part, the EC announced that it would propose multilateral negotiations with the United States on the Airbus issue under the GATT Aircraft Committee in order to introduce more stringent international disciplines on all forms of government intervention in support of the aircraft sector. In response to US action in the GATT, the EC stated that it would be counterproductive because the EC had expressed the desire to reinforce existing international commitments. Again, the referral of another bilateral trade dispute to the uncertainty of the Uruguay Round may be a convenient but dangerous action if negotiations collapse.

Soybeans (1988–Present)

Perhaps for the United States the most sensitive farm export to the EC is soybeans. Any attempt by the EC to impair the 1962 GATT-bound zero-duty rate on imports of oilseeds from the United States infuriates the US government and industry. The US got the young EC to grant it a tariff exemption on soybeans in 1962, not knowing that in the future the EC would want to support its own domestic production.

The dispute began in 1988 when the American Soybean Association (ASA) filed a petition with the USTR alleging that the EC unfairly subsidised its domestic production and processing of oilseeds and charging that these subsidies were inconsistent with the GATT because they impaired the duty-free binding granted to the US; and that subsidies to processors of oilseeds encouraged the purchase of EC oilseeds at the expense of imported oilseeds, particularly US soybeans. US soybean producers argued that the EC rule that payments to oilseed processors were conditioned on the purchase of oilseeds originating in the EC was also illegal under the GATT.

As a result, the USTR initiated a section 301 investigation on 5 January 1988. Subsequent bilateral consultations under GATT rules failed to resolve the dispute, which then led to the request for the establishment of a GATT dispute settlement panel to address the issue. The EC blocked formation of the dispute panel, noting that under GATT complaint procedures it is only after bilateral talks have collapsed that a dispute panel is formed. EC officials claimed that they were still awaiting a response from the US to several questions, including the extent of injury to the US soybean producers. The ASA estimated that the value of lost trade because of the EC subsidies amounted to $1.5 billion annually. The second request from the US came in June 1988 and the dispute panel was approved but not established before the end of the year on procedural grounds.

The panel's final report in 1989 supported the US position. The panel reported that EC payments to oilseed processors conditioned on the purchase of oilseeds grown in the EC are inconsistent with the GATT and that EC subsidies to oilseed producers impaired benefits accruing to the US under its zero-duty binding for oilseeds. The EC indicated its willingess to comply with the GATT panel's conclusions but only within the framework of the negotiations leading to the conclusion of the Uruguay Round. Since the Uruguay Round has stalled over lack of agreement on cuts in farm subsidies, the EC has delayed implementing the GATT report. It has maintained all along that the real problem facing the US industry is the loss of the oilseed market to Latin American producers.

The EC's failure to implement the findings of the GATT panel prompted strong criticism from the US side, including threats of retaliation. The EC remained committed to implement the GATT findings only in the context of the Uruguay Round. On the one hand, the EC has accepted the findings of the committee and has stated that it will implement those findings. On the other hand, the EC, by linking implementation with completion of the Uruguay Round, is rebuffing the GATT and the United States. Here the EC is blocking necessary reform and may engender a US retaliatory response (which would be legal under GATT rules) if action is not taken. If the US shows it is serious about retaliation, and if that retaliation appears to heavily damage EC trade interests, then the EC can be expected to belatedly and grudgingly implement the GATT findings. Until then, the ASA's victory is an empty one.

Apples (1988–Present)

On 3 February 1988 the EC Commission unilaterally imposed an import licensing scheme on dessert apples from nonmembers. In defence of the measure, the EC stated that it was necessary to monitor imports because of the increased internal production leading to oversupply and depressed producer prices. On 20 April 1988 the EC Commission unilaterally imposed import quotas on dessert apples that fixed overall targets for imports until August 1988. Supplier countries were each given targets for imports. In June 1988 the US held consultations with the EC under GATT Article 23: 1 at which it charged that the EC quotas violated GATT rules and not only harmed US apple exporters but resulted in diversion of southern hemisphere apples to the US market. In July the US requested that a dispute panel be formed under GATT Article 23: 2 to review the US complaint.

ANALYSIS OF THE TYPOLOGY

The rise in the number of disputes parallels the shift in US–EC interdependence from its asymmetric form, dictated by the cold war and the unequal shares of power in the bilateral partnership, to its complex and more symmetric form, ushered in by the end of the cold war, the ascendancy of the EC itself, and the rise of a post-hegemonic order. Part Two has revealed that the EC's new-found assertiveness and confidence in retaliating against adverse US actions or counter-retaliating against US measures has occurred only recently. For example, it was 1985 when the EC counterretaliated against the United States when the US restricted EC steel exports and 1986 when the EC counterretaliated against United States actions taken against EC Mediterranean tariff preferences. Trade disputes of the 1980s were handled not with silk gloves but with neo-mercantilist determination to press hard to 'protect' domestic producer interests until an eleventh-hour compromise was necessary or when punitive action was delivered or sustained. The literature on neo-mercantilism provides rich explanations for the specific disputes that have entailed punitive actions because these disputes merely reflect the state of competition that exists between the US and EC. Indeed at the level of sectoral disputes the neo-mercantilist recognises the importance of governments protecting and asserting specific trading interests. Yet despite the tough stances and hostile actions the partnership was strong and durable enough to withstand the strains and to go on to expand bilateral trade and investment. Yet the seventeen disputes during the period 1962–90 represent only the rough edges of the US–EC economic relationship not its core. As previously mentioned, the US–EC partnership reflects neo-mercantilism at one level (sectoral trade conflict), but this is set in a wider environment possessing other characteristics. Although the US initiated the lion's share of trade disputes against the EC, the reader ought not to interpret this as hegemonic behaviour. The large number of US-initiated trade disputes with the EC testifies to the power, influence and weight of the EC relative to the US domestic economy and the symmetry of power that emerged in the 1980s within the partnership.

This section has also shown that despite some very difficult trade disputes, with conflict in one sector spilling over into two or three others, when put into the broader perspective of three decades and when set against the total value of two-way trade ($184 billion in 1990), the seventeen disputes appear neither dominant nor excessive. Finally, Table 4.19 shows that of the seventeen disputes, four remain unsettled. While no new specific outbreaks of trade disputes have occurred since 1988, the ones that remain to be resolved in addition to those on the horizon will keep trade diplomats working in overtime well into the 1990s.

CONCLUSIONS

Finally, what does the future hold for the economic dimension of US–EC relations? Chapter 6 explores the policy responses necessary to ensure maintenance of the partnership. For the purposes of this chapter, the following may be surmised. Despite the increase in trade disputes, the US–EC commercial partnership, more balanced now than in the 1980s, continues to flourish. Despite the growing importance of the Pacific Rim to US commercial interests and Eastern Europe and the Mediterranean to EC interests, the United States will remain a Pacific and an Atlantic commercial power, just as the EC will remain an Atlantic as well as a Mediterranean power. Since the

US and EC own a piece of each other's economies, they will remain intimately acquainted with domestic policies and feel deeply their adverse effects. The key to the future of US–EC relations is not the level of economic interdependence which has grown so complex, but the will and capability of US, EC and EC member-state leaders to adapt to change, handle trade disputes judiciously to avoid widespread damage, and indeed to proactively work to steer away from confrontation.

One of the key problems of US–EC economic relations, then, is not the content of those commercial flows but the question of how to manage complex interdependence in a post-hegemonic world. There are three key problems policy-makers need to address. First, the early post-war institutions that affect international trade and economics, the GATT, NATO, IMF, etc., are past their prime and need to be reformed. Second, since these organisations provide the institutional structure of US–EC relations, if they do not work as they should then that deficit will adversely affect US–EC relations. Third, given the fact that trade disputes will increase exponentially with the increased interdependence, the US and EC will need to work more closely together given the inevitability of conflict. These questions will be addressed in Chapter 6.

NOTES

1. Based on figures provided by the US International Trade Commission, the US Department of Commerce and the Congressional Research Service.
2. European Communities (1972: 301).
3. Cafruny argued just the opposite – that 'even as the American economy has weakened, the fundamental asymmetry in power between the United States and Europe has become more striking' (Cafruny, 1989: 112).
4. Data derived from *Historical Statistics of the OEEC* (Paris: OECD, 1988).
5. Raymond Vernon has defined the MNC as a cluster of corporations of diverse nationalities joined together by ties of common ownership (Goodman, in Mally, 1974: 243).
6. The US Government defines foreign direct investment as the ownership or control, direct or indirect, by one foreign person (individual, branch, partnership, association, government, etc.) of 10 per cent or more of the voting securities of an incorporated US business enterprise or an equivalent interest in an unincorporated US business enterprise. (Jackson, 1991: 5).

7. According to Harrison, foreign direct investment appears to be poorly understood when considered in the context of general trade relations. Of the $59.7 billion in total US exports to the EC in 1987, nearly one-third or $19.4 billion was purchased by majority owned affiliates of US companies. Further, US direct investment in the EC is overwhelmingly focused on producing goods and services for the EC market. Only 4 per cent of sales by affiliates of US firms in the EC of $15. 8 billion were made to the US. Thus, when measured in terms of trade flows, US direct investment in the EC generated a net trade surplus of $3.6 billion in 1987 (Harrison, 1990: 5).
8. Harrison (1990: 4). However, Japanese investment in the EC has grown from $7 billion in 1984 to $30 billion in 1988. Japanese investment is expected to continue to grow rapidly in the 1990s as Japanese firms seek to establish a presence in the EC in order to take advantage of the expected post-1992 economic expansion and the time left to set up production plants in advance of new EC rules restricting imports. Historically, Japan has been one of the largest targets of EC antidumping duties. This leaves one observer to point out that, in the not too distant future, Japanese investment in the EC may overshadow US investment.
9. Harrison (1990: 6). The question of balance in US–EC investment is of concern to US policy-makers. Foreign direct investment in the US is primarily oriented toward selling in the US domestic market rather than producing for export. When exports and imports associated with US foreign direct investment in the EC are balanced against exports and imports associated with foreign direct investment in the US by EC firms, the result is a net deficit of $20.8 billion for the US (1987). The bulk of this deficit, however, is related to EC investment in wholesale trade, an activity principally concerned with the marketing and distribution of products. Wholesale trade, of course, includes automobiles, which generate a substantial portion of the overall US trade deficit.

Most of the 62 per cent of imports generated by foreign direct investment by the EC in the US is accounted for by goods for resale without further manufacture. In 1987 this category accounts for $24.6 billion out of $39.5 billion of imports. West German motor vehicles and equipment accounted for $9.8 billion out of $244.9 billion of this total while imports, presumably goods for resale without further manufacture, associated with EC investments in wholesale trade probably accounted for nearly one-half to two-thirds of the imports associated with EC direct investment in the US. Thus a more intensive focus on wholesaling activities, especially automobiles, by EC investors largely accounts for the large overall net trade deficit that results from foreign direct investment.

If only those exports associated with investment in manufacturing are considered, the deficit disappears entirely. For Europe as a whole, US direct foreign investment in manufacturing resulted in US exports of $11.3 billion and imports of $7.8 billion for a trade surplus of $3.5 billion in 1987. Direct foreign investment in the US by European firms generated US exports of $8.5 billion and US imports of $11 billion for a trade deficit of $2. 5 billion in the same year. The net effect in terms of trade of the US and Europe for investment in manufacturing is a surplus of about $1 billion.

10. Thiel (1990).
11. US International Trade Commission (1990). In addition, the US Department of Commerce has estimated that 21,900 jobs are associated with each $1 billion in US manufactured exports.
12. Ibid.
13. Besides currency fluctuations, monetary interdependence is manifested in ways too numerous to be included here: e.g. stock market interactions (sudden massive dips in the Dow-Jones Industrial Average) and banking integration (the BCCI scandal). On 18 October 1987 ('Black Monday') Wall Street experienced its largest one-day fall in stock prices in US history, triggering large-scale disinvestment from US equities and a crisis in equity markets worldwide. Stock exchanges around the world suffered large losses in the value of their stocks in the wake of the US crash.
14. Kyriazis and Chryssanthou (1986: 25).
15. For further analysis of the impact of the Plaza Accord on the EC see Kyriazis and Chryssanthou (1956).
16. Cafruny (1989: 118).
17. Thygesen (1986: 17).
18. Gleske argues that inflationary forces and an expansionary US fiscal policy in the 1980s produced huge account deficits financed by imported capital, upset the savings–investment balance, and undermined the internal stability and strength of the dollar. As a result, an eroded dollar could no longer function as an anchor of stability for the international monetary system to the extent it did previously (Gleske, 1990: 13). According to Kashiwagi, in 1987 up to 62 per cent of the US current accounts deficit was financed by the inflow of private foreign capital. Although by the end of 1988 world foreign currency reserves included 63.3 per cent in US dollars, 16.2 per cent in German marks and 7.2 per cent in Japanese yen, the domination of the dollar has been steadily reduced and 'a secular trend toward a more diversified set of international currencies is unmistakable'. The US dollar share in international bond issues in 1989 was only one-half (Kashiwagi, 1990: 9).
19. There is already a trend for money managers to diversify their holdings between more currencies. This trend has benefited the EC at the expense of the US (Emerson and Huhne, 1991: 121).
20. Henning questions the seriousness of the Bush Administration with regard to G7 co-operation and the lack of interest in doing what is necessary to breathe meaning into G7's work., i.e. reducing the US budget deficit. Henning also states that the undisclosed but widely recognised currency target ranges of the G7 unravelled in 1989–90. Despite opportunities for co-ordinated action, the G7 responded belatedly and minimally to sizeable swings in interest rates. He sees no signs that G7 will shift away from a reactive to a forward-looking strategy (Henning, 1990: 20).
21. This section on the external implications of EMU is gleaned in part from predictions of Emerson and Huhne (1991), Stokes (1991), Thiel (1990), Henning (1990) and Pierre Ifri (1990).
22. US Trade Representative (1990).
23. In August 1991 the National Governors' Association (US) voted in support of the withdrawal of 'Buy American' or 'Buy Local' public

procurement requirements in response to the USTR's initiative to convince them that their interests lie in accessing the EC's public procurement market. The EC will only widen access to utilities contracts if US states permit foreigners to bid on state and local contracts. For more information see 'US Nearer to Dropping Buy Local Policy', *Financial Times*, 23 August 1991, p. 6.
24. Commission of the European Communities (1991).
25. Corn gluten feed is a high-fibre NGFI, a co-product of the maize refining process, used as a cheap animal feed.

REFERENCES

Ball, George W. (1976) *Diplomacy for a Crowded World* (Boston: Little, Brown).

Blake, David H. and Walters, Robert S. (1987) *The Politics of Global Economic Relations* (New York: Prentice-Hall).

Cafruny, Alan (1989) 'Economic Conflicts and the Transformation of the Atlantic Order', in Stephen Gill (ed.), *Atlantic Relations Beyond the Reagan Era* (New York: St Martin's).

Commission of the European Communities (1991) *Report on United States' Trade Barriers and Unfair Practices, 1991: The Problems of Doing Business with the US* (Brussels: Commission of the European Communities).

Czempiel, Ernst-Otto and Rustow, Dankwart A. (1976) *The Euro-American System: Economic and Political Relations Between North America and Western Europe* (Boulder: Westview).

Directorate-General for Information (1982) *The European Community and the United States* (Brussels: Commission of the European Communities).

Emerson, Michael and Huhne, Christopher (1991) *The ECU Report* (London: Pan).

European Communities, *General Report of the Activities of the European Communities* (Brussels: European Communities, 1972).

General Accounting Office (1990) *European Single Market: Issues of Concern to US Exporters* (Washington: GAO).

Gill, Stephen (ed.) (1989) *Atlantic Relations Beyond the Reagan Era* (New York: St Martin's).

Gilpin, Robert (1987) *The Political Economy of International Relations* (Princeton: Princeton University Press).

Ginsberg, Roy H. (1991) 'EC–US Political and Institutional Relations', in Leon Hurwitz and Christian Lequesne (eds), *The State of the European Community: Policies, Institutions, and Debates in the Transition Years* (Boulder: Lynne Rienner).

Ginsberg, Roy H. (1989a) *Foreign Policy Actions of the European Community: The Politics of Scale* (Boulder: Lynne Rienner).

Ginsberg, Roy H. (1989b) 'US–EC Relations', in Juliet Lodge (ed.), *The European Community and the Challenge of the Future* (New York: St Martin's).

Gleske, Leonhard (1990) 'Dollar–EMS–Yen: Changes in the Relationships', *Dollar–EMS–Yen: An Evolving Partnership* (Berlin: Japanisch-Deutsches Zentrum).

Goodman, Elliot R. (1978) 'The Impact of the Multinational Enterprise Upon the Atlantic Community', in G. Mally, *The New Europe and the United States: Partners or Rivals* (New York: Lexington Books).

Harrison, Glennon J. (1990) *European Community Trade and Investment with the United States: CRS Report for Congress*, 90–128 E (Washington: Congressional Research Service, 7 March).

Haus, Leah (1991) 'The East European Countries as the GATT', *International Organization*, vol. 45, no. 2.

Henning, C. Randall (1990) 'The United States and the Group of Seven', *Dollar–EMS–Yen: An Evolving Partnership* (Berlin: Japanisch–Deutsches Zentrum, 1990).

Ifri, Piere Jacquet (1990) 'EMS and EMU: The International Dimensions of European Economic and Monetary Integration', *Dollar–EMS–Yen: An Evolving Partnership* (Berlin: Japanisch–Deutsches Zentrum).

Jackson, James K. (1989) *The European Community's 1992 Plan: Effects on American Direct Investment* (Washington: Congressional Research Service, 2 June).

Jackson, James K. (1990) *Foreign Direct Investment: Why Companies Invest Abroad* (Washington: Congressional Research Service, 7 December).

Jackson, James K. (1991) *Foreign Direct Investment in the US: A Decade of Growth* (Washington: Congressional Research Service, 12 April).

Jannuzzi, Giovanni (1991) 'Europe and a Security Dimension', *NATO Review*, vol. 39, no. 2 (April) pp. 3–7.

Japanese–German Center (1990) *Dollar–EMS–Yen: An Evolving Partnership* (Berlin: Japanisch-Deutsches Zentrum).

Kashiwagi, Yusuke (1990) 'Multi-Currency Paradigm and the Future of the International Monetary Regime', in *Dollar–EMS–Yen: An Evolving Partnership* (Berlin: Japanisch–Deutsches Zentrum).

Krause, Laurence B. (1968) *European Economic Integration and the United States* (Washington: Brookings, 1968).

Kyriazis, Nicholas and Chryssanthou Nicholas (1986) *US–EC Monetary Relations: Research and Document Papers* (Luxemburg: European Parliament Secretariat).

Mally, George (1974) *The New Europe and the United States: Partners or Rivals* (New York: Lexington Books).

Milward, Alan S. (1984) *The Reconstruction of Western Europe, 1945–51* (Berkeley: University of California Press).

Morgan, Roger (1976) 'The Transatlantic Relationship', in Kenneth J. Twitchett (ed.), *Europe and the World: The External Relations of the Common Market*, (London: Europa).

Odell, John and Matzinger-Tchakerian Margot (1989) *EC Enlargement and the United States* (Pittsburgh: Pew Charitable Trust).

Schaetzel, J. Robert, Jr. (1975) *The Unhinged Alliance: America and the European Community* (New York: Harper and Rowe, 1975).

Spero, Joan Edelman (1990) *The Politics of International Economic Relations* (New York: St Martin's).

Stokes, Bruce (1991) 'Fading Greenback', *National Journal*, 12 December, pp. 3013–5.
Tarr, David G. (1988) 'The Steel Crisis in the US and EC', in Robert E. Baldwin, *et al.* (eds), *Issues in US–EC Trade Relations* (Chicago: University of Chicago Press, 1988).
Thiel, Elke (1983) 'Trade Conflicts and Western Cooperation', *German Foreign Affairs Review*, vol. 34 (4) pp. 372–81.
Thiel, Elke (1990) *Western European Economic and Monetary Integration and Atlantic Relations* (Washington: West European Studies Program, Wilson Center for International Scholars).
Thygesen, Niels (1986) 'Flexible Exchange Rates and National Monetary Policies, in Loukas Tsoukals (ed.), *Europe, America, and the World Economy* (Blackwell).
US International Trade Commission (1985) *Review of the Effectiveness of Trade Dispute Settlement Under the GATT and the Tokyo Round Agreements* (Washington: US International Trade Commission, December).
US International Trade Commission (1989) *The Effects of Greater Economic Integration Within the European Community on the United States* (Washington: US International Trade Commission, July 1989).
US International Trade Commission (1990a) *Operation of the Trade Agreements Program: 41st Report* (Washington: US International Trade Commission, 1990).
US International Trade Commission (1990b) *US Trade-Related Employment: 1978–84* (Washington: US International Trade Commission).
US International Trade Commission (1990c) *1992: The Effects of Greater Economic Integration Within the European Community on the United States, First Follow-Up Report* (Washington: US International Trade Commission, March).
US Trade Representative (1990) *1989 National Trade Estimate Report on Foreign Trade Barriers* (Washington: Office of the United States Trade Representative).
Warnecke, Steven J. (1976) 'The Political Implications of Trade of European-American Relations', in Ernst-Otto Czempiel and Dankwart A. Rustow (eds) *The Euro-American System: Economic and Political Relations Between North America and Western Europe* (Boulder: Westview).
Yannopoulos, George N. (1988) *Customs Unions and Trade Conflicts: The Enlargement of the European Community* (London: Routledge).

5 The Social Dimension

INTRODUCTION

While 'economic interdependence' is a term readily understood and often applied to US–EC relations, the contribution made by socio-cultural factors in international relations is often neglected. 'Social interdependence' has little meaning, yet few would deny that socio-cultural factors affect relations that are close enough to be termed 'interdependent'. Interdependence is an inherently multidimensional phenomenon: economic relations typically parallel political and social trends. Socio-cultural factors can greatly strengthen bilateral international ties. The postwar Atlantic alliance is frequently identified with common social and cultural heritages. But in the midst of the dramatic changes that have affected the international system at the start of the 1990s, how strong are the social foundations of the US–EC relationship? Are the two sides growing closer together or drawing apart?

This chapter focuses on the changing political culture of both the US and the EC nations. Bilateral contrasts are drawn between the US and the 'European' traditions: this allows the distinctiveness of the US to be highlighted. Intra-European contrasts are less relevant here, though they are certainly not denied. The concern is with general European patterns drawn from individual national circumstances. The chapter covers a variety of domestic factors affecting the relations between both sides.

'Political culture' is broadly conceived here: the analysis has four major components covering political development, transnational social trends, public policy traditions and public opinion. Firstly, the chapter contrasts the political development of the US from that experienced by Western Europe. It relates these long-term differences to evidence of current public attitudes. Secondly, the chapter considers the impact of shared socio-cultural changes on bilateral US–EC links. Thirdly, the analysis examines how contrasting domestic policy traditions affect US–EC relations, and give rise to transatlantic trade disputes. At the same time, evidence of 'policy transfer' is cited as a symptom of interdependence: both sides attempt to learn from each other's experiences. Fourthly, evidence of public support for US–EC relations is examined. To what extent does this offer a firm foundation for transatlantic co-operation? This series of comparisons allows conclusions to be drawn on how far domestic policial inputs might foster or hinder closer US–EC relations in the 1990s.

The evidence suggests a complex picture: a consequence no doubt of US–EC relations becoming more intense, but less unique. Differences of political culture might have been overlooked in the era of reconstruction, but in more recent years complex interdependence has given them a greater profile. Current policy differences often stem from long-term contrasts that seem set to endure. More importantly, closer economic interdependence means domestic policy differences become more consequential: mutual sensitivities arise from a broad range of policies. Socio-cultural changes apparent in the US and the EC are also felt in other Western nations. It is thus the West as a whole – covering the total OECD area – that is changing and drawing closer together. In cultural terms, the US may be closer to other nations than to those of the EC. At the level of the mass publics, both the US and the EC nations remain friends, yet both have found other friends further afield. As in other spheres, the ties have become less exclusive.

PATTERNS OF POLITICAL DEVELOPMENT

Contemporary politics owes much to long-term traditions. The distinctiveness of the United States's political development has been well-charted in earlier historical works. The relevance of such contrasts can easily be neglected, however, in discussions of US–EC relations. Moreover, old assumptions need updating to keep pace with changes in attitude, and new generations need to be reminded of the legacies of the past.

Initially, the 'first new nation' was built on values and practices brought over from Europe in the eighteenth century (to use Lipset's phrase: 1963). Yet, subsequently, the course taken by the US came to differ from that of Western Europe in a number of key aspects. By the late twentieth century, the 'Atlantic community' rested on the ambiguous foundations of partially shared values mixed with different conditions and experiences. To stretch Oscar Wilde's well-worn aphorism, the US and Western Europe had become two partners separated by 'common' values.

The US was founded on liberal values imported from seventeenth- and eighteenth-century Europe. Louis Hartz described this as 'an absolute and irrational . . . attachment' to the philosophy of John Locke (1955: 6). Yet US experience has differed substantially from that of Western Europe, prompting attention to its 'exceptionalism'. In the US the feudal and clerical oppressions of the Old World were non-existent (1955: 3). The absence of a feudal past in the US is used by Hartz and others to explain the lack of both a conservative and a socialist movement there. Without a feudal inheritance, neither reaction seemed relevant to US circumstances. Class-based politics never emerged as strongly as in Europe. The constraints and attacks on organised labour in the US may also have been 'exceptional', however (Sexton, 1991). In any event, the two dominant ideologies, 'American liberalism' and 'American conservatism', can be seen as variants of the European liberal philosophy imported by the Founding Fathers.

Liberalism had emerged from an Old World built on social conflict. When transplanted to the new world, however, it could flourish in a more harmonious environment. In eighteenth-century Europe, modernisation required the centralisation of the state and the supremacy of its authority in order to break with the feudal power structure (Hartz, 1955: 43). In the US, however, the absence of feudalism made the centralisation of power unnecessary at the founding of the new nation. With a stronger social consensus, government could remain divided. Few other nations have adopted the US model of a separation of powers (Huntington, 1968: 138). 'Divided societies', comments Huntington, 'cannot exist without centralised power; consensual societies cannot exist with it' (1968: 125). The new nation imported the principles of pre-modern Europe, especially Tudor England, where 'harmony and unity (had) made it unnecessary to fix sovereignty in any particular institution' (1968: 124). Indeed, without the constraints of feudalism, only the power of government might coerce the individual. It therefore had to be limited, to give freedom from government. This left the freedom of the individual as the prime political value.

The liberal absolutism of the new nation created a pervasive 'American ideology'. Those who reject its values are 'un-American', in a manner other Western nations cannot understand (Hartz, 1955: 11–12). As Hofstadter has commented, 'It has been our fate as a nation not to have ideologies but to be one' (cited in Lipset, 1990: 19). Antistatism left only the law sovereign, creating a legalistic and litigious culture.

Antistatism and the assertion of individual rights also meant a *laissez-faire economy.* Moreover, antistatism has existed alongside a stronger affirmation of the values of capitalism than has been the case in post-war Europe. US elites and the mass public have generally been more comfortable with the operation of the market than have their European counterparts. The US political culture has not displayed the same urge to 'manage capitalism'.[1]

Individualism in a growing economy fostered the belief that the US was a land of opportunity, based on meritocracy rather than privilege. Individualism has affected even radical opinion in the US, which has been more sympathetic to anarchism, syndicalism and libertarianism than to the state (Lipset, 1990: 27). The belief in individual opportunity and limited government has meant there has been much less support for welfare and redistributive policies than is typically found in Europe. There is a strong commitment to equal opportunity, but this is to be in the competition of a *laissez-faire* economy, and not via strong government.

Many writers have also noted a heavily populist strain in the American ideology, emanating from a belief in the sovereignty of the people. This has led to an explosion of elections: according to Lipset, there were some 504,404 elected public officials in the US in 1987. Yet, participation (turnout) in elections remains exceptionally low. Overall, the inclusiveness of the American ideology has fostered a popular pride in what 'the First New Nation' stands for, making it a more patriotic society than is typically found today in Western Europe (Lipset, 1963; Inglehart, 1990). Indeed, the belief in limited government generally coexists with a relatively strong sense of civic pride: the reverse condition to that found in some southern European political cultures in recent times (cf. Almond and Verba, 1965).

The dominance of shared values has not been without challenge, however. Racism sustained slavery at home beyond the time when the major European powers had abandoned it abroad. Hartz notes, however, that the South fought the Civil War claiming to defend liberal values rather than those of racism (1955: 168). Yet, racism also denied civil rights in the South until the 1960s. Some radicals define racism as being part of the American ideology (Dolbeare and Edelman, 1974). Today, the US continues to face the challenge of the politics of race, as it also responds to new issues based on gender and on ecology. Each set of issues also forms part of the current agenda of European polities, but differences in history give them a distinct setting and interpretation in the US.

Of course, to argue that the US experience has been distinct is not to suggest that there has been a uniform pattern of political development in Europe. Important contrasts can be drawn between the European nations. The conception of the state has taken various forms, for example. Dyson has contrasted the 'Anglo-American' tradition from that of the rest of Europe, in this respect. The conception of the 'state' is alien to the Anglo-American experience (Dyson, 1980: 4). The British state tradition could thus be regarded as a middle-case placed between those of the US and continental Europe.[2] Moreover, further differentiation could be drawn between the state traditions in France and Germany, and between northern and southern Europe.

Yet, in a study of US–EC relations, it is the differences in political development between the US and Western Europe which are of most concern. Hartz, Huntington, Lipset and others distinguish the US experience from that of European nations in general. In a number of important respects there are discernable differences in political attitudes, ideology, organisation and policy approach between the US on the one hand and most of Western Europe on the other. Even with respect to the role of the state, general bilateral contrasts can be drawn in terms of market intervention and corporatist traditions. The values of the free economy, individualism and limited state welfare are stronger in the US than in Western Europe. Such differences still find expression in bilateral trade disputes and contrasting public attitudes.

Today public opinion continues to display differences of attitude across the Atlantic on a range of issues, which can be explained, in part by the contrasts in historical development between the US and Western Europe. Survey evidence illustrates these divergences. In a report based on polls conducted in 1987, Smith contrasted the public attitudes existing in the US and Australia with those found in five European nations (Smith, 1989). His findings are summarised in Table 5.1. He reported a greater affinity between the US and Australia than between the US and the EC nations. Public opinion in the US and Australia was more hostile to redistributive programmes carried out by government. Americans and Australians were also much more optimistic about their own chances of achieving economic success. It was the evaluation of inequality that varied enormously: how unfair it was felt to be, and whether it was the job of government to do something about it. Interestingly, class differences seemed to play

TABLE 5.1   *Public attitudes towards inequality and welfare**

	Support for welfare state[†] (%)	Support government action to reduce income inequalities (%)	Agree that 'people like me have a good chance of improving standard of living' (%)
Hungary	79	77	33
Italy	76	81	43
West Germany	64	56	36
Britain	63	63	36
Netherlands	60	64	23
Australia	42	42	58
USA	38	28	71

* The surveys were conducted in 1987.
† Combines responses to five different questions on a similar theme.

SOURCE   See T. W. Smith article in R. Jowell (1989: 59–77).

little part: in Europe, both middle and working-class respondents were more in favour of welfare and redistribution than were their counterparts in the US and Australia. To Smith,

> the lower level of support among Americans for redistributive measures, and the relatively greater enthusiasm for measures that allow scope for individual opportunity, suggest that an ideology of opportunity plays a key role. Australians also . . . appear to conform to this pattern. Given their similarities as 'pioneering' and 'immigrant' nations, one might wonder whether the experience of nation-building or the influx of immigrants in search of a better life (or both), might have helped to create an enduring ethos of 'individualism'. In contrast, citizens of Hungary and (Britain, West Germany, Italy, and the Netherlands) are more supportive of an egalitarian ideology, and of government programmes designed to lessen inequality and provide for at least some of the citizen's basic needs . . . we have also found that those nations with well-established welfare states are more in favour of welfare state provision. In that sense we are all products of our experience (Smith in Jowell, 1989: 74).

Lipset also noted these differences of attitude:

> The United States continues to be exceptional among developed
> nations in the low level of support it provides for the poor in
> welfare, housing and medical care. As a result, though the weal-
> thiest country in the world, the proportion of its people living in
> poverty is the highest among the developed nations . . . (Lipset,
> 1990: 39).

Contrasts in the 'ideology of opportunity', and in attitudes towards
inequality and the role of the state, can be explained by reference to
the differing patterns of historical development outlined earlier.

Yet these differences in public values ought not to be exaggerated.
Evidence drawn from other spheres suggests counter-trends. In the
same volume as Smith's report, Taylor-Gooby concluded from his
own survey work that the Atlantic nations shared a broad public
consensus on basic principles of economic policy (Taylor-Gooby,
1989: 51). The public seemed to reject ideas of radical economic
change, be they of the left or the right. Analyses of electoral behaviour have also noted similarities in recent trends on both sides of
the Atlantic. The party identification of voters is weakening as they
focus more on individual issues (Crewe and Denver, 1985). Recent
political activity has centred on new social movements and forms of
political action (based on women's rights, peace, the environment)
much more than in the past, when political parties played a more
dominant role (Inglehart, 1977). The fact that movements promoting
these issues can be identified both in the US and in most of the
Western European countries indicates the existence of common social trends.

Changes at a more general level are said to be affecting both sets of
nations, as well as others. 'Post-Fordism' refers to a transition in
advanced industrial societies from the old structures of mass production (as used by Ford) to a new pattern of social organisation,
involving diverse economic, social and political changes (Stoker,
1990; Jessop, 1988). Such changes range from the impact of new
technology, the increased importance of the service sector, a growth
in small and medium-sized companies, and more flexible patterns of
production. These economic changes have various social and political
effects: for example, in patterns of work and also in the role of the
state. The transition to post-Fordism is seen as being gradual and as
yet incomplete. Evidence for its existence, however, is drawn directly

from the current experience of the US and the Western European nations: both sides of the Atlantic are said to be displaying similar developmental trends. Yet, this experience is shared not only by the Atlantic nations but also more generally by most advanced Western economies. In not being exclusive to the US–EC nations, its impact on their relations remains unclear.

An equally general shift in political culture may be occurring in each of the advanced economies. Inglehart has charted such common trends in Western societies: firstly towards 'post-materialism' and more recently in the direction of a broader 'syndrome of cultural change' (1977, 1990). In the past few decades, economic, technological and sociopolitical changes have been gradually transforming the political cultures of the advanced industrial nations. The public is placing a greater emphasis on the quality of life and they are also becoming more skilful in a political sense. According to Inglehart,

> The implications are far-reaching. Cultural change is shaping both the economic growth rates of societies and the kind of economic development they are pursuing. It is reshaping the social bases of political conflict, the reasons people support political parties, the kinds of parties they support, and the ways in which they try to attain their political goals. It is also changing population growth rates, family structure, and church attendance rates (1990: 4).

Each of these changes is affecting Western nations to varying degrees.

It would thus be wrong to ignore the dynamism in modern societies. Western nations have experienced profound changes since 1945: economically, socially and politically. Further, they have also displayed some important common trends. Social interactions between nations have greatly increased (cf. Taylor and Hudson, 1972). A high proportion of the various national populations have travelled to foreign countries, and many have foreign ties. Popular culture has become more transnational, partly as a result of technological change, but also because of shared experiences. The US has been the most dynamic society of all and also the most economically powerful. Its international influence has served to promote a transnational culture that accepts change. Parallel changes have occurred in Western Europe and the US; in some instances there have probably been reciprocal influences across the Atlantic. Reference to the '1960s culture' or the spirit of 1968 evokes common understanding across the Western world. In television, films, pop music, fashions, student culture, personal health and fitness and many more areas, Western societies have increasingly shared common products and experiences. Indeed, it is tempting to deny centripetal social trends at all when the world is watching *Dallas* on television or listening to a world-wide pop concert.

Yet these social trends are common to most Western societies, not just the US or the nations of the EC. Their effect may not make the US–EC relationship exceptional in the context of the Western world as a whole. Transnationalism here is a broad phenomenon. Moreover, common cultural changes may not easily overcome differences in political attitudes. While culture may becoming more transnational, political attitudes continue to display major differences in distinct settings: a phenomenon of fundamental importance (Hartz, 1964). Different public policy traditions persist. Governments continue to set varying agendas and approach common problems differently. Clashes of attitude and policy endure between the US and the EC governments.

Current changes in the international system might lead to an increasing divergence. Vlahos has argued that it was the cold war which allowed the US to assert its cultural influence over the rest of the world (1991). With the demise of the cold war, he argues, there has emerged a greater independence on the part of other, distinct 'culture-areas'. Neither the Europeans nor the Japanese ever believed in 'the West': they had no choice other than to mouth the rhetoric. 'Now they do' have a choice, however, and that is 'to go their own ways and assert their own culture-area independence' (Vlahos, 1991: 61). The new world order will be dominated by three culture areas (the US–Canada, Western Europe and Japan) but 'at best they will be associates, not friends' (Vlahos, 1991: 68).

There is some inconsistency and exaggeration in such arguments, however. Vlahos concentrates on the 'West' and neglects the influence of culture-areas based on the former Soviet Union or China, for example, which may also be important in an interdependent world. He dismisses the importance of international media and communication encouraging convergence among 'culture-areas' (1991: 69), but he suggests that these same factors have promoted a greater homogeneity within the US itself (1991: 77). Moreover, the assertion of ethnic and cultural diversity in Eastern Europe should not obscure other, wider trends. Vlahos's culture-areas may be less distinct today than, for example, sixty years ago. He does not succeed in proving the opposite.

Socio-cultural explanations are an important element in understanding the domestic context within which policies are formulated.
Inglehart, for example, stresses that culture 'is an essential causal
element that helps shape society' and one that is often underestimated (1990: 14). Yet socio-cultural explanations have limitations in
accounting for specific policy outcomes or for policy differences between nations. By their very nature, socio-cultural explanations
relate to general-level phenomena, rather than to the particular
characteristics of the public policy process.

The contrasting forms of political development between the US
and the EC nations highlight other features of relevance here: differences in the role of the state, the impact of ideology, the strength of
organised labour and of social democracy, among others. Such features are compatible with other explanations for policy differences.
Various approaches exist to 'comparative public policy' (Heidenheimer *et al.*, 1990: 7–9). Approaches stressing the importance of
party government, the strength of organised labour, neo-corporatism
and the position of the state in society each help to account for the
continuing differences in the policy traditions found among the US
and the EC nations. In each of these societies, the public policy
process is likely to be diversified and complex: not only between
sectors but also within the same sector. Different types of policy can
also promote different kinds of policy process. Richardson *et al.* have
discussed the extent to which national processes might reflect a
collective 'policy style' (Richardson, 1982). There may be a common
European 'policy style', but national processes are likely to change
and vary over relatively short periods. The EC itself hardly exhibits a
uniform policy style, as noted in Chapter 2. In sum, the concept of
policy style remains loosely formulated.

Differences between national settings are important: the distinction between foreign and domestic policy is increasingly blurred in a
world of interdependence. As Katzenstein has noted, 'To a greater
extent than in the 1950s and 1960s the strategies of foreign economic
policy of advanced industrial states now reflect their domestic structures . . . the divergences in foreign economic policies in the 1970s is
due principally to differences in domestic structures' (Katzenstein,
1978: 297). Moreover, change in foreign economic policy 'partly
results from conflict in domestic politics' (Katzenstein, 1978: 22).

Yet, the explanation for policy differences among nations (and
between the US and the EC) will be complex and multifaceted.
Charting trends based on a single variable risks neglecting other

important factors (Heidenheimer *et al.*, 1990: 9). Aspects of long-term development need to be combined with short-term and specific characteristics. An all-encompassing analysis is beyond the scope of this study. Progress can be made, however, by relating the long-term patterns of political development to specific examples of policy differences between the US and the EC. This will illustrate how and why policy differences have arisen, without purporting to establish a full explanation.

PUBLIC POLICY: CONFLICT AND LEARNING

In the sphere of public policy, the US and the EC nations exhibit contradictory trends. Differences in their respective public policy traditions are manifest; they cannot be easily set aside. In an increasingly interdependent world, domestic policies have external implications which affect trade and investment flows. Much publicity is given to disputes based on issues of market access, yet such clashes contrast with cases of one side 'copying' policies from the other. For example, the US and the EC nations do make attempts to learn from each other's domestic policy experiences. Such interactions are a further manifestation of the multiple channels associated with interdependent relations. Thus before examining how and why differences in domestic policies affect bilateral relations it is instructive to consider the nature of such bureaucratic exchanges.

Interactions between nations prompt a learning process on the part of a variety of actors. Both Keohane and Nye (1987) and Haas (1991) have emphasised the importance of this process, as have others (Lasswell, 1951). Elite perceptions of national interests affect foreign policies; these perceptions are themselves shaped by political cultures and subcultures. Yet the learning process also involves bureaucracies in one nation borrowing policies from their counterparts in another national setting. Where such policy borrowing occurs, it can be assumed that it has important consequences for transnational understanding and that it offers scope for policy collaboration. Unfortunately, the learning process in general, and the phenomenon of policy borrowing in particular, has been a neglected area of research in international relations.

With respect to policy borrowing, the more general process of transfer can be distinguished from that of diffusion. The latter 'consists of the communication of a new idea in a social system over time'

(Gray, 1973: 1175). Policy transfer involves not only the borrowing of specific policy designs by public officials in distinct national settings, but also the process by which different concepts and approaches are learned (Wolman, 1990). In the context of urban policy studies, focusing on the US and the UK, Wolman has concluded that 'Policy transfer is not an isolated endeavour, but an integral part of the policy development process' within national bureaucracies (1990: 25).

Though not a new phenomenon, policy transfers among Western nations, including the US and the EC, may be on the increase. A number of writers suggest this as a consequence of growing interdependence (Wolman, 1990; Heidenheimer *et al.*, 1990: 2; Heclo, 1974; Waltman, 1980). The nature of the policy transfer process, particularly between the US and the EC nations, almost certainly remains 'unsystematic and unstructured' (Wolman, 1990: 18). The process is neither one of perfect fungibility nor of perfect blockage, rather it is conditional, comments Wolman,

> Policymakers thus learn about the policies of other countries through trips abroad by individual ministers and civil servants (sometimes for general reconnaissance purposes and sometimes organised around a specific problem or policy); more formal fact-finding missions, usually by groups of civil servants; reports from civil servants who participate in formal exchange programmes involving a stay of substantial duration in another country; formal and informal contacts with foreign visitors; and, advice and information from academics, think tanks, consultants, and journalists, both through personal contact and through reading their reports, articles, and books. (Wolman, 1990: 16)

Evidence of the patterns of policy transfer is very limited; in the absence of further research there is only speculation. It would be useful to know the scope of policy transfer between the US and France or Germany, for example. Valuable historical trends could be charted. Moreover, the EC nations as a group have undoubtedly become closer and more interconnected in this respect. Further, the US and the EC do not only seek to learn from each other: both have been attracted by the economic success of Japan, for example. Policy transfer is important: a key assumption is that there is a sufficient convergence of national circumstances to justify a transfer. Policy transfer may foster a recognition of interdependence and a will to collaborate. As a phenomenon, policy transfer falls outside the purview of realism or neo-mercantilism: it does elaborate, however, on the processes of interdependence.

In contrast to such cases of domestic policy transfers and convergence are the better-known examples of external trade conflict between the US and the EC. It is in the sphere of agricultural trade that most of the serious US–EC disputes have occurred. After 1958 the EEC quickly developed its Common Agricultural Policy (CAP) to encourage domestic production and to ensure a fair income for farmers (Marsh and Swanney, 1980). The CAP combines internal market support to ensure food security, with protection against cheap imports and subsidies for exports. By the 1970s the CAP was increasingly criticised as an expensive mechanism for collecting and dumping surpluses, and one which was not doing enough to restructure the EC's agricultural production. The consequences of the CAP for US farmers were that it challenged their historic market shares in the EC and, later, in increasingly competitive third markets (notably in North Africa, the Middle and Far East, and in the USSR). Chapter 4 discussed the evolution of disputes between the US and the EC in agriculture.

In reality, the EC has not been alone in offering massive subsidies to farmers. OECD calculations of the percentage of farmers' incomes that come from direct subsidies and from protection against imports suggest levels of 30 per cent in the US, 48 per cent in the EC and 68 per cent in Japan in 1990 (*Financial Times*, 5 June 1991). The US at one stage sought to match EC subsidies: both the US and the EC have spent billions of dollars on grain export subsidies.[3]

US policy in agriculture has differed from that of the EC. It is not designed to support rural development and employment, nor does it guarantee a return on the costs of production for items covered under price supports. Instead, US farm policy seeks to enable farmers to meet production costs through price supports, as well as set aside, storage and other programmes. To meet the competition from EC producers in certain third-country markets, the US government offers an export enhancement programme. US food aid is an important purchaser of farm products (through Public Law 48). US agricultural policy is thus not enmeshed with social objectives. The number of US farmers has dropped sharply over the last twenty years, so that they now represent 2.9 per cent of the US workforce (*Basic Statistics of the EC*, 1988). In the EC, the proportion of workers employed in agriculture across the member states varies between 2.2 per cent in the UK and 20.7 per cent in Portugal (*Basic Statistics of the EC*, 1988).

Agriculture has long played a special economic, social and political role in Europe. The CAP developed with the legacy of starvation and shortages still fresh in the minds of policy-makers. Economic security interests encouraged market intervention. French farmers also needed new markets for their produce. Farmers are an important part of the social structure of their local communities. From the start, the CAP was seen as having a social as well as an economic role. It should provide farmers with decent incomes comparable with those of their manufacturing counterparts, and it should offer a planned management of the shift of workers from agriculture into urban employment. Still in the 1990s, subsidising farmers is seen by policy-makers in many EC states as 'taking from the rich and giving to the poor'. Even in Germany, efforts to reform agriculture by the EC have been mitigated by increased domestic state help. A 1991 GATT study reported that Germany had adjusted VAT rates and greatly expanded federal aid to 'disadvantaged regions' which made up half its total agricultural area: the effect was to further favour agriculture (*Financial Times*, 17 April 1991). In addition, the electoral influence of farmers is much larger than their numbers might suggest. This affects not only local and national politicians wary of a voter backlash, but also Commissioners and Members of the European Parliament. The establishment of a common policy for agriculture has created, moreover, a powerful lobby organisation (Committee of Professional Agricultural Organisations (COPA)) which is able to doggedly promote its vested interests at the EC level. The CAP turned into a 'sacred cow' as the symbolic foundation of European economic integration, buttressed by a panoply of different interests. Even when the issue of agricultural subsidies threatened the GATT Uruguay Round trade negotiations in 1990–91, the EC maintained its resolve and defended the CAP. The policy has taken deep root.

European agriculture is a prime example of domestic constraints prompting conflict in international trade. The policy philosophy behind the CAP rests on intervention to regulate the market, to produce not only economic gains but also social benefits as well. It is the result of a long tradition of protection, prompted by state paternalism and mixed with a little electoral populism. It is the sector least affected by the urban bourgeois revolution of liberal economics. Though at various stages the US has also given huge help to agriculture, the long-term uniqueness of the CAP is symptomatic of the differences between the respective policy environments that exist in the US and the EC.

A second area of conflict has concerned US–EC trade in steel. Again, differences in domestic policies have been cited as affecting fair trade; the domestic environment has external consequences. The European Coal and Steel Community (ECSC) originated from the desire to take iron, steel and coal policy out of the hands of national governments so as to promote the interests of peace on the continent. A common system of market intervention and regulation was the specific European response to the experience of war. From the start, the ECSC was 'not based on free trade principles' (Messerlin, 1986: 36). The ECSC Treaty gives the EC Commission considerable powers over investments by companies, state aids, production levels and selling prices. Such powers are far more extensive than those available to the US administration. The Commission also has the financial capacity to provide limited aid for the modernisation of the steel industry, the retraining of redundant workers and regional redevelopment. EC steel policy from the beginning has thus had a political and social dimension as well an economic one. Amid the crisis in the steel industry, following the 'oil shock' of 1973–4, the EC adopted 'a variety of measures to protect, restructure and cartelise the industry' (Crandall, 1986: 34). The Commission acted as the head office for the EC steel cartel: it 'became a prisoner of the very cartel it created, providing a new example of the well-known role of the "regulator regulated"' (Messerlin in Tsoukalis, 1986: 40).

During the 1970s and 1980s, the US and the EC pursued 'two diametrically opposed approaches to the same fundamental industrial problems' in steel (Benyon, 1986: 47). Unlike the EC, the US administration chose

to avoid government-established rationalisation cartels. There are no minimum prices, no direct government subsidies, no forced rationalisations and no incentives to reduce employment. Rather, the US government has been a passive recipient of difficult foreign trade suits from which it must continually extricate itself. (Crandall in Tsoukalis, 1986: 29)

The nature of the US–EC steel disputes was discussed in Chapter 4. US policy under Reagan involved managing an import cartel. In October 1989 the US and the EC agreed new quota arrangements guaranteeing European exporters a 7 per cent share of the US market.

As with agriculture, the case of steel illustrates highly contrasting policy approaches between the US and the EC. On the European side, both sectors involve EC– level regulation, rather than national government autonomy. Like agriculture, steel has been one of the cornerstones of the European integration process. Domestic political and social pressures have fundamentally shaped the EC's policies in both areas. As a result, the integration process has been bound up with managing markets in order to achieve desired objectives. For its part, the EC Commission has been given the major role in matching domestic pressures to external trade flows, allowing it to affect both the internal and world markets.

The cases of both agriculture and steel have arisen in the context of a more pervasive difference between the US and at least most EC states with regard to economic planning and market intervention. In the US, 'only in wartime has the national government been equipped with tools for detailed economic intervention' (Heidenheimer *et al.*, 1990: 155). It has found it expedient to rescue particular sectors from financial crisis (Lockheed, Chrysler, savings and loans associations) but these have been isolated actions. Some interventionist programs have a long history: federal military support for R and D, and 'a broad range of regulatory, tax, credit, subsidy, and other instruments' at federal and state level to effect the market (Heidenheimer *et al.*, 1990: 155). None of this, however, adds up to active state intervention on behalf of a 'coherent industrial policy' (Heidenheimer *et al.*, 1990: 155). Unlike most EC governments, the US does not have a member of the Cabinet responsible for public policy in this area.

Though the contrasts with the US are far from uniform or stable, EC governments have generally pursued a very different approach to industrial policy. The European economic structure differs from that of the US. Despite a recent trend towards 'privatisation', two of the top ten EC companies in 1989 were state-owned (IRI: Instituto per la Riconstruzione Industriale in Italy and Deutsche Bundespost in Germany) and other public sector firms also figured prominently (ENI: Ente Nazionale Idrocarburi in Italy and Elf Aquitaine in France) (*The Times 1000*, 1989). Data illustrating the differences in the role of the public sector are given in Tables 5.2 and 5.3 (size of public sector; the scope of public utilities). Of the four largest EC states, France and Italy remain the most statist in their domestic economic policy. Greece, Portugal and Spain have also had strong statist traditions, however. In France, *dirigisme* (state direction of economic activity) has involved both indicative economic planning and extensive public ownership (Wright, 1989: 101–108). In Italy, the partitocrazia (party

TABLE 5.2 *Size of general government as a percentage of GDP*

	Total expenditure	
	1985	1989
Denmark	59.3	59.9
Netherlands	59.6	56.9
Greece	48.1	53.9
Belgium	55.8	51.2
Italy	50.8	51.2
Luxembourg	51.1	51.1
France	52.1	49.8
W. Germany	47.5	45.1
Ireland	53.7	44.3
Portugal	43.5	41.7
Spain	42.1	40.7
UK	44.1	37.1
EC12	49.0	46.3
USA*	20.1	19.8

* US figures are based on GNP not GDP.

SOURCES *European Economy*, 2 February 1990; US figures adapted from Hall (1991: 43–4) and Barron *et al.* (1989: 25)

state) exerts its influence through major state holding companies (ENI, IRI) and other undertakings (LaPalombara, 1987).

Yet contrasts can also be drawn between both the UK and Germany, and the US. Katzenstein has noted the similarities in UK and US external trading policies and domestic economic controls (1978: 20–1). The domestic UK tradition is quite distinct, however: corporatism in Britain in the 1970s was very different from US experience and, while the Thatcher governments of the 1980s sought to imitate US conditions, Britain in the 1990s is increasingly subject to common EC policies. West Germany (prior to unification in 1990) was close to the UK position in external trade questions in the EC, but its '*sozialmarktwirtschaft*' (social market economy) created a very different business environment from that associated with neo-liberalism. Extensive legal controls, codetermination in industry, and wide-ranging welfare provision contrast the German situation with that of the US. Moreover, 'it would be wrong to conclude that Germany resembles the approach of the United States in its instruments of economic management' (Heidenheimer *et al.*; 1990: 157).

TABLE 5.3 *Extent of public ownership in key industries, by country: figures below show the extent of public enterprise as a percentage of each industry*

	Post	Telecom	Electricity	Gas	Oil	Coal	Rail	Air	Car*	Steel	Shipbuilding
United States	90	0	25	0	0	0	25	0	0	0	0
Canada	100	25	100	0	0	0	75	75	0	0	0
Japan	100	33	0	0	n.a.	0	25	0	0	0	0
Germany	100	100	75	50	25	50	100	100	25	0	25
France	100	100	100	100	n.a.	100	100	75	50	75	0
Italy	100	100	75	100	n.a.	n.a.	100	100	25	75	75
UK	100	0	100	25	25	100	100	0	0	75	50

* Motor industry as a whole.

SOURCE OECD data reported in *Financial Times*, 12 February 1991.

Set against this background, policies at the levels of both the EC Commission and the EC national governments have targeted certain domestic industries so as to improve their competitive position and structure.[4] The EC Commission targets coal and steel, but traditionally where significant targeting has existed it has almost always been carried out by the national governments (USITC Report, 1984). The EC Commission has the authority to disapprove state aids to industry if these distort competition within the Community. EC national governments have been allowed to target several declining industries (shipbuilding, textiles, clothing and cars), and they have agreed programmes to boost the international competitiveness of Community firms in high-technology industries (aircraft, computers and telecommunications equipment). The EC itself funds research and development projects, in whole or in part, over a range of sectors.[5] The French government has traditionally been most active in targeting: it has used government ownership, financial subsidies, cash grants and, in a much less specific manner, tax policy (USITC Report, 1984). It has also been one of the strongest advocates of targeting being conducted at the EC level, a trend reinforced by Edith Cresson as Prime Minister in 1991–2.[6] Overall, the existing targeting policies of the EC and its member governments again reflect the stronger European desire to 'manage capitalism'.

Yet state intervention poses particular problems for foreign trade and investment. Public subsidies can distort international competition, protectionism can bar foreign access to markets, company law can be used to hinder domestic acquisitions by foreign companies, and high company taxation levels can affect investment plans. Recent examples illustrate the relevance of these effects, which contrast domestic objectives with external trade consequences. The Mitterrand administration's approach to the public sector in France has brought it into repeated conflict with the EC Commission, which has effective regulatory powers over competition policy. The administration fought a long-running (though unsuccessful) battle with the EC Commission at the end of the 1980s to subsidise the Renault car firm and thereby improve its competitive position. In 1991, a series of fresh initiatives provoked the EC Commission to scrutinise French action: firstly over government plans to invest $976 million in the Thomson and Groupe Bull companies, and secondly as a result of a government bid to merge Commissariat à l'Energie Atomique (the nuclear energy group) with Thomson Consumer Electronics and SGS-Thomson (consumer electronics and semiconductor groups) to create a giant high-technology concern under majority state own-ership. The EC Commission was concerned that these moves might involve unfair competition as a result of state aid (*Financial Times*, 8 April 1991; *Independent*, 20 December 1991). Six French state com-panies also faced charges in 1991 of chanelling funds to smaller companies in depressed regions in order to help boost their economic prospects (*European*, 26–28 April 1991). Such aid policies distort internal competition within the EC and also external trade. Other national differences also affect competition. The EC nations have very different legal provisions governing domestic acquisitions by foreign firms. Under the internal market programme, the EC Com-mission plans to reduce this variation; but what access might be given for non-EC predator companies remains unclear. Similarly, US firms have lobbied very strongly for open access to the public procurement market in the EC after its liberalisation (Featherstone, 1990: 165–9).

Thus, by its very nature, state intervention can restrain inter-national competition and provoke trade disputes between the US and the EC. 'Internal' economic policies have 'external' implications: the distinction between the domestic and the international system is less sharply focused in a world of interdependence. The contrast between 'high' and 'low' politics is also less meaningful. The differences of policy approach reflect enduring values and traditions, as suggested by the contrasts in their forms of political development. Whatever the differences within Europe, the EC and the US have developed distinct sets of policy choices in contrasting environments, which have significant external consequences for their bilateral economic relations.

PUBLIC ATTITUDES

So far, the focus has been on differences between national (and regional) contexts, but what of attitudes towards bilateral co-operation? To what extent might public opinion serve to enhance or hinder closer US–EC relations? The role of public opinion in this regard is a complex phenomenon: it both affects and is itself affected by foreign policy. The attitudes and influence of elites may be more influential, though little research has been undertaken on this in recent years in both the US and the EC (cf. Lerner and Gorden, 1969). Yet survey evidence of popular attitudes can also act as a bar-ometer to suggest the scope for either co-operation or estrangement.

Here, evidence of public attitudes towards US–EC relations will be analysed both historically and between national settings. The focus is first on European views of the US, and then on US attitudes towards the EC and the European nations.

EUROPEAN ATTITUDES TOWARDS THE US

In the post-war era, the most significant contrasts in European attitudes towards the USA have been between France, on the one hand, and most of her neighbours, on the other. For much of the period, French public opinion has been noticeably less sympathetic to the United States than have its British, German or Italian counterparts. However, during the 1980s these differences were noticeably reduced, partly as a result of an increase in pro-American attitudes in France, and partly because of increased criticism elsewhere of US defence policy. Survey data illustrating these trends are given in Table 5.4; the data cover the period 1954–87.

The attitudes of the French public can be differentiated not only over time, but also by reference to the impact of other national images. Rupnik and Humbertjean (1990) have charted the evolution of French attitudes and have explained that

Thirty years ago the French were not only the most anti-American people in Europe, they were also the most pro-Soviet. Today's anti-Sovietism is accompanied by a refurbishment of the USA's image which would seem to be unique in Europe. (1990: 81)

They also suggest that

The attitudes towards the USSR and the USA at the time of the Liberation was [sic] marked by an inferiority complex. Sixties' anti-Americanism had more to do with a certain idea of 'grandeur'. The recent decline in anti-American feeling goes hand in hand with a more realistic image of France's position in the world. (1990: 83)

French public attitudes – and indeed party and elite opinion – have oscillated between aversion and fascination, support and hostility, with respect to the US.

Certainly, after the initial euphoria of liberation had abated,

TABLE 5.4   *Public attitudes in Western Europe towards the USA, 1954–87*

Figures show percentage favourable minus percentage unfavourable to the question 'Do you have a very good, good, neither good nor bad, bad or very bad opinion of the United States?'

Nation	1954	1955	1956	1957	1958	1959	1960	1961
West Germany	57	56	55	58	65	65	65	71
Britain	40	54	51	41	52	65	49	56
Italy	49	57	65	62	53	68	57	53
France	0	17	6	4	23	31	33	42

	1962	1963	1964	1965	1969	1971	1972	1973
West Germany	68	75	84	73	63	51	46	45
Britain	52	44	66	57	41	37	49	—
Italy	61	68	74	62	52	—	60	57
France	36	36	41	28	38	32	38	—

	1976	1978	1981	1982	1984	1985	1987
West Germany	50	81	45	43	37	37	42
Britain	24	63	14	20	20	37	40
Italy	25	64	39	39	31	47	48
France	28	49	31	25	18	31	37

SOURCE   R. Inglehart (1990: 394). Taken from surveys conducted by the US Information Agency, and Eurobarometer (EC).

French public attitudes in the 1950s became distinctly less favourable to the United States. French public support for the Atlantic Alliance from the 1940s to the 1960s remained low and there was little recognition of common interests with the US. Opinion of the USA was barely more favourable than that towards the USSR. By contrast, French attitudes towards the USA became much more positive in the early 1980s, just as the opinion of the Soviet Union declined. Somewhat surprisingly, this shift occurred during the relatively 'hawkish' presidency of Ronald Reagan.

Public opinion in Britain prior to the 1980s was typically much more pro-American and anti-Soviet than were popular attitudes in France. Support for Atlanticism was relatively high, while the Soviet Union was distrusted. Some sections of British public opinion turned more critical of the US during the Vietnam War era, but this only had a limited impact on overall levels of support. UK support ebbed after Watergate and defeat in Vietnam in the mid-1970s, and more noticeably during Reagan's term of office in the 1980s. Prior to the 1980s, British public attitudes were largely compatible with the actual policies pursued by successive UK governments: Thatcher's support for Reagan's foreign policies, by contrast, created a more significant divergence, as Atlanticism had by then become more controversial.

For much of the post-war period, the highest levels of public support for the US were found in West Germany. As noted in Chapter 3, Atlanticism became a cornerstone of the new nation's foreign policy under Adenauer. It was not until the 1970s that these values were challenged. In the 1980s, the NATO decision to place intermediate-range nuclear missiles in West Germany met with strong popular protests, as the peace movement opposed Reagan's 'new cold war'.

A similar trend to that found in both Britain and West Germany is recorded in Italy. Public opinion on the US has fluctuated. Yet the general level of support is much lower from 1976 onwards than in the previous two decades. Christian Democratic governments have consistently supported the general aims of US policy in Europe, but in the early Reagan years Italian voters appeared to share the concerns of others that Washington was threatening the prospects for peace.

The evidence presented here of public support in Europe for the US suggests a notable general decline over the course of the post-war period. Majorities expressing pro-American attitudes can still be found today in Western Europe – indeed they remain the norm, as will be noted in a moment – but the long-term deterioration is significant. As Inglehart has commented, 'despite the complexities of detail and the contrast between trends in France and elsewhere, there is an overall downward trend' which is to be explained by a shift in deep-rooted cultural orientations (Inglehart, 1990: 395). He cites two changes as being of prime importance in this regard: the rise of post-materialism and the decline of nationalism and patriotism among West European publics (Inglehart, 1990: 408). He describes post-materialists in Western Europe as being less Atlanticist than others. NATO, he argues, bases its appeal on nationalistic and patriotic sentiments that developed 'during the balance of power era', but these have significantly eroded over the years (Inglehart, 1990: 409). Elsewhere in his study, Inglehart reports that in terms of the level of public trust 'the relative position of the United States has declined greatly' in Western Europe (Inglehart, 1990: 402). Clearly a change

TABLE 5.5   *Public attitudes in the European Community towards the US, 1987*

	(1) Opinion of US very good/ good	(2) EC–US ties matter	(3) Present US policy	(4) EC–US ties closer
Belgium	42	62	43	48
Denmark	45	64	55	39
West Germany	51	59	55	48
Greece	34	56	27	46
Spain	33	44	32	32
France	49	63	43	35
Ireland	73	62	52	45
Italy	60	63	49	44
Luxembourg	68	71	62	51
Netherlands	54	65	59	40
Portugal	54	56	41	39
UK	63	63	61	48
EC12	52	60	49	43

(1) Column gives percentage saying opinion of US is 'very good' or 'good', November 1987.
(2) Column gives percentage saying EC ties with US 'matter a great deal', November 1987.
(3) Column gives percentage saying present US policy towards Western European unification is 'favourable', November 1987.
(4) Column gives percentage saying EC ties with US are 'closer' than ten years previously, November 1987.

SOURCE   Eurobarometer surveys, EC, Brussels.

in public attitudes towards the US has occurred, and this is to be explained in terms of wider political and social developments.

A more complete picture of recent attitudes (1987) is given in Table 5.5, drawing upon surveys conducted for Eurobarometer. The survey results reported in the table indicate the following:

(a) There is positive support for the US among a majority of the EC public.

Only in Greece and Spain was noticeably low support recorded in November 1987. Both cases reflect special circumstances. In Greece, the governing party, PASOK, had pursued foreign policies regarded as 'anti-American' after disputes over US policy towards the Greek junta, Cyprus, and US military bases in Greece. In Spain there had also been controversy over US bases there and Spanish participation in NATO.

Despite earlier contrasts, the support for the US in France in 1987 now matched that found in West Germany. The strongest support for the US was found in Ireland, Luxemborg, Britain and Italy. Long-term cultural and immigration factors may well help to explain this differentiation in most cases, along with the absence of recent intense political disputes with the US.

(b) While most Europeans view the US as supporting European unity, a sizeable minority believes Washington is 'opposed, but not actively working against it'. A further small minority believes that the US is 'actively working against' European unity.

This suggests that Europeans have responded to the heightened political and economic disputes between the US and Western Europe in the 1980s. Though substantial numbers of Europeans felt that US–EC relations in 1987 were closer than ten years previously, approximately one-third of British, Dutch and French voters felt they were not as close.

(c) However, a substantial majority of Europeans believe that EC–US ties 'matter a great deal'.

Only in Spain was this not the majority view. In Britain, France, Germany and Italy approximately two out of three voters believed relations with Washington to be very important.

(d) Other evidence suggests that there is only minority support in the major European countries to replace NATO with an East–West European alliance which would exclude the US and the Soviet Union. Only in Italy was there more support than opposition to this idea.

US ATTITUDES TOWARDS EUROPE AND THE EC

Given the complexity of European political structures and the diverse forms of US–European co-operation, the analysis of US attitudes towards Western Europe in the post-war world must make various distinctions. There are three broad dimensions of relevance here: the political and the security, the economic, and the social. Attitudes along one dimension can be assumed to affect the others. Evidence of US attitudes is available for both elites and the mass public.

Hitherto, it has been Atlanticism and NATO which have dominated the political and security relations of the US with Western Europe. Moreover, US opinion has traditionally placed prime emphasis on this dimension. Gill has distinguished between different forms of Atlanticism among US elites (Gill, 1989). The traditional bastions of Atlanticism are to be found in 'the liberal flanks of both major parties, in much of Ivy League corporate America, particularly in Wall Street and New York city, and in prestigious, blue-chip inter-nationalist associations and policy planning groups, such as the . . . Council on Foreign Relations, the Committee on Economic Develop-ment, and the Atlantic Council of the United States' (Gill, 1989: 16). Atlanticism is also strong in the major liberal foundations (Ford, Rockefeller, Carnegie, the German Marshall Fund) and think-tanks (the Brookings Institution). The election of Ronald Reagan as Presi-dent in 1980 was interpreted as symbolising a shift of orientation in the US from the east to the west coast, and the Pacific Basin. As regards the EC, the Reaganite establishment in the 1980s expressed a more realist–mercantilist vision which was 'more coercive, seeking to reassert American prerogatives within alliance policies' (Gill, 1989: 17). Smith has also noted the 'secular decline' in the Atlanticism of the Reaganites (1985). This reinterpretation of Atlanticist values was best expressed by the Hoover Institution (Stanford), (some theorists in) the Center for Strategic and International Studies, Georgetown University, and the Heritage Foundation (Gill, 1989: 17). Kelleher has offered further differentiation between 'old' and 'new' Atlanti-cists, and between those who are 'non-Atlanticists' owing to dis-appointment, disinterest, or a unilateral mentality (1983: 61–5).

At both the elite and the mass level it is important to distinguish between a 'surface' Atlanticism and the emergence of new concerns (Kelleher, 1983: 45). There is some evidence that US attitudes have shifted in response to the new international situation after the end of the cold war. The Chicago Council poll on US attitudes, conducted in late 1990 (see Table 5.7), suggested that 'Americans enter this new era with increased confidence about their military pre-eminence, but with a growing sense of economic vulnerability' (Rielly, 1991: 79). This is expressed in changing attitudes towards the Soviet Union, Western Europe and Japan.

Changes in Eastern Europe have led to an astonishing rise in public warmth towards the Soviet Union. The Chicago Council poll placed the Soviet Union in the fourth highest position in public esteem. In parallel to this, the US public was found to support substantial troop cuts in Europe. Yet the basic Atlanticist premise still held: majority

TABLE 5.6 *Public attitudes in the US towards the EC*

(a) *Public awareness of the EC and of the 1992 programme*
> Q. 1: 'Do you happen to have read or heard anything about the European Community, or the Common Market, as it's also called?'
> Q. 2: 'Have you heard or read anything about the so-called Europe 1992 Project – that is, about the plan to create a single trading market for all European Community member countries by the year 1992?'

	Question 1			Question 2
	1973	1987	1990	1990
Yes	45	29	47	28
No	55	67	47	67
Don't know	—	4	6	5
Total	100%	100%	100%	100%
	N = 1030	N = 1300	N = 1001	N = 1001

(b) *Public feelings towards the EC*
> Q. 1: 'Do you have a very good . . . opinion of the European Community?'
> Q. 2: 'As you may know, the European Community is an association of 12 Western European countries which are working toward closer integration with one another. . . . In general, would you say you are for or against efforts being made to unify Western Europe?'

	Question 1		Question 2	
	1987	1990	1990	
	Those aware of EC		*Total*	*Aware*
Very good/very much for	27	17	37	48
Fairly good/somewhat for	63	54	36	35
Neither good nor bad (volunteered)	4	15	—	—
Rather bad/somewhat against	2	5	8	8
Very bad/very much against	2	3	3	3
Don't know	2	6	16	11
Total	100%	100%	100%	100%
	(N = 440)	(N = 503)	(N = 1001)	(N = 503)

Note: The results for question 1 refer only to those respondents who indicated that they were 'aware' of the EC. The results for question 2 differentiate between all respondents and those who were 'aware' of the EC.

continued on page 231

TABLE 5.6 *continued*

(c) *Perceptions of trading fairness*
    Q. : 'Some people believe that some of our country's trading partners
           use unfair practices that make it difficult for Americans to sell
           products there. From what you know or have heard, tell me if you
           think the following trading partners are fair or unfair to the US
           when it comes to trade?'

	1987		1990	
	Unfair	*Fair*	*Unfair*	*Fair*
W. Europe	30	47	22	40
Japan	65	25	63	24
Canada	11	72	8	69
S. Korea	42	29	32	20

SOURCE   Surveys conducted by Gallup Organisation for EC Commission.
Fieldwork: March–April 1973, November–December 1987, February–March
1990.

---

support was expressed for the use of troops in a crisis situation in
Europe.

By contrast, US attitudes towards Japan have hardened both
among elites and the mass public. Only a minority in the Chicago
opinion survey supported the deployment of US troops to defend
Japan. Moreover, 'By substantial margins, both the public and the
leaders believe the economic power of Japan will be a more critical
threat to American vital interests in the next few years than will
Soviet military power' (Rielly, 1991: 80).

US concern over relations with the EC is much less pronounced
than for Japan. Survey evidence of recent public attitudes in the US
towards the EC is given in Table 5.6. The results suggest that the US
public continues to be favourable towards the EC, with even a slight
fall in the number believing the EC to be an unfair trading partner.
The extent of public awareness of the EC has recently increased,
although it has merely recovered to the level recorded in 1973. In
1990 there were as many Americans who were aware of the existence
of the EC as those who were not (47 per cent). Two-thirds were
unaware of the EC's '1992' programme. A large majority of Americans express support for the principle of Western European unity
(73 per cent). More notably, the 1990 survey records a drop in the
number of Americans believing the EC's trading policy to be unfair
(just 22 per cent believe this). In both 1987 and 1990, the number of

TABLE 5.7   *US public attitudes towards selected countries (mean ratings)*

	1990	1986	1982
Canada	76	77	74
Great Britain	74	73	68
W. Germany/Germany	62	62	59
Soviet Union	59	32	26
Italy	59	58	55
Poland	57	54	52
Mexico	56	59	60
France	56	58	60
Brazil	54	54	54
Israel	54	59	55
Japan	52	61	53

Original reported as 'Thermometer Ratings for Countries – 'The Public', showing 'Mean Temperatures (degrees)'. Figures thus indicate levels of public support for each country.

SOURCE   Adapted from Chicago Council on Foreign Relations poll, reported in Rielly (1991). No other European nation cited in original source.

voters believing the EC's trading policy to be fair was notably higher than for Japan or South Korea (though less than for Canada, with whom the US had recently signed a free trade agreement). Moreover, the responses to other survey questions indicate an increasing belief that EC integration will benefit the US. In 1973, 42 per cent believed that the 'Common Market' would benefit the US: in 1987, this had risen to 51 per cent; in 1990, 61 per cent thought that the '1992' programme would 'improve relations' with the US.

US support for the EC has to be qualified, however. Though the level remains high, it has fallen recently: from 90 per cent in 1987 to 71 per cent in 1990. It seems to be much more conditional than in the past. Short-term fluctuations can be prompted by highly publicised differences.

US images of other societies have changed. American public support for Britain after 1945 was extended, though not completely, to other major European nations as the cold war created a common sense of identity. Over the course of the post-war period, favourable opinions of each of the major European nations have increased (*Gallup Opinion Index*, November 1976 and May 1989; *Harris Survey*, December 1984). This is most notable in the cases of West Germany after 1945, and of France since the 1950s. The evaluation of

Italy has fluctuated over the post-war period. Britain has enjoyed consistently greater support than either France or West Germany, however, and this was particularly notable in the 1980s. Some of the smaller European nations have also enjoyed high support (the Netherlands, Sweden, Switzerland). Moreover, it is also probably true to say that US opinion today distinguishes between individual European nations much less than in the past. In recent years the tendency is increasingly to refer to what the Europeans, collectively, want, think, resist, fear (Kelleher, 1983: 44). The rise of the EC has had an effect in this respect.

Moreover, the US public has also shown a high regard for other, non-European nations. To some extent, an Anglo-Saxon heritage still holds: the favour shown towards Britain is matched by that for Canada and Australia also. In addition, wider affinities have developed: high approval ratings have been recorded for a variety of countries (depending on the survey), though attitudes towards Israel and Japan suffered somewhat at the end of the 1980s. The affinity with Western Europe is by no means exclusive. The shift of orientation away from the traditional East Coast establishment to the West and the Pacific basin has been widely noted, while generational change has meant that now fewer Americans in elite positions personally experienced the Second World War in Europe. The 'successor generation' has had different experiences and concerns.

US elites and public are probably less 'European' in outlook than in earlier periods. At the surface, Atlanticist values remain prevalent (probably more in the political and social sphere than in the economic), but changes in the international system have produced a less exclusive orientation on the part of the majority of Americans. 'Atlanticism' is being gradually overtaken by new, wider concerns in an increasingly multipolar world. US favour is not limited to Europe and there is a heightened sense of economic vulnerability.

The 'comparative favourability ratings' across the Atlantic provide interesting contrasts. While in 1987 90 per cent of US respondents had a 'very good' or 'good' opinion of the EC, only 52 per cent of Europeans felt the same way about the US. European support for the US is much lower than in previous periods, while US support for Europe has also declined. Thus, neither the Americans nor the Europeans place each other in such privileged positions today as in earlier times. A special US–EC relationship is unlikely to be sustained by unambiguous public support on either side of the Atlantic.

CONCLUSION

How strong are the socio-cultural foundations of the US–EC relationship? Are the two sides growing closer together or drawing apart? The evidence of this brief survey paints a complex picture.

At a general level, long-term differences in political development between the US and the EC are reflected in contemporary contrasts of values and policies. Attitudes towards the role of the state and market intervention differ, leading to distinct policy approaches towards agriculture, steel and industrial policy generally. In a highly interdependent economic relationship, these domestic policy differences often have external consequences, creating problems in their bilateral economic and trade relations. Such disputes stem from deeply rooted differences sustained over many decades. It is not so much that the two sides are growing apart, as that their increasingly close economic relationship is serving to expose, and even magnify, their historic domestic differences. Separate traditions are being penetrated more extensively than in earlier periods. Such effects reflect the 'complex interdependence' discussed in Chapter 2.

In other respects, the US and the EC, along with other Western societies, may well be drawing closer together. Common cultural trends are discernable, and social interactions have greatly increased. Yet the effect of such changes may be to swamp the US–EC bilateral relationship within a new milieu, with unpredictable consequences. Socio-cultural relations are difficult to evaluate over the long term. Yet the US–EC relationship may be losing its exclusivity amid wider, multilateral trends. The US and the EC dominate the 'West' in many respects (depending on how broadly 'the West' is defined), but there is a distinction to be drawn between the two sets of nations. This distinction may prove to be important in the minds of policy-makers and the public. Public attitudes in both the US and the EC still display strong affinities for each other and for Atlanticism, but public support seems more conditional than in the past and it has shown signs of falling. New external orientations are apparent on both sides. Moreover, a combination of international developments in politics, policy and culture may be encouraging identifications by groups of nations, rather than individually. Transatlantic relations are increasingly seen in terms of the US and 'Europe', rather than by national subdivisions. The instincts of the past are being affected by changes in the international system.

The US and the EC remain distinct in a variety of ways. Werner Link's comment made in 1976 still seems to hold true for the 1990s:

> in spite of all that Europe and the US have in common in regard to important social issues, nonetheless a line of demarcation and distinction separates the societies of Western Europe and the US. Thus the goal of initiating a process of true Euro-American homogenisation and integration is probably unrealistic. At best, a Euro-American system could perhaps be organised – in both senses of the word – elliptically; it would be a system evolving around two focal points and would remain, for the forseeable future, incomplete. (1976: 189)

NOTES

1. We are grateful to Larry Mead (New York University) for having raised this point with us.
2. Again, this point emerged in discussion with Larry Mead.
3. Subsequently, the Bush administration changed course and announced that the long-term aim should be a complete dismantling of all agricultural support, protection, and export subsidies (the so-called 'zero-option'). The EC has strongly resisted such plans: it sees free trade in agriculture as nonsense as it risks dangerous market fluctuations.
4. Industrial targetting is defined as 'co-ordinated government actions that direct productive resources to give domestic producers in . . . selected industries a competitive advantage' (US International Trade Commission report, 1984).
5. For example, in coal, steel, textiles, footwear, data-processing, information technologies, biotechnology, nuclear and solar energy, nuclear fusion and telecommunications.
6. Other EC governments pursue industrial targetting: for example, in June 1991, the EC Commission approved an exceptional aid plan (of $34.3m) by the German government to the electronics company, Siemens, for research into semiconductor technology.

REFERENCES

Almond, G. A. and Verba, S. (1965) *The Civic Culture* (Boston: Little, Brown).
Barron, J. M. Loewenstein, M. A. and Lynch, G. J. *et al.* (1989) *Macroeconomics* (Reading, Mass.: Addison-Wesley).

Basic Statistics of the EC (1988) Luxembourg: Official Publications of the European Communities.

Benyon, F. (1986) 'Comment' in Tsoukalis, L. (ed.) *Europe, America and the World Economy* (Oxford: Blackwell).

Chicago Council on Foreign Relations: survey reported in Rielly (1991).

Crandall, R. (1986) 'The EC–US Steel Trade Crisis' in Tsoukalis, L. (ed.) *Europe, America and the World Economy* (Oxford: Blackwell).

Crewe, I. and Denver, D. (eds) (1985) *Electoral Change in Western Democracies: Patterns and Sources of Electoral Volatility* (London: Croom Helm).

Czempiel, E-O. and Rustow, D. A. (1976) *The Euro-American System: Economic and Political Relations between North America and Western Europe* (Boulder, Colo: Westview Press).

Dolbeare, K. and Edelman, M. (1974) *American Politics: Policies, Power and Change* (Lexington, Mass.: D.C. Heath).

Dyson, K. H. F. (1980) *The State Tradition in Western Europe: A Study of an Idea and Institution* (New York: Oxford University Press).

The European, London: issues as indicated in text.

Eurobarometer: Public Opinion in the European Community, Commission of the EC, Brussels. Various issues as indicated.

Featherstone, K. (1990) *The Successful Manager's Guide to 1992: Working in the New Europe* (London: Fontana).

Featherstone, K. (1991) 'Greece and European Integration in the 1990s', paper delivered to *Modern Greek Studies Symposium*; Gainesville, Florida, 31 October–3 November.

Financial Times, London: issues as indicated in text.

Freedman, L. ed. (1983) *The Troubled Alliance: Atlantic Relations in the 1980s* (New York: St Martin's).

Gallup Polls, March–April, 1973, November–December 1987, February–March 1990, Gallup Organization, Princeton, New Jersey.

Gallup Opinion Index, Gallup Organization, Princeton, New Jersey, November 1976, May 1989.

Gill, S. ed. (1989) *Atlantic Relations: Beyond the Reagan Era* (New York: St Martin's).

Grant, W. (1990) 'Government–Industry Relations', in D. W. Urwin and W. E. Paterson (eds), *Politics in Western Europe Today* (London: Longmans).

Gray, V. (1973) 'Innovation in the States: A Diffusion Study', *American Political Science Review*, vol. 67, pp. 1174–85.

Haas, E. B. (1991) *When Knowledge is Power: Three Models of Change in International Organization* (Berkeley: University of California Press).

Hall, R. E. and Taylor, J. B. (1991) *Macroeconomics* (New York: Norton).

Harris Survey, 27 December 1984; reported in D. A. Gilbert, *Compendium of American Public Opinion* (New York: Facts on File).

Hartz, L. (1955) *The Liberal Tradition in America* (New York: Harcourt).

Hartz, L. (1964) *The Founding of New Societies* (New York: Harcourt, Brace & World).

Heclo, H. (1974) *Modern Social Politics in Britain and Sweden* (New Haven: Yale University Press).

Heidenheimer, A. J., Heclo, H. and Adams, C. T. *et al.* (1990) *Comparative Public Policy: The Politics of Social Choice in America, Europe, and Japan*, 3rd ed. (New York: St Martin's).

Huntington, S. P. (1968) *Political Order in Changing Societies* (New Haven: Yale University Press).

Inglehart, R. (1977) *The Silent Revolution: Changing Values and Political Styles Among Western Publics* (Princeton: Princeton University Press).

Inglehart, R. (1990) *Culture Shift in Advanced Society* (Princeton: Princeton University Press).

Jessop, B. (1988) 'Regulation Theories in Retrospect and Prospect', paper presented to the International Conference on Regulation, Barcelona, 16–18 June.

Jowell, R., Witherspoon, S. and Brook, L. *et al.* (1989) *British Social Attitudes: Special International Report* (Aldershot: Gower).

Katzenstein, P. J. (1978) *Between Power and Plenty: Foreign Economic Policies of Advanced Industrial States* (Madison: University of Wisconsin Press).

Kelleher, C. McArdle (1983) 'America Looks at Europe', in L. Freedman, (ed.) *The Troubled Alliance: Atlantic Relations in the 1980s* (New York: St Martin's).

Keohane, R. and Nye, J. S. (1987) *Power and Interdependence: World Politics in Transition* (Boston: Little, Brown).

LaPalombara, J. (1987) *Democracy Italian Style* (New Haven: Yale University Press).

Lasswell, H. (1951) 'World Organization and Society', in D. Lerner and H. Lasswell (eds), *The Policy Sciences* (Stanford: Stanford University Press).

Lerner, D. and Gorden, M. (1969) *Euratlantica: Changing Perspectives of the European Elites* (Cambridge, Mass.: MIT Press).

Link, W. (1976) 'The Euro-American Society', in Czempiel, E-O. and Rustow, D. A.

Lipset, S. M. (1963) *The First New Nation: The United States in Historical and Comparative Perspective* (New York: Basic Books).

Lipset, S. M. (1990) *Continental Divide: The Values and Institutions of the United States and Canada* (New York: Routledge).

Lowi, T. S. (1969) *The End of Liberalism: Ideology, Policy and the Crisis of Public Authority* (New York: Norton).

Marsh, J. S. and Swanney, P. (1980) *Agriculture and the European Community* (London: Allen & Unwin).

Meny, Y. and Wright, V. (1986) *The Politics of Steel* (Berlin: de Gruyter).

Messerlin, P. (1986) 'Comment' in Tsoukalis, L. (ed.) *Europe, America and the World Economy* (Oxford: Blackwell).

OECD (1980) *Steel in the 80s*; OECD Symposium, Paris.

Richardson, J. ed., (1982) *Policy Styles in Western Europe* (London: Allen & Unwin).

Rielly, J. E. (1991) 'Public Opinion: The Pulse of the 90s', *Foreign Policy*, vol. 82 (spring).

Rupnik, J. and Humbertjean, M. (1990) in D. Lacorne, *The Rise and Fall of Anti-Americanism: A Century of French Perception* (London: Macmillan).

Sexton, P. C. (1991) *The War on Labor and the Left: Understanding America's Unique Conservatism* (Boulder, Col.: Westview).

Smith, M. (1985) *The Reagan Administration and Western Europe: The*

Shifting Domestic Foundations of Policy Making (UK: Political Studies Association, American Politics Group, occasional paper).

Smith, T. W. (1989) 'Inequality and Welfare' in Jowell, R., Witherspoon, S. and Brook, L. (ed.) *British Social Attitudes: Special International Report* (Aldershot: Gower).

Stoker, G. (1990) 'Regulation Theory, Local Government and the Transition from Fordism', chapter in D. King and J. Pierre (eds), *Challenges to Local Government* (London: Sage/European Consortium for Political Research).

Talbot, R. (1978) *The Chicken War: An International Trade Conflict between the United States and the EEC* (Ames: Iowa State University Press).

Taylor, C. L. and Hudson, M. C. (1972) *World Handbook of Political and Social Indicators* (New Haven: Yale University Press).

Taylor-Gooby, P. (1989) 'The Role of the State', in Jowell, R., Witherspoon, S. and Brook, L. (ed.) *British Social Attitudes: Special International Report* (Aldershot: Gower).

The Times 1000 (1989) (London: Times Books).

Tsoukalis, L. (1986) *Europe, America and the World Economy* (Oxford: Blackwell).

USITC Report (1984) *Foreign Industrial Targeting and its Effects on US Industries; Phase II: The European Community and Member-States*, United States International Trade Commission, April 1984, Washington, DC.

Vlahos, M. (1991) 'Culture and Foreign Policy', *Foreign Policy*, vol. 82 (spring).

Waltman, J. (1980) *Copying Other Nations' Policies* (Cambridge, Mass.: Schenkman).

Wolman, H. (1990) 'Understanding Cross National Policy Transfers: The Case of Britain and the US', unpublished paper, Wayne State University, Detroit.

Wolman, H. (1991) 'Cross-National Comparisons of Urban Economic Programs: Is Policy Transfer Possible?', in D. Fasenfest (ed.), *Local Economic Development Policy Formation* (London: Macmillan).

Wright, V. (1989) *The Government and Politics of France* (London: Unwin Hyman).

Section Three

Research and Policy Implications

6 Conclusions

This book has offered an overview of US–EC relations in the contemporary world. It has argued that the importance and complexity of this relationship raises a variety of questions, for both the policy analyst and the student of international relations. Both the US and the EC, as well as the wider international system, are undergoing major changes and observers need to be able to place this dynamism in context. US–EC relations in the 1990s are entering a critical new phase: in the conditions of post-hegemony, their future relations may develop according to one of a number of alternative scenarios, each with different implications. Moreover, understanding the specific components of their vastly more intense bilateral relationship has never been more difficult: moving between their micro and macro-levels presents a variety of analytic problems.

In this final chapter, the major analytical and policy questions are re-examined in the light of the empirical investigations undertaken in the previous chapters. The intention is not to summarise what has gone before, but rather to highlight those issues that seem to be most pertinent to future policy and theoretical investigation.

THE ANALYTIC PROBLEM RECONSIDERED

A major concern of this book has been with the question of how to study US–EC relations. Chapter 2 surveyed the relevance of different types of explanatory frameworks to these bilateral relations. It contrasted realism and neo-mercantilism with the concept of interdependence. It concluded that the totality of US–EC relations was best captured by the notion of interdependence, but that specific components of the relationship – such as trade disputes, or security co-operation under NATO – might be better illuminated by realism and neo-mercantilism. Chapters 3, 4 and 5 have analysed empirical evidence concerned with the political, economic and social dimensions of US–EC relations with a view to evaluating the relevance of these different explanatory frameworks.

What conclusions can be drawn? Undoubtedly, the overall picture of US–EC relations requires a broad and diverse perspective. The magnitude of the subject-matter is so great as to warrant a focus almost at the level of the international system as a whole. The concept of interdependence – and of 'complex interdependence' – lends itself to this general level of analysis. Yet as a result it lacks specificity; indeed, it may be too malleable. It leaves unclear orders of magnitude, in terms of actors, issues, channels and results. The full picture needs to be brought into sharper relief.

The present study has sought to take such a first step. The purpose here has been not to investigate one narrow subset of US–EC relations, but rather to focus on the overarching conceptual and policy frameworks. In short, an attempt has been made to map out the general terrain of US–EC relations. As part of this process, it is appropriate to draw together some of the analytical implications from the political, economic and social chapters.

In the political domain, the multidimensional nature of Europe's international relations creates a profound analytic complexity. For the EC, foreign relations increasingly involve both national governments and the EC institutions. This dualism means that traditional realist assumptions emphasising government-to-government relations are no longer valid. The EC itself has emerged as an important international actor in matters of trade politics but also in 'high politics'. Complex and varied political channels involve different types of actors, issues and interests. Action by the EC institutions in the external world cannot be adequately understood in terms of bargains struck between national government leaders alone.

Overall, US–EC political relations do constitute an environment of interdependence. There has been a notable growth in bilateral and multilateral interactions, in part intended to achieve closer co-ordination. Even in the less tangible political sphere, policy sensitivities and mutual effects can be identified. Yet US–EC political relations display little formal organisation, parsimony or exclusivity. This is, in part, a reflection of the wider changes that have occurred in the international system.

In the economic sphere, highly intense trade and investment relations between the US and the EC are the foundations of their closely woven interdependence. On this basis, policy sensitivities and mutual effects abound, as government actors are all too well aware. Such intense economic interactions are arguably the most notable defining characteristics of the contemporary international system.

Yet in both the economic and political spheres the analyst is left with a macro–micro linkage problem. Interdependence highlights essential characteristics of US–EC relations and helps to chart the overall macro picture. At the micro level, however, it cannot easily account for different policy outcomes. General perspectives neglect specific types of interaction. In the economic domain, much attention has been given to US–EC trade conflicts. Here the concept of interdependence has important limitations: at best, it needs to be refined. Alternative perspectives are suggested.

Neo-mercantilism, in parallel to realism in the political sphere, posits that governments pursue their economic self-interests in trading relations and that these lead to the occurrence of 'trade wars'. Chapter 4 analysed the actual experience of trade disputes between the US and the EC since the 1950s. These cases were distinguished according to whether one side or the other threatened or took punitive action to press its claims. Such instances of conflict represent, at one level, neo-mercantilist clashes of economic interest. If the focus is exclusively on governments engaged in trade conflict then almost by definition their behaviour is consistent with the basic tenets of neo-mercantilism.

In reality, though, the situation is more complex even in this partial sphere of trade conflict. The explanation for trading clashes must relate the power and interests of particular producer groups (in pluralistic societies) to the response and action taken by national governments and EC institutions. In some instances, the complaints of producers have led to government action, but not in others. The differences in how governments respond to producer group pressure are important: they indicate varying priorities (the absence of a consistent hierarchy of issues) on agendas comprised of different types of issues (trade and investment, but also politics and security). More fundamentally, the interactions between producer groups and governments suggest the varied types of domestic actors important in international economic relations. Governments are decision-takers, but their decisions and behaviour are affected by a complex policy process involving actors operating inside and outside their administrative structures.

No student of public policy in a modern liberal democratic system would assume in the domestic context today that governments were either unitary or autonomous actors, nor ones which pursued a consistent set of priorities. Similarly, there is little value in assuming this in the external sphere of international relations. Locating instances of trade conflict in the wider environment of bilateral interdependence requires a greater analytic complexity to be accepted. This is one sphere in which simplification is dangerous.

Economic relations which are as intense as those which exist between the US and the EC must inevitably impinge on domestic sensitivities and vulnerabilities, provoking reactions from those sectional interests most affected. In a sense, such conflict parallels that which often occurs in a single national economy when producer groups and sectional interests react to changed economic conditions or altered government policy (e.g. the allocation of regional development aid, revised tax rates, fluctuations in interest rates). Environments of intense economic 'integration' and competition (national or international) give rise to conflicts of interest.

A neglected and equally interesting question to that of trade conflict is, why are so many US–EC economic interactions conducted without significant political controversy? The magnitude of change over the course of the twentieth century is impressive: far more trade and investment flows between the US and the EC today than ever before. This is an important change to the character of their respective economies. Yet, actual trade disputes are relatively few: only seventeen were reported in thirty years. Economic interdependence has grown in the environment created after the end of the Second World War; thereafter it has faced little political interruption. Shared values and interests have sustained economic interdependence. The economic sphere is nevertheless one closely affected by political action: international regimes have been created and frequent intergovernmental interactions sustain its basic conditions (e.g. Group of Seven meetings). Indeed, political action in the economic sphere has created a certain system of international management to help tackle disturbances (e.g. Group of Seven finance ministers meetings). Such organisation contrasts with the different arrangements which pertain in the political sphere of US–EC relations.

The social dimension of US–EC relations illustrates the extent to which increasingly intense political and economic interactions impinge upon domestic sensitivities. The respective societies have become more open and more deeply penetrated than ever before as a result of such interactions. This has exposed the external trading consequences of different domestic policy traditions. These traditions have been built up over many years and they reflect differences in political development and political culture. Interdependence challenges national autonomy: it serves to break down national economic barriers and intensify international ties. It is not so much that the US and the EC societies are growing apart, as that increasing interdependence is penetrating more deeply into areas previously left untouched and creating new sensitivities and controversies. For its part, public opinion may not readily accept or understand the consequences of increased interdependence, thus raising further questions as to the domestic–external linkages of political and economic interdependence.

Taken together, the political, economic and social evidence of the previous chapters sustains the notion that the totality of US–EC relations are best placed in an analytical framework which recognises their mutual interdependence. Indeed, they approximate to the Keohane and Nye formulation of 'complex interdependence' discussed in Chapter 2. Inevitably, the nature of bilateral interdependence varies and takes different forms in different policy sectors. The US–EC relationship is such a mosaic. Yet, there remains a fundamental analytical difficulty in overcoming the limitations of an interdependence approach. 'Interdependence' lacks parsimony and specificity; it is most suited to macro-level descriptions. By contrast, realism and neo-mercantilism are straitjackets, too narrowly conceived to accurately reflect important features of US–EC relations. There is thus a need for theorising which goes beyond the generalised concept of interdependence.

Interdependence needs to be refined so as to take better account of several specific aspects of bilateral relations. Firstly, it needs to be more closely related to the results of interdependence: the outcomes of international trade negotiations, and political consultations, for example. Trade negotiations represent something of a 'black box' for an interdependence approach. Here, an approach based on the concept of bargaining may be the way forward. The question of who wins and why is crucial to any set of political interactions. Moreover, future case studies might usefully focus on particular types of mutual policy sensitivities and effects. As noted in Chapter 3, however, empirical investigation of this type is likely to be very difficult. Secondly, the responses of key actors to interdependence must be distinguished. How have government actors responded to the international management and policy implications of interdependence and why do their responses differ? In particular, contacts between governments vary across policy sectors – both in their form and their intensity – to what extent do these variations reflect interdependence, as suggested here in Chapter 3? Thirdly, there is a more general problem involving the perceptions and acceptance of interdependence, both on the part of elites and the mass publics. A distinction may be drawn between the objective reality of interdependence and the subjective evaluation of it. At a research level, the latter could be usefully related to different value-choices and cultural traditions. Finally, in combination with the above, case study research might enhance understanding of the relative importance of certain types of actors, issues and channels under particular conditions, as previously suggested. The scope for such empirical research may be limited, however, not least by the availability of appropriate types of information.

The study of US–EC relations is complex and daunting. Its relative importance offers a firm justification for attempting it, however. It has been argued here that the bilateral relationship will be better understood with further theoretical refinement of the concept of interdependence, linked with more detailed case study investigation of its actual nature and form for the US and the EC. In the context of the current changes occurring in the international system, further research on US–EC relations is both a necessary and an exciting task.

THE POLICY PROBLEM RECONSIDERED

This section (a) considers the difficulties entailed in US and EC foreign policy decision-making as a source of friction in bilateral relations and (b) weighs the opportunities to reshape bilateral relations at a crucible of change. The US and the EC are engaged in wholesale rethinking about their relations with one another: outcomes at this point can only be surmised. Modest adjustments have been made but the broad outlines of bilateral military, trade, and monetary relations are still left undefined. US–EC economic interdependence has never been more mutually advantageous and this is a source of stability in a changing world. Yet the organisation and process of the US–EC relationship have not been fundamentally altered by the end of the cold war. The relationship is highly problematic:

- adjustment in the process and organisation of bilateral relations was never fully made in the transition from hegemony to hegemonic decline in the 1960s. That previous inertia is compounded by the current adjustment lag as relations merge out of hegemonic decline into post-hegemony; and
- the multilateral institutions which provided a structure for US–EC relations in the past may no longer serve that function in the same

way in the post-cold-war world, leaving the US and EC without the kind of binding multilateral commitments that have ungirded bilateral relations for over forty years.

Much unfinished business remains. Besides risking inaction or maladjustment, the US and the EC could: (a) seek to breathe new life in such multilateral institutions/regimes as the GATT, NATO, OECD and G7 (assuming the political will exists); and/or (b) create new bilateral institutions or procedures (given the difficulty of reaching global agreement on issues of major importance to the US and EC). A dual approach would strengthen international co-operation as well as US–EC relations: in case one fails, the other can help compensate.

Chapter 4 showed that potentially disruptive trade and subsidy disputes lurk over the horizon, with too many of them referred to the Uruguay Round for settlement. By 'passing the buck', the US and EC risk postponing painful decisions should the GATT negotiations not yield desired results. Even if the MTNs are finally concluded sometime in 1992, not all outstanding bilateral commercial disputes will be resolved. The GATT as it stands cannot be a panacea for all the problems of US–EC trade relations. Complex interdependence as a framework of US–EC relations can be a shield against neomercantilism because it places commerce in a broader set of relationships. Indeed the political framework of US–EC relations provided by the existence of the Atlantic Alliance has helped contain the spread of trade disputes into other bilateral areas. Yet the difficulty of the 1990s will be for the US and EC to maintain the benefits of complex interdependence at a time when the overarching cold-war-era political framework provided by the Atlantic Alliance is undergoing drastic change.

NATO's future too is a problem for US–EC relations. Its role in those relations has always been an intimate and prominent one, tempering commercial and other disputes with broader military–security concerns. Now that NATO – and the US – are likely to play a much reduced role in Europe as an EC defence identity gains currency, a forty-three year old edifice of US–EC relations is being questioned: with it will go some of the binding legal commitments and habits of co-operation upon which the Atlantic Alliance has rested. Until there is an institutional link between the US and the EC, the US will want to retain its influence in Europe through NATO, but since NATO's future as it has been known is so uncertain that link in effect may be short-lived. The future of NATO is tied not only to EC movement toward a defence identity – which will eventually determine what place, if any, the US and NATO will have in European defence – but to the future of the GATT and the international trade order. If the US perceives that the EC is not committed to the GATT, then it will question the logic behind maintaining a military presence in the EC through NATO (assuming the Europeans want it). Without NATO or a new meaningful institutional link between the US and EC, the framework of complex interdependence is stripped of a very important political–military component.

Many on both sides of the Atlantic are now asking what is left to US–EC relations after the cold war. It has been a primary task of this book to show readers that the bases for US–EC relations are deeply and broadly rooted in mutual political and economic advantages lodged in a framework of complex interdependence that will outlive the cold war. Common interests in the management of the international political economy, in maintaining the advantages of the world's largest economic partnership and in responding to threats to, or breaches of, world peace and security are likely to be powerful reasons behind continual engagement and co-operation even if the EC replaces NATO as the primary defender of Western European security. However, despite what is at stake, it remains to be seen if the two will be able to address change constructively, acting to balance their own needs with those of common Western interests. Indeed, it will take not one but both to make the necessary adjustments.

Despite mercurial positions toward the EC since the Nixon administration, the United States government since 1989 has made significant strides toward adjusting its EC policy from one of hostility and lingering hegemony to one of post-hegemonic co-operation under complex interdependence conditions. As Chapter 3 indicated, the Bush administration undertook a major review of US policy towards the EC during its first three months in office in 1989. However, while the broad reevaluation of US relations with the EC is attributed to the Bush administration, the origins of an emerging new policy towards the EC go back to the US response to the EC's implementation of the Single European Act in 1987 and the enhanced position of the EC Council Presidency, the codification of EPC and the establishment of an EPC secretariat which followed. A much more rounded and proactive approach to the EC emerged. The US response was (and remains) pragmatic. It needs the EC as a potential partner in an otherwise dangerous world characterised by regional conflicts, national extremism, nuclear proliferation, terrorism, the drug trade and social and political instability unleashed by the growing North–South chasm. Although the EC is not yet willing or able to act in all areas of international relations with the unison and weight of a single powerful state, its diplomatic, political and economic weight can be brought to bear in Eastern Europe, the new Commonwealth of Independent States, Lebanon, the Mediterranean Basin and Africa. The EC is being transformed by its own internal dynamic and external stimuli. The United States has had to adjust more to the new EC than the new EC has had to adjust to the United States. Yet why, then, does the Bush administration focus on the old familiar order – NATO and the GATT – to cope with change at a time when these organisations may have outlived their original purposes?

The Bush administration is in a quandary. It offered the idea of a treaty with the EC to pave the way for a new relationship and as a hedge against the eclipse of NATO by the EC and of the GATT by regionalism/protectionism. However, as mentioned, the EC was neither ready nor willing to oblige the United States. Since the EC at Maastricht postponed the hard decision of how to provide for its defence beyond a commitment to work towards a common defence policy, it cannot yet initiate a new defence relationship with the United States. As a result, it is not really very surprising that the Bush administration has opted to back NATO as the continuing key US–European link until something else can be agreed upon. The Bush administration has concluded that NATO as a link to the EC is better than no link at all, but that approach could be fleeting should NATO's relevance suffer from decline relative to the EC. Ironically, the traditional British policy of upholding NATO at the expense of participation in an alternative European defence system could serve to hinder the US administration in adapting to these new circumstances. The future of US–EC relations beyond the economic realm will depend very much on whether or not the EC will adopt a common defence in the 1990s and how that new position will affect the United States. By 1996, the EC states are expected to decide whether or not the WEU will be incorporated into the EC. The Brussels Treaty (of the WEU) expires in 1998. An affirmative decision by the EC to incorporate the WEU into the EC will require NATO–EC consultations and adjustments. If handled judiciously, it may be possible to retain NATO alongside the EC–WEU link, but the role of NATO (and the United States) in Europe's defence will, of course, never be the same.[1]

The EC – preoccupied with EMU, civil war in Yugoslavia and the mammoth challenges it faces from Central and Eastern Europe – is neither ready (nor willing in some quarters) to reach out to the United States in any new bold action that would put bilateral relations on a new post-cold-war footing. Its resources and attention are fully usurped by these fast-breaking developments. The US is much farther removed than the Europeans from some of the hard decisions, high costs, and security threats posed by the eclipse of Soviet power, the break-up of Yugoslavia and the potential for social collapse in parts of the Commonwealth of Independent States. The United States and the US–EC relationship are not in crisis. In contrast, the EC's eastern flank is in crisis and the EC faces a likely rapid expansion of membership and other forms of engagement to pull as many as possible of the existing and emergent states of the region into its orbit in order to stave off economic, social and political instability and the return of dictatorship.

Thus, for the United States, the EC's future occupies a very high place on the foreign policy agenda as NATO takes a less prominent place in US–European relations. For the EC, the relationship with the United States is less urgent and the need to tailor EC–US relations to the post-cold-war world is being postponed until the EC gets its own house in order, although there can be no certainty that adjustment will take place even when the dust settles. The risk of inaction or maladjustment within the US–EC relationship is likely to adversely affect the US–EC partnership should remedial action not be taken in the 1990s. Given that the expectations of the EC to act with economic and political leadership in the old Soviet bloc are so high, a close and beneficial relationship with the United States would seem to be welcome so long as a convergence of interests based on a rough symmetry of power is maintained.

Before outlining policy scenarios, two structural problems which adversely affect bilateral relations are identified: (a) the foreign policy decision-making process on both sides of the Atlantic which are not conducive to rapid adjustment to change, and (b) the organisation and processes of US–EC relations which depend heavily on outdated cold war-era multilateral institutions. Adjustment to change, which has underlined most of the chapters of this book, is tempered by outdated processes and institutions that need overhaul.

DECISION-MAKING PROCESSES IN THE UNITED STATES AND THE EC

An enduring problem in bilateral relations has to do with the distinctive policy-making processes of the US and EC. Both are pluralist democracies, with multiple access points into the policy-making process by groups representing special interests. The US and EC are not monolithic decision-makers: their policy actions take into account varied interests at many different levels. Indeed the failure to act, when action appears necessary and in the national (or European) interest, can be traced to the power of opposition in democratic government. Cogent leadership, singularity of purpose and swift and constructive responses to change often elude pluralist democracies. There is a diffusion of power between different types of governmental structure, coalition governments, and party systems. Policy proposals in the US and in many of the EC states, especially those where there are coalition governments, must pass through many hurdles before being realised. Outcomes often reflect the lowest common denominator. Often times progressive policies cannot be successfully engineered because of domestic opposition. The challenge before the US and EC states is to successfully balance domestic interests with international (and US–EC) interests. It is in the nature of democratic government that the domestic inputs into policy-making often prevail over global commitments that may seem abstract to the unemployed steelworker in Pittsburgh or to the unemployed shipbuilder in Liverpool. Although this book has focused chiefly on policy outputs, the structure of US and EC foreign policy decision-making warrant attention as they affect the ability of each partner to respond with one voice and in timely fashion to external stimuli. The analysis shows that despite all intentions, present and future, there will be built-in limits to speedy constructive change in US–EC relations which in part are due to the decision-making quirks that are unique to both.

In the United States government no one agency nor person has the responsibility of co-ordinating US policy toward the EC. There is no EC 'tsar' in the federal government. The President is ultimately responsible for setting US policy toward the EC but implementation and execution of Presidential policy directions are dependent on multiple bodies and individuals – political appointees and career civil servants – throughout government. Before the 1970s, the State Department reigned supreme over US foreign policy towards the EC within the executive branch. As the substantive content of US–EC relations has grown, so too have the number of US government agencies involved in making EC policy. Fifteen Federal agencies are involved in interagency or other deliberations concerning US relations with the EC.[2] While the State Department takes the lead on the daily relationship with the EC, and manages the growing number of consultations that draw on personnel from other government agencies, other powerful departments with an interest in the EC jealously guard their prerogatives, e.g. Treasury, Commerce, Agriculture and the Office of the US Trade Representative (USTR). The Treasury Department, covetous of its own domain (US representation in the G7), expunged from the draft Transatlantic Declaration any of the proposed references to US–EC monetary co-operation. Other agencies are very powerful in the making and implementation of US policy. For examples, the Justice Department is regularly involved with the EC in anti-terrorist matters; the Justice Department and the Federal Trade Commission are involved with the EC in anti-trust matters; the USTR is the principal agency involved in US trade policy towards, and negotiations with, the EC; and the Commerce Department and US International Trade Commission are responsible for antidumping and countervailing duty investigations into allegations of unfairly traded EC products in the US and EC markets.

Since the EC is such a diverse body whose work touches on nearly all major US federal agencies, policy-making within the Executive Branch is very decentralised, indeed compartmentalised. Regular and *ad-hoc* interagency deliberations bring together the segments of US policy interests. Over time, expertise on the EC has expanded within the various agencies of government and this has been reflected in the quality of interagency deliberations. The interagency approach to US policy-making toward the EC reflects a democratic society, but the cost in pluralist decision-making is a less cohesive foreign policy. The net result of pluralism and diffusion as attributes of US policy-making toward the EC is a process not terribly dissimilar to the kinds of deliberations that transpire among the member governments and institutions of the EC as they make policy.

Executive authority over US policy with the EC is not only constrained by a complex and diffuse interagency process of decision-making but is dependent on congressional legislation. Legislation is needed to govern import and export policy, mandate foreign trade negotiations for the executive to enter into, and determine the stationing of US troops abroad (e.g. in Western Europe). The Senate Foreign Relations Committee and House Foreign Affairs Committee, with their oversight and appropriations powers, are indispensable to the ability of the executive branch to make policy toward the EC. All federal agencies are responsive to congressional queries and concerns because Congress determines their budgets. Presidential appointees who will have a major input into EC policy, e.g. the Secretary of State and the US Trade Representative, face confirmation hearings and votes in the US Senate. In addition to these powers, Congress also reflects US public opinion and, given economic hardtimes, it could pass protectionist legislation that adversely affects EC interests. However, despite the importance of Congress as a barometer of US public opinion, and the use of hearings to investigate government policies and international developments, Congress remains on the periphery of the daily functioning of US relations with the EC. For example, the drafting of, and negotiations for, the 1990 Transatlantic Declaration was wholly an executive branch affair. Since it was not a treaty, it did not go to the Senate for ratification; yet the President committed the United States to an expansion of cooperation with the Europeans with no significant input from Capitol Hill. Finally, the impact of special interest groups who lobby both Congress and the executive can be very strong and affect policy outcomes.

Despite the diffusion of US foreign policy decision-making, the United States is still a unitary international actor capable of taking purposeful actions. The EC's decision-making structure is much more complicated and this makes it much more difficult for the EC to act as a coherent foreign policy unit. When one considers the multiple inputs into the EC decision-making process, it is rather striking when the EC does speak with one voice and acts as one in international affairs. The difficulty encountered by the EC in making a 'US policy' is further compounded by twelve national governments elected into office at different times and by twelve separate historical relationships with the United States.

EC foreign policy actions must first take into account subnational constituent interests that are fleshed out at the member government levels before member governments in the Council of Foreign Ministers, Council Presidency or EPC flesh out a common position. In areas where the EC Commission has constitutional powers to act on behalf of the twelve, EC policy-making takes on not an intergovernmental but a supranational authority. Relations with the

United States, then, fall under both the Rome Treaty powers of the Commission and the Council of Ministers (trade, diplomacy) and the Council Presidency and EPC (high–level political consultations, joint policies).

The inputs into decision-making matters pertaining to the United States are far more numerous than those that go into EC policy-making in the United States. No one agency or person is responsible for EC policy toward the United States; there is no 'US tsar' in the EC. The EC Commission External Relations Directorate-General (DG-I), like the US Department of State, is responsible for the day-to-day relationship with the United States. The EC Commission, like the US President, has the power to initiate policy actions. Again, like the US executive branch, the EC Commission is responsible for implementation of policy decisions. The European Parliament has limited foreign policy powers (e.g. on questions related to enlargement and association) and plays an important consultative role in the decision-making process. The Economic and Social Committee plays a consultative role as well. The Committee of Permanent Representatives assists the EC members' Foreign Ministers with preparations for meetings and attempts to deal with skirmishes and differences to avoid crowding the agenda of the Foreign Ministers. At the EC level of decision-making, pan- European interest group associations lobby the EC institutions with their foreign policy concerns.

Within the EC Commission and Council there is fragmentation. The EC Commission is divided into separate directorates-general. Although the Directorate-General I (DG-I) is responsible for external relations, other directorates-general have inputs into foreign policy-making, e.g. Agriculture and Development. As in the US Executive branch, these agencies are highly covetous of their own domain and guard it jealously. Within the Council, presidencies come and go every six months. Although the troika concept and the establishment of an EPC secretariat were designed to provide more continuity in EC policy-making, the top leadership of the EC is highly transitory. The lack of a longer-serving EC executive has been a major sore point in US–EC relations. In the past, the United States has complained about the difficulties of attempting to co-ordinate policy and negotiate with the EC because of the variability in the top EC leadership and multiple layers of decision-making authority that must be dealt with. This, of course, is the same complaint the EC refers to when it deals with the Executive branch agencies.

An irony of EC foreign policy decision-making is that the EC has the potential to make a unified US policy. The EC has well-formed policies toward many other countries in the world, albeit some of them weaker and more dependent (on the EC) than is the United States, and it has treaties and other institutional arrangements with the Lomé countries, the Mediterranean Basin states, and regional bodies in South-East Asia and Central America. However, the size of the United States, its role in the affairs of Europe since the Second World War, and the divergent interests the separate twelve EC member governments have in their relations with the United States, all deny the EC the ease with which it develops coherent policies towards many other countries and regions.

In sum, it is thus clear that the US and EC have remarkably diffuse decision-making processes. In the EC's case, decision-making occurs at both the national and subnational as well as EC levels. There has never been a consensus in the EC as to what its US policy should be because the members are split. A federal system with separation of powers, the United States has multiple points of access for those wishing to influence policy outputs and a distribution of power among different levels of government. The EC's embryonic federal structure permits some foreign policy decision-making to occur at the EC level, while member governments maintain sovereignty and foreign policy activities at their level as well. Both sides lack central authorities to preside over US–EC relations. The US President is not, in practice, supreme, yet neither is the EC Commission President nor Council President. While it is more likely that the US can make unified policy than the EC – albeit unsteadily – the EC of the past could not reach agreement on what its policy should be towards the United States. That may change as further foreign policy homogenisation occurs among the twelve EC member governments. Indeed the EC may be better able to act in unison *vis-à-vis* the United States after it achieves EMU and aspects of political union later in the decade. The inputs into policy-making will be a constant source of frustration, however, for the US in its relationship with the EC and for the EC in its relationship with the United States.

ORGANISATION AND PROCESSES OF US–EC RELATIONS IN FLUX

US–EC relations have been adjusted to accommodate change. Not only has there been a jump in the number of consultations at the highest levels but there has been an expansion of co-operation in functional areas traditionally kept outside the US–EC framework. However, US–EC relations cannot be further revised to accommodate change without the US and EC working in concert and with resolution to

- strengthen existing multilateral institutions and/or regimes, and
- move toward a US–EC treaty which would bring defence co-operation and bilateral trade and/or monetary relations under an overarching framework.

At the least, if US–EC relations are not to lapse into a neo-mercantilist mentality, they will need strengthened multilateral and bilateral political frameworks. The preference here is for both multilateral and bilateral relations to be strengthened, because in the event of a shortfall in one the other could then help compensate and thus work in tandem.

Management of US–EC relations is tied heavily to the future of multilateral co-operation. Appendix 1 shows that eighteen multilateral institutions provide a critical management function for US–EC relations. In contrast, there are seven bilateral processes which help structure US–EC relations but there are no bilateral institutions. Several functional agreements tie the US and EC into co-operation, but they are disjointed and not brought into any unified framework (e.g. one similar to the EC–Canada co-operation agreement). That US–EC relations have been maintained with a minimum of bilateral structures is remarkable, but during the cold war multilateral co-operation was sufficient compensation. The dearth of institutional development in US–EC relations is made more clear now because the US and EC may not be able to depend on multilateral co-operation as much as they used to. Since the US and EC are not the exclusive members of multilateral organisations, their bilateral relationship is captive to other countries, with the inevitable complexities and difficulties in reaching agreements. The lack of institutionalisation of US–EC bilateral relations is in stark contrast to the sophisticated contractual relations which the EC has with EFTA, the Mediterranean and Lomé Convention states, and many other countries, and to the contractual relations that the United States has developed with Canada and Israel and may be developing with the North American Free Trade Area (NAFTA).

Of the many multilateral organisations and regimes on which the

US and EC depend for a management function, some are under siege (GATT), threatened with diminished relevance (NATO), under-utilised (OECD) or too *ad hoc* (G7). Concomitantly, US–EC bilateral arrangements are underdeveloped. Assuming that new multilateral organisations are very difficult to construct in global peacetime, the US and EC will want to review very carefully their own bilateral processes to determine which of them can be beefed up to compensate for the loss of cohesion, authority, and/or relevance of some of the multilateral organisations.

POLICY SCENARIOS FOR THE 1990s

US–EC relations in the 1990s could go in one of two directions. One scenario, based on a neo-mercantilist assumption, is for an increase in fracticidal trade wars to occur as the cold war ends. The fabric of ties could unravel as the politico-security framework – which once tempered economic nationalism – is unveiled from bilateral relations. The end of the cold war could unleash neo-isolationist tendencies in the United States and regional protectionism in the EC. It is not difficult to see that such forces lurk just beneath the surface in both the EC and US. Indeed, both partners already act in ways which distort trade to protect politically powerful market interests (voluntary restraints, orderly market agreements, export subsidies). Yet these actions are still the exceptions to the overarching liberal framework of US–EC trade relations. It has been shown in this book that the vast flow of goods, services and capital across the Atlantic is untouched by neomercantilist controversy. Trade discord, none the less, is still potentially damaging.

It was shown in Chapter 4 that the number of commercial disputes over trade-distorting policies rose with the decline of hegemony and that the majority of bilateral disputes was settled only after confrontation had occurred. Most of the trade disputes occurred in the 1980s during the transition from hegemonic decline to post-hegemony, suggesting that the frequency of disputes may continue to rise as hegemonic vestiges are completely expunged from US–EC relations. In addition, the number of outstanding or potential trade disputes is on the rise and could risk trade wars if the GATT round collapses or a new GATT accord falls short of needed reform.

Although there are many exceptions to the extent to which US–EC relations are framed by a liberal approach, with the lid off the cold war, a 'no-holds-barred' approach could replace previous constraints. Indeed a major impetus behind the European project has been to achieve independence from not only the old Soviet Union but also the United States. The neo-mercantilist scenario does not seriously entertain the possibility that common interests would force the US and EC leaderships to construct a new structure of bilateral relations because the press of national economic interests would prevail over the will to change. If the past is prologue, then the potential for constructive adjustment is not sanguine. There can be no certainty that what the two sides have built up since the 1940s will not be torn down in the 1990s.

The other scenario, based on a liberal assumption, is for the US and EC to continue to entertain, at times rather uneasily, both co-operation and conflict within the context of complex interdependence. Sectoral disputes are considered inevitable by-products of complex interdependence, yet the US and EC will continue to contain specific disputes from poisoning overall relations given the costs of a breakdown in complex interdependence. It was only four years ago that the complaints in the US of a 'Fortress Europe' were being uttered with some ferocity in response to the 1992 programme, only to be reduced to a murmur once the EC produced reassurances and actions to the contrary. Without the overriding defence alliance tempering other disputes, it will be more difficult for the US and EC to contain disputes. Yet the end of the cold war also unleashes new opportunities to fashion bilateral relations on a new and more enduring symmetric basis.

In this scenario, the US recognises that the EC must move toward more self-sufficiency in military security terms because this is generally consistent with the interests of the EC member states; and the EC member states recognize they must take into account the security interests of the United States as they redefine their own defence needs. One of the early objectives behind US support for a united Europe was to strengthen the independence and security of what became the EC. Now that the EC is on the threshold of developing its own security identity, the US should welcome this as an outcome in part of its earlier policy (assuming the transition meets mutual needs).

This scenario also assumes that the US and EC will have to exercise joint leadership in a post-hegemonic relationship to maintain mutual interests. The quest to co-manage the world political economy, along with the Japanese, is weighed against the alternative scenario and is determined to be more beneficial than costly. Chapters 3–5 revealed the breadth and depth of US–EC interdependence from the economic, political and social dimensions.

The second scenario is the more likely of the two because the benefits of continued constructive engagement outweigh the costs. The emergence of the post-hegemonic period in US–EC relations offers new opportunities for long-overdue policy adjustment. The logic of complex interdependence points to co-operation despite the inherent difficulties. The US and EC are in essence 'condemned' to co-operate because of:

- the interlinkage of their economies;
- mutual dependence on order in the international political economy;
- mutual dependence on international political order; and
- common interests in avoiding social collapse in the former Soviet bloc.

Contrary to the neo-mercantilist scenario, and despite the increase in trade disputes, the US–EC commercial partnership is more balanced now than in the 1980s. Commercial relations continue to flourish despite the growing importance of the Pacific Rim to the US and Eastern Europe and the Mediterranean to the EC. The US will remain a Pacific and an Atlantic power just as the EC will remain an Atlantic and a Mediterranean power. Since the two own a piece of each other's economies, they will remain intimately acquainted with each other's domestic politics and deeply feel their adverse effects. Given these assumptions, how can policy be adjusted so that the US and EC leaderships can plan proactively to deal with the coming of post-cold-war commercial disputes? How can the US and EC remain engaged in one another's overall security, both military and economic, to retain the benefits that have been reaped for over four decades, yet provide flexibility and enhance security?

The key to future US–EC relations is the adequacy of a framework within which policy co-ordination (on defence, economic, commercial and monetary matters) and dispute settlement (in case the GATT can no longer serve that function) can be achieved. Bilateral processes are growing anachronistic and will need to take into account post–hegemonic dynamics. The dependence on multilateral fora as a structure of bilateral relations is outdated and dangerous because it subjects US–EC ties to wider problems. Multilateral institutions that date back to the 1940s have provided a structure for US–EC relations but that structure may no longer be adequate. The US and EC need to strengthen bilateral relations to compensate for, or enhance, multilateral structures.

US policy towards the EC in the 1990s will continue to adjust to the growing weight and role of the EC in the international system, not so much by choice (nor by solidarity with the European project) but by pragmatic necessity and self–interest. It is pragmatic for, and in the interests of, the US to accept and work with the EC as a partner in dealing with international problems too big for itself or any other single state to solve. Given the EC's wealth and its potential external cohesion, it is an indispensable partner of the United States in maintaining post-hegemonic co-operation in the vein of Robert Keohane's *After Hegemony*. The US should consistently support the EC's aid efforts in Eastern and Central Europe given (a) the EC's proximity to the scene of potential social instability, (b) the EC's resources and interests, and (c) limitations of the financial and political reach of the United States. Beyond a pragmatic approach, the current US administration is not likely to develop a resolute proactive and visionary approach that could, for example, draw from the work on domestic choices found in Joseph Nye's *Bound to Lead* or Henry Nau's *The Myth of America's Decline*. In a US presidential election year, no major foreign policy breakthroughs are expected. Protectionist pressures will make their imprint on election politics, but are not expected to alter fundamentally present US policies toward the EC, barring, of course, the collapse of the GATT negotiations. Yet the legacy of the Bush administration to future Administrations is the Transatlantic Declaration. Despite falling short of US expectations, it is a document that both US and EC officials use as a point of reference and as a means with which to regularise consultations. US–EC relations have become less *ad hoc* as a result.

As much as this book has sought to highlight the importance of the EC to the United States, an example of how absorbed US public opinion can be in either domestic or other international events can be found in the US press coverage of the run up to, and negotiations during, the Maastricht Summit. Not only was there thin press coverage to inform Americans of the effects of the European debates and decisions on them, but US administration officials only reiterated their support in general for EC integration with the usual caveat that support is contingent on there being no adverse effects of that integration on US interests. It is clear that despite the Bush administration's positive engagement of the EC since 1989, the US Government does not appear willing to go beyond the usual rhetoric at a turning point in European history, nor does US public opinion make demands as such.

Bilateral relations between the US and the major EC states will continue to be very important but, as the purview of the EC grows from economics to defence and foreign policy, the US relationship with the EC will by necessity become even closer. The Bush administration has already responded to the new powers of the EC by beefing up co-operation and consultations. The United States government is more ready now than ever to accept and work with the EC. However, US overtures will have to await EC developments that could facilitate more timely and meaningful responses. If US overtures continue to meet with the EC's passiveness, disinterest or unwillingness in responding in constructive terms over the long term then Atlanticism as a cornerstone of US foreign policy could come under attack by protectionist and neo-isolationist forces. Future US foreign policy actions could reflect impatience with the course of European unity.

Whereas the EC used to take its lead in foreign policy from the United States during the hegemonic period, the US now awaits EC reforms and developments to determine how to tailor its relations with the EC. A more assertive EC has forced the United States to adjust its policy. However, the EC must itself not put relations with the United States on the back burner for too long or give US interests short shrift. Although the EC has the power to take actions that could adversely affect US interests, it would be wise to act judiciously. After all, any EC actions that could hasten the collapse of NATO or the GATT would have adverse effects not only on the US but on the EC and the wider international order as well. Although the Soviet threat to the EC is gone, the uncertainties of ethnic unrest, as seen in Yugoslavia, the ever-constant fear of massive east-to-west immigration flows and the possible rise of new nuclear powers out of the old Soviet Union mean that the EC is faced with new potential threats to its security. The EC could be reassured if US engagement in European defence is maintained.

Although it has been inconsistently applied, the US has had a single policy toward the EC since its inception. However, the EC has never been able to formulate a common 'US policy'. Despite the difficulties of forging such a common policy out of twelve separate policies, the EC cannot expect to engage the US constructively without being able to act in unison. So long as the EC fails to reach some internal consensus on what its US policy should be it cannot expect to develop a full-blown symmetric and post-hegemonic relationship with the United States it has so long sought. A future common defence policy without a common US policy would be folly and could sour US–EC political relations.

EC foreign policy cohesiveness is not a certain thing. Although the EC acted in unison and with resolution in Yugoslavia, trying as it did to broker peace, even at the loss of life of five EC peace monitors, Germany asserted its national interests and broke ranks with the EC by recognising the independence of Slovenia and Croatia on 23 December 1991. The EC had planned to move in that direction in mid-January but only after tying recognition to certain criteria on human rights and other international legal standards. The German action could either be an exception to the rule (that Germany works within the EC on a consensual basis) or be the harbinger of a new assertive and independent German foreign policy. Clearly the German action violated established EPC practices under the stipulations of the Single European Act. The German move was opposed by France, the UK, other EC members and the United States. The action throws into question the kinds of problems that the EC faces as it attempts to adopt a common foreign and security policy. It shows the potential of one EC member state to move unilaterally against the will of the others and probably does not bode well for an emergent common foreign policy should the German action be more than just an exception to previous practices.

To further complicate matters for the EC, several member governments face parliamentary elections between 1992 and 1994 so the remarkable confluence of interests at this point in EC history is not a perennial thing. As mentioned, between the time of this writing and 1996, when the EC will hold its next intergovernmental conference on defence union, the future of the EC's political and defence union will be determined. An international or European crisis could trigger the first usage of the WEU–EC military link. How and if the EC would respond to a military action will have to await judgment. It is therefore rather difficult to predict the future form of EC policy towards the United States, given the lack of previous policy cohesion and the uncertainty over EC defence policy. A key to easing EC relations with the US over the future EC defence policy would be to strengthen US–EC commercial relations by beefing up bilateral as well as multilateral management of the international trade order. The largest contribution the EC can make to improve relations with the

United States at this point would be to muster up the political will to move ahead with more substantial cuts in agricultural export subsidies. That would help pave the way for the conclusion of the GATT round, stabilise the international trade order from the chaos of the collapse of the GATT system and prepare the US–EC agenda to tackle defence issues without connecting them to trade issues.

Bilateral relations in the 1990s cannot continue to depend as heavily as they have in the past on the structure provided by multilateral organisations. Given the problems and constraints of international co-operation, and despite the difficulties on the EC side of forming a consensus when it comes to relations with the US, the Transatlantic Declaration should form the basis of a future US–EC treaty. Such a treaty would be between two equals and would bring defence, economic and monetary co-operation, and trade management and dispute settlement under one rubric. It would provide, for the first time in the history of US–EC relations, a legal rubric under which the myriad component parts could be related to a coherent whole. The parts would consist of the existing bilateral agreements and consultative arrangements, which would expand to include dispute settlement and collective self-defence, and the whole would comprise the overarching principles and objectives of the US and EC in not only bilateral relations but in international relations. Such a treaty could serve as a model for broader international co-operation if the US and EC can show others the benefits of managing complex interdependence over the costs of economic nationalism.

In sum, the US and the EC in the 1990s will want to maintain maximum flexibility as they adjust to changes in their relative roles. The EC is struggling to adjust to a position of economic and political leadership within Europe. The United States is struggling to adjust its former global position to one which reflects more accurately the trajectory of power in a plural world. The US and EC adjustment processes have been encapsulated in part by the Transatlantic Declaration but hard decisions about the future management of complex interdependence, multilateral co-operation and bilateral defence issues have been postponed. It would be ironic if both partners risk inaction or maladjustment at a time when US–EC relations have never been more symmetric, when the stifling effects of hegemonic decline have been replaced by the symmetry of post-hegemony, and when the remnants of the Soviet empire are looking to the West for their salvation. A critical juncture for the US–EC partnership has arrived. This book has attempted to show that the benefits of constructure change outweigh the costs of discord. US–EC relations can and should withstand the shock of the end of the cold war despite the uncertainties that lie ahead.

NOTES

1. The Treaty on European Union's provisions for a common defence policy, however tentative, are significant for US interests. The desire of Europeans to protect their own security interests should be viewed as neither anti-NATO nor anti-American, but rather as indigeneously European. It has strong links to European history and civilisation. When viewed in this perspective, NATO and the EC represent two distinct dynamics. NATO was formed as a result of the cold war, and has achieved its objective of deterring an attack on any of its members. The EC is a movement for European unity that transcends the cold war. Its members view it as a means to enhance their power and influence in Europe and the world through joint action.

   In the Treaty on European Union, and especially in the WEU Declaration appended to the Treaty, the signatories took pains to link the WEU's development to the strengthening of the European pillar of NATO. For the US and many Europeans, the key question is whether the EC–WEU link with NATO is transitional or whether over time the two organisations will emerge as parts of a larger whole. Although both organisations are concerned with collective security, their compositions, histories and functions are different. Maintaining links between NATO and EC–WEU in the face of changing security needs will test political will on both sides of the Atlantic. NATO and the EC–WEU could both serve as Western security organisations, but the growth of the EC–WEU operation could cause some in the United States to question the US commitment to European defence at a time when many believe Europeans could easily defend themselves.

   The primary mission of the new EC–WEU link is to enhance the security of the EC; any complementarity of the WEU with NATO is likely to be a secondary objective of the WEU. Despite language in the new Treaty that connects the development of a EC–WEU defence policy with NATO, the main thrust is not to revitalise NATO but to create an independent European force that would defend EC interests in non–NATO Europe (at the least) and outside Europe (at the most). The EC–WEU link could potentially give the EC a much wider latitude than NATO provides.

2. US agencies dealing with the EC number fifteen; their areas of concern are listed opposite.

US Government Department/ Agency	Area of EC Concern
Department of State	Diplomatic relations, initiating and executing policy, negotiations, representation
Department of the Treasury	Monetary relations, fiscal policy
Department of the Defense	Security relations
Department of Commerce	Trade relations, representation, antidumping and countervailing duty investigations
Department of Agriculture	Trade relations, representation
Department of Labor	Labour relations
Department of Justice	Anti-trust relations; anti-terrorism co-operation
Department of Energy	Energy relations
International Trade Commission	Antidumping and countervailing duty investigations
Federal Trade Commission	Anti-trust relations
US Federal Reserve Board	Setting interest rates, monetary policy
US Trade Representative	Co-ordinates US trade policy, negotiations
National Security Council	Overall US foreign policy interests
Office of Management and Budget	Budgetary implications of all US Government programmes
US Information Agency	Handles information exchanges with EC

Appendix 1: Fora and Content of United States–European Community Relations

Name/year/type frequency	Subject participants	Economic content	Political content
1. ILO/'19/multilateral annual	EC members, US, EC Commission observer	Adopts codes governing living and working conditions	Little
2. IMF/'44/multilateral annual	EC members, US, EC Commission observer	Promotes international currency stabilisation	Little
3. IBRD/'44/multilateral annual	EC members, US, EC Commission observer	Provides loans for purposes of economic development	Little
4. UN Security Council '45/multilateral annual/ as needed	UK, France, US	May call for economic sanctions against state threatening or violating international peace and security	May call for military sanctions against state threatening/violating international peace/security
5. UN General Assembly '45/multilateral annual	EC members, US, EC Commission observer	Debates international issues; considers resolutions; promotes functional co-operation	Considers political resolutions; EC Council Presidents address body on EC positions

6.	FAO/'45/multilateral annual	EC members, US, EC Commission observer	Promotes food production in the LDCs	Little
7.	IAEA/'45/multilateral annual	EC members, US, EC Commission observer	Promotes safeguards in use of atomic energy	Little
8.	GATT/'48/multilateral ongoing	EC members, and EC Commission, US	Negotiates trade liberalisation; provides dispute settlement mechanism, global trade rules	Little
9.	OEEC/OECD/'48/ multilateral/annual	EC members, US, EC Commission observer	Promotes economic cooperation/ reconstruction; succeeded by OECD in 1961. OECD pro-economic co-operation; prescribes policy; develops policy on social/economic/scientific issues; monitors export credits and civil aircraft codes	Designed to stabilise European states through regional cooperation to stem communist tide; OECD has little political content beyond the political goal of promoting economic growth and non-discriminatory world trade; could serve as model for economic development in post-cold-war Eastern Europe
10.	NATO/'49/multilateral annual	11 EC members; US	Promotes scientific/ technological/ environmental knowledge	Provides for collective self-defense
11.	COCOM/'49/ multilateral/regular	11 EC members, US; EC Commission observer	Restricts militarily useful exports to communist states	Designed to obstruct military capabilities of communist states

continued on page 270

Appendix 1: *continued*

	Name/year/type frequency	Subject participants	Economic content	Political content
12.	US–EC diplomatic relations/'51/bilateral	EC Commission, US	Missions represent respective economic interests	Missions represent respective political interests
13.	Group of 10/'62 multilateral/biennial	6 EC Members, EC Commission, US	Members co-operate on international lending/bank issues	None
14.	Congress–European Parliament meetings '72/bilateral/annual	Members of European Parliament and US Congress	Discuss economic issues, build understanding, seek co-operation	Discuss political issues, build understanding, seek co-operation
15.	IEA/'74/multilateral/ regular	11 EC members, EC Commission, US	Co-ordinates energy policy of oil importing states	Designed in part to serve as counterweight to OPEC
16.	UNCTAD/'74/ multilateral/every 4 years	EC members, US, EC Commission observer	Promotes economic/trade development in LDCs; framework for GSP, commodity agreements	Is a political forum for Group 77 to promote ideas of a North-South dialogue leading to reform
17.	US–EC High-Level Meetings/'74/bilateral/ originally biannual (then annual in '81 with return to annual in '90)	EC Commission President and Commissioners, US Secretary of State, members of the cabinet	Discuss outstanding bilateral trade and other economic issues; seek co-operation in trade, science/technology, economic, farm, monetary, educational,	Talks have expanded to cover international political and security issues; discussion of/ co-operation in combatting drug trade/money laundering/ consumption; combatting terrorism; reconstruction of

			cultural, environmental, and Third World debt relief issues/areas	Eastern Europe; preventing nuclear proliferation
18.	EPC–US consultations/ '74 bilateral periodic	EC Council presidency, US	Little	Sprang from US pressure on EC over development of EPC and the effects of EPC on US interests; led to EC's response or the 'Gymnich Formula'; EC Council President informs US on EPC matters of interest to it; US makes demarches
19.	Economic Summit/'74 multilateral/annual	4 EC members, EC Commission, EC Council President, US	Seeks consultation on/co-operation concerning macroeconomic/trade/ monetary policies	Discusses/makes statements on international crises/drug trafficking/energy/human rights/environment/terrorism
20.	Group of 7/'75 multilateral/biannual and as needed	4 EC members, EC Commission, US	Finance ministers meet to co-ordinate/monitor exchange rates and co-operate on international economic/monetary issues	Little other than the politics that undergird economic/ monetary co-operation and recent co-ordination of policy toward Soviet economy
21.	CSCE/'75/multilateral/ regularly	EC members, EC Commission, US	Promotes East–West co-operation in trade, science, industry and the environment	Promotes security, conflict prevention, confidence-building measures, human rights

continued on page 272

Appendix 1: *continued*

Name/year/type frequency	Subject participants	Economic content	Political content
22. US–EC Summits/'91 bilateral/annual	EC Council and US Presidents and EC Commission President	Discuss/consult on outstanding bilateral problems/issues; international developments	Discuss/consult on outstanding bilateral problems, issues; international developments
23. US–EC foreign ministerial consultations '90/bilateral/biannual	EC foreign ministers and US Secretary of State with EC Commission	Little	Discuss/seek co-operation on foreign policy issues of common concern
24. US–EC Task Force on Biotechnology Research/'90/bilateral/ biannual	EC Commission, US	Aims to increase US and EC in biotechnology research; holds workshops	Little
25. EBRD/'91/multi/ London/ongoing	EC members, EC Commission, EIB, US	Provides loans to Eastern Europe	Encourages political pluralism and market economics in Eastern Europe

Appendix 2: The Transatlantic Declaration on EC–US Relations

The United States of America on one side and, on the other, the European Community and its member states:

- mindful of their common heritage and of their close historical, political, economic and cultural ties,
- guided by their faith in the values of human dignity, intellectual freedom and civil liberties, and in the democratic institutions which have evolved on both sides of the Atlantic over the centuries,
- recognising that the transatlantic solidarity has been essential for the preservation of peace and freedom and for the development of free and prosperous economies as well as for the recent developments which have restored unity in Europe,
- determined to help consolidate the new Europe, undivided and democratic,
- resolved to strengthen security, economic co-operation and human rights in Europe in the framework of the CSCE, and in other fora,
- noting the firm commitment of the United States and the EC member states concerned to the North Atlantic Alliance and to its principles and purposes,
- acting on the basis of a pattern of co-operation proven over many decades, and convinced that by strengthening and expanding this partnership on an equal footing they will greatly contribute to continued stability, as well as to political and economic progress in Europe and in the world,
- aware of their shared responsibility, not only to further common interests but also to face transnational challenges affecting the well-being of all mankind,
- bearing in mind the accelerating process by which the European Community is acquiring its own identity in economic and monetary matters, in foreign policy and in the domain of security,
- determined to further strengthen transatlantic solidarity through the variety of their international relations, have decided to endow their relationship with long-term perspectives.

Common Goals

The United States of America and the European Community and its member states solemnly reaffirm their determination further to strengthen their partnership in order to:

273

- support democracy, the rule of law and respect for human rights and individual liberty, and promote prosperity and social progress world wide;
- safeguard peace and promote international security, by co-operating with other nations against aggression and coercion, by contributing to the settlement of conflicts in the world and by reinforcing the role of the United Nations and other international organisations;
- pursue policies aimed at achieving a sound world economy marked by sustained economic growth with low inflation, a high level of employment and equitable social conditions, in a framework of international stability;
- promote market principles, reject-protectionism and expand, strengthen and further open the multilateral trading system;
- carry out their resolve to help developing countries by all appropriate means in their efforts towards political and economic reforms;
- provide adequate support, in co-operation with other states and organisations, to the nations of Eastern and Central Europe undertaking economic and political reforms and encourage their participation in the multilateral institutions of international trade and finance.

Principles of US–EC Partnership

To achieve their common goals, the European Community and its member states and the United States of America will inform and consult each other on important matters of common interest, both political and economic, with a view to bringing their positions as close as possible without prejudice to their respective independence. In appropriate international bodies, in particular, they will seek close cooperation.

The EC–US partnership will, moreover, greatly benefit from the mutual knowledge and understanding acquired through regular consultations as described in this Declaration.

Economic Co-operation

Both sides recognise the importance of strengthening the multilateral trading system. They will support further steps towards liberalisation, transparency, and the implementation of GATT and OECD principles concerning both trade in goods and services and investment.

They will further develop their dialogue, which is already under way, on other matters such as technical and non-tariff barriers to industrial and agricultural trade, services, competition policy, transportation policy, standards, telecommunications, high technology and other relevant areas.

Education, Scientific and Cultural Co-operation

The partnership between the European Community and its member states on the one hand, and the United States on the other, will be based on continuous efforts to strengthen mutual co-operation in various other fields which directly affect the present and future well-being of their citizens, such as exchanges and joint projects in science and technology, including, *inter alia*, research in medicine, environment protection, pollution prevention, energy, space, high energy physics, and the safety of nuclear and other installations, as well as in education and culture, including academic and youth exchanges.

Transnational Challenges

The United States of America and the European Community and its member states will fulfil their responsibility to address transnational challenges, in the interest of their own peoples and of the rest of the world. In particular, they will join their efforts in the following fields:

- combatting and preventing terrorism;
- putting an end to the illegal production, trafficking and consumption of narcotics and related criminal activities such as the laundering of money;
- co-operating in the fight against international crime;
- protecting the environment, both internationally and domestically, by integrating environmental and economic goals;
- preventing the proliferation of nuclear armaments, chemical and biological weapons, and missile technology.

Institutional Framework for Consultation

Both sides agree that a framework is required for regular and intensive consultation. They will make full use of and further strengthen existing procedures, including those established by the President of the European Council and the President of the United States on 27 February 1990, namely:

- biannual consultations to be arranged in the United States and in Europe between, on the one side, the President of the European Council and the President of the Commission, and on the other side, the President of the United States;
- biannual consultations between the European Community Foreign Ministers, with the Commission, and the US Secretary of State, alternately on either side of the Atlantic;
- *ad hoc* consultations between the Presidency Foreign Minister or the Troika and the US Secretary of State;
- biannual consultations between the Commission and the US Government at Cabinet level;
- briefings, as currently exist, by the Presidency to US Representatives on European Political Co-operation (EPC) meetings at the Ministerial level;

Both sides are resolved to develop and deepen these procedures for consultation so as to reflect the evolution of the European Community and of its relationship with the United States.

They welcome the actions taken by the European Parliament and the Congress of the United States in order to improve their dialogue and thereby bring closer together the peoples on both sides of the Atlantic.

Index